T0330396

Entrepreneurial Ecosystems Meet Innovation Systems

NEW HORIZONS IN REGIONAL SCIENCE

Series Editor: Philip McCann, *Professor of Urban and Regional Economics, University of Sheffield, UK*

Regional science analyses important issues surrounding the growth and development of urban and regional systems and is emerging as a major social science discipline. This series provides an invaluable forum for the publication of high quality scholarly work on urban and regional studies, industrial location economics, transport systems, economic geography and networks.

New Horizons in Regional Science aims to publish the best work by economists, geographers, urban and regional planners and other researchers from throughout the world. It is intended to serve a wide readership including academics, students and policymakers.

Titles in the series include:

Entrepreneurial Ecosystems Meet Innovation Systems

Synergies, Policy Lessons and Overlooked Dimensions

Edited by

Alexandra Tsvetkova

Spatial Productivity Lab, the OECD Trento Centre for Local Development, Italy

Jana Schmutzler

Department of Economics, Universidad del Norte, Colombia

Rhiannon Pugh

Centre for Innovation, Research and Competence in the Learning Economy (CIRCLE), Lund University, Sweden

NEW HORIZONS IN REGIONAL SCIENCE

Edward Elgar
PUBLISHING

Cheltenham, UK • Northampton, MA, USA

Published by
Edward Elgar Publishing Limited
The Lypiatts
15 Lansdown Road
Cheltenham
Glos GL50 2JA
UK

Edward Elgar Publishing, Inc.
William Pratt House
9 Dewey Court
Northampton
Massachusetts 01060
USA

A catalogue record for this book
is available from the British Library

Library of Congress Control Number: 2020938613

This book is available electronically in the **Elgar**online
Economics subject collection
DOI 10.4337/9781789901184

ISBN 978 1 78990 117 7 (cased)
ISBN 978 1 78990 118 4 (eBook)

Printed and bound by CPI Group (UK) Ltd, Croydon CR0 4YY

Contents

Figures

Tables

About the editors

Rhiannon Pugh is a senior lecturer in innovation studies at CIRCLE (Centre for Innovation, Research and Competence in the Learning Economy) at Lund University. With a background in economic geography, she previously worked at Örebro and Uppsala Universities in Sweden and Lancaster University in the UK. She is interested in researching policies and programmes for regional economic development, innovation, and entrepreneurship. She is also an editor of the early career section of the journal *Regional Studies, Regional Science.*

Jana Schmutzler is Assistant Professor of Economics at the Universidad del Norte in Barranquilla, Colombia. She holds a PhD in economics from the Schumpeter School of Business and Economics at the Bergische Universität Wuppertal, Germany. Her research interest centers on innovation processes and entrepreneurial behavior with a focus on developing countries. Specifically, she explores the role a context plays in fostering (or hindering) these vital economic behaviors. She has published in internationally recognized journals in the field of entrepreneurship and innovation such as *Entrepreneurship: Theory and Practice* and *Industrial and Corporate Change*. In addition, she has co-edited the book *Innovation in Developing and Transition Countries* published by Edward Elgar Publishing.

Alexandra Tsvetkova is Economist and Policy Analyst at the Organisation for Economic Co-operation and Development (OECD) Trento Centre for Local Development, Italy, where she manages activities of the Spatial Productivity Lab. Before joining the OECD, Alexandra was affiliated with the Ohio State University and George Mason University. Her research on drivers of regional and local growth in the United States has appeared in *Small Business Economics*, *Energy Economics*, *Regional Science and Urban Economics*, *Economic Development Quarterly* and other journals. She is co-editor of the book *Innovation in Developing and Transition Countries* published by Edward Elgar Publishing.

Contributors

Veneta Andonova is Dean and Associate Professor of Business Strategy in the School of Management at Universidad de los Andes, Colombia. Previously, she has worked at Universitat Pompeu Fabra, ITAM and the American University in Bulgaria. Her research focuses on business strategy internationalization and innovation-driven entrepreneurship in emerging markets. It has appeared in *Entrepreneurship Theory and Practice*, *Journal of Development Economics*, *Journal of Business Research* and *Journal of Development Studies* among others. Recently, she has co-authored two books: *Multilatinas: Strategies for internationalization* (2017) and *Entrepreneurial Ecosystems in Unexpected Places* (2019).

Maksim Belitski is Associate Professor in Entrepreneurship and Innovation at the Henley Business School, University of Reading, United Kingdom. He is Research Fellow at the Institute for Development Strategies, Indiana University Bloomington, United States. He has worked for the University of Bolzano, Italy, Loughborough University, University College London and University of Leicester, United Kingdom, University of Economics Bratislava, Belarusian State University. His research interests lie in the area of entrepreneurship, innovation and regional economics, with a particular focus on entrepreneurship as a spillover of knowledge and creativity. He is Editor of *Small Business Economics: An Entrepreneurship Journal*, *E-commerce Journal* and *Journal of Management Development*.

José Eduardo Cassiolato is an economist. He gained his postdoctorate at Université Pierre Mendes-France, France and PhD in Development, Industrialization and Scientific and Technological Policy, Science Policy Research Unit, Sussex University, United Kingdom. He has been a professor at the Institute of Economics of the Federal University of Rio de Janeiro, RedeSist coordinator and general secretary at the Global Network on the Economics of Learning, Innovation and Capacity Building Systems and chairman of the Council of the Center for High Studies Brazil 21st Century. He is a member of the Superior Council of Fiocruz.

Antonio Pedro da Costa e Silva Lima holds a BSc in economics at the State University of Rio de Janeiro, a BA in social sciences from the Federal University of Rio de Janeiro and an MSc in public policies, strategies and development from the Federal University of Rio de Janeiro. Currently, he is a PhD student in the Public Policies, Strategies and Development Program at the Institute of Economics of the Federal University of Rio de Janeiro.

Claudia De Fuentes is Associate Professor of Innovation and Entrepreneurship at the Sobey School of Business at Saint Mary's University, Canada. Her research experience includes innovation in firms, systems of innovation, the creation and use of knowledge in a globalized economy, innovation in global value chains, new forms of academia–industry collaboration and science, technology and innovation policy. Her work has circulated internationally. She has collaborated with several research groups to work on projects in Canada, Mexico and the European Union. She has worked on research projects for the Treasury Board of Canada Secretariat, Inter-American Development Bank, Foro Consultivo científico y tecnológico in Mexico and for the International Development Research Centre.

Nikolay A. Dentchev is Associate Professor of CSR and Entrepreneurship at the Vrije Universiteit Brussels (VUB), Belgium. He holds the Solvay Business School Chair of Social Entrepreneurship at the same, with founding partners Close the Gap, BNP Paribas Fortis and Euroclear. Nikolay has been involved in initiatives supporting student entrepreneurship for more than ten years and is coaching about ten students a year to develop their business. He has (co-) authored more than 40 scientific publications, published in various indexed journals such as *Business and Society*, *Journal of Business Ethics* and *Business Ethics: A European Review*. Nikolay serves occasionally as a guest editor of special issues in journals such as *Business and Society* and *Journal of Cleaner Production*. He also serves at the executive board of two international associations, International Association for Business and Society and New Business Models. Nikolay is a co-founder of Equalisi BVBA, a social enterprise that commercializes products of vulnerable entrepreneurs.

Abel Diaz Gonzalez is a PhD candidate at the Vrije Universiteit Brussels (VUB), Belgium. His research focuses on the supportive function of social entrepreneurial ecosystems. For his doctoral dissertation, Abel has conducted field research in Bolivia, Ecuador, Colombia and Belgium. His research has been presented at different international conferences (among which are the Academy of Management, International Association for Business and Society, EMES and New Business Models). Abel has acted as a reviewer at various conferences and for journals, and as co-organizer of numerous events (e.g. the VUB Social Entrepreneurship Fair and the Social Entrepreneurship Summit). Abel is a co-founder of Equalisi BVBA, a social enterprise incorporated in 2019 in Belgium, aimed at supporting vulnerable entrepreneurs from Latin America to commercialize their products in alternative markets.

Juan Federico holds a PhD in entrepreneurship and management, Autonomous University of Barcelona, an MSc in industrial economics and development, with emphasis on small and medium-sized enterprises (SMEs), and a BA in economics. He works as Assistant Professor and Researcher at Prodem (Entrepreneurial Development Program), Institute of Industry, National University of General Sarmiento, Argentina. His main research interests are on entrepreneurship and development, young business growth, entrepreneurial ecosystems and policies. He is currently Academic Coordinator of the master's course in industrial economics and development with emphasis on SMEs. He was president of the Argentinean Affiliate of the International Council for Small Business and is now President of the Mercosur's SME network.

Andrew Godley is Head of Leadership, Organisations and Behaviour. He is Professor of Management and Business History and Academic Director of the Henley Centre for Entrepreneurship. His research interests lie in the areas of the economics of entrepreneurship and business history, with a particular focus on the historical evolution of the international food and pharmaceutical sectors. He has published in journals ranging from *Economic History Review*, *Business History Review*, *Journal of Management Studies* and *Strategic Entrepreneurship Journal* and has won research grants from the Economic and Social Research Council, the Leverhulme Trust and British Academy among others. He has also been a consultant to several leading firms and government departments and is a frequent commentator in the broadcast and written media on trends in entrepreneurship. He is Senior Fellow of the Higher Education Academy and Visiting Professor at Zhejiang University, China.

Manuel Gonzalo holds a PhD in economics from Universidad Federal de Rio de Janeiro, an MSc in industrial economics and development from Universidad Nacional de General Sarmiento (UNGS) and a BA in economics from Universidad de Buenos Aires. He is Researcher-Professor at ProDem, Institute of Industry, UNGS and at the School of Economics, Universidad Nacional de Chilecito, Argentina. He is also Researcher at RedeSist, Institute of Economics, Federal University of Rio de Janeiro, Brazil. He mainly does research on the innovation and entrepreneurial systems in the Global South. He teaches comparative development and industrial organization at both the undergraduate and the postgraduate levels. He belongs to the following research networks: Globelics, Lalics, Red Pymes MERCOSUR, Young Scholars Initiative Economics of Innovation and India and South Asia CARI's working group.

Andres Guerrero Alvarado is Director of the Entrepreneurship Center at the Universidad de los Andes School of Management. He currently teaches entrepreneurship and innovation, business planning and entrepreneurship financing. His research examines the finance process in early-stage ventures, entrepreneurial ecosystems, impact investing and sustainable entrepreneurship. His research has developed from a practice approach based on his approximately 15-year career in the private and public sectors before beginning his academic career.

Sabrina Ibarra Garcia holds an MSc in industrial economics and development with emphasis on small and medium-sized enterprises from Universidad de General Sarmiento, Argentina and a BA in economics from Universidad de Buenos Aires. Sabrina is currently pursuing her PhD in economic development at Universidad Nacional de Quilmes. She joined Prodem in 2008 as a research assistant and lecturer. Since then, she has been involved in several research projects in quantitative data processing and analysis. Her main research interests are the determinants of dynamic new ventures (especially in Latin America), the elaboration of composite indicators of entrepreneurship and quantitative research methods.

Hugo Kantis is Director and Professor of the master's in industrial economics and development with emphasis on small and medium-sized enterprises, Universidad de General Sarmiento, Argentina and Director of Prodem. He holds a PhD degree in entrepreneurship and small business management (Universitat Autonoma de Barcelona, Växjö University) and a BA in economics and business administration. He has more than 15 years of experience designing, advising and evaluating entrepreneurship policies and programs throughout Latin America. He is a member of the editorial boards of several journals such as *Venture Capital* and *Journal of Small Business Management*. He has authored several articles, books and chapters focused on entrepreneurship in Latin America and is Director of *Dinamica Emprendedora*, the newsletter of Prodem. He is a 2016 recipient of the Start Up Nation Award for Groundbreaking Policy Thinking granted by the Global Entrepreneurship Network.

Renata Lèbre La Rovere holds a BSc in economics at the Pontifical Catholic University of Rio de Janeiro, Brazil, a specialization degree in industrial economics at the Federal University of Rio de Janeiro (UFRJ), Brazil, a diplôme d'etudes approfondies in productive structures and global systems at the Université Paris 7, France and a PhD in economic sciences at the Université Paris 7. After getting her PhD, she worked as an invited researcher at the Management of Information Systems Department at the University of Arizona, United States, between 1991 and 1992. In 1993 she became a professor of the Institute of Economics at UFRJ. She did a postdoctoral study on technology policies for small and medium-sized enterprises at the Management of

Information Systems Department at Rostock Universitaet, Germany, between 1995 and 1996. She is currently Associate Professor at the Institute of Economics at UFRJ and at the Public Policies, Strategies and Development Program. She is a researcher of the Economics of Innovation Group of the Institute of Economics at UFRJ. Her main research interests are in the fields of economics of innovation, regional development and entrepreneurship.

Maria Cecília Junqueira Lustosa, PhD in economics, is a professor at Post-Graduate Program in Intellectual Property and Technology Transfer for Innovation at the Federal University of Rio de Janeiro, and was a postdoctoral researcher at Bordeaux IV University, France. She is currently a researcher at the Research Network on Local Productive and Innovative Systems as well as the Environmental Economics and Sustainable Development Research Group, both at the Federal University of Rio de Janeiro, Brazil. She is on the board of directors of the Brazilian Society for Ecological Economics and her main areas of interest are regional development, innovation and environment.

Helena Maria Martins Lastres is Researcher and Associate Professor at the Institute of Economics of the Federal University of Rio de Janeiro (UFRJ) and Co-coordinator of the Research Network on Local Innovation and Production Systems. She holds a PhD in development and science and technology policy from Science Policy Research Unit, Sussex University; a master's in technology economics from COPPE, UFRJ and a BA in Economics from UFRJ. She has also held a postdoctorate position in innovation and local productive systems at Université Pierre Mendès-France. Her main areas of interest are development and science, technology and innovation economics and policies; innovation and knowledge economy; local innovation and production systems; and regional and territorial development.

Félix Modrego is Assistant Professor at the Institute of Social Sciences of the University of O'Higgins, Chile. He has been an assistant professor at the Department of Economics of the Catholic University of the North, Chile, postdoctoral research fellow in applied economics at the Gran Sasso Science Institute, Italy and a researcher at the Latin American Center for Rural Development, Chile. He holds a PhD in spatial sciences from the University of Groningen, the Netherlands and an MSc in agricultural economics from the Pontifical Catholic University, Chile. His current research interests are the economic geography of entrepreneurship and innovation, spatial economics and regional development, particularly in Latin America.

Guilherme de Oliveira Santos holds a BA in social sciences and an MSc in public policies, strategies and development from the Federal University of Rio de Janeiro (UFRJ). Currently, he is a PhD student in the Public Policies,

Strategies and Development Program at the Institute of Economics of UFRJ and a researcher at the Innovation Economics Group.

Jahan Ara Peerally is Associate Professor of International Business at HEC Montréal, Canada. Her research interests encompass mainly the activities of multinational and social enterprises in developing and emerging economies. Her publications have focused on technological capability creation in foreign multinational and domestic enterprises located in developing countries and other issues related to the socio-economic development effects of multinational enterprises in developing and emerging economies. She has published scientific articles in peer-reviewed books and journals and teaching case studies with accompanying teaching notes in peer-reviewed journals as well.

Jonathan A. Perez-Lopez holds a BSc in industrial engineering from Universidad Pontificia Bolivariana. Currently, he is a PhD student in the School of Management at the Universidad de los Andes, Colombia, where he has also worked as research assistant in different entrepreneurship-related projects. He recently co-authored a book chapter in *Entrepreneurial Ecosystems in Unexpected Places* (2019, edited by Andonova, Nikolova and Dimitrov). His research interests encompass entrepreneurship, entrepreneurial and innovation ecosystems and regional development studies.

Marcelo Gerson Pessoa de Matos holds a BSc in economics from the Federal University of Rio de Janeiro, an MSc and a PhD in economics from the Fluminense Federal University. He is currently Professor at the Economics Institute of the Federal University of Rio de Janeiro and the Public Policies, Strategies and Development Program. He is Researcher at the Research Network on Local Productive and Innovative Systems and member of the Scientific Board of the Latin American Network for the Economics of Learning, Innovation, and Competence Building Systems. He coordinates and develops research in the area of innovation, innovation systems, local productive and innovative systems and arrangements, regional and local development, micro and small enterprises, cultural and creative industries, industrial dynamics and industrial and innovation policy.

Maria Giulia Pezzi is Postdoctoral Research Fellow at the Gran Sasso Science Institute, Italy. She has been a research fellow at Università degli Studi di Bergamo, Italy and holds a PhD in anthropology from KF-Universität in Graz, Austria. Her research interests include local development strategies, tourism development, entrepreneurship and innovation.

Maria del Carmen Roman Roig earned a BSc in psychology from the University of Barcelona and an MSc in management from the Vrije Universiteit Brussels, Belgium. She wrote her master's thesis about the role of universities in support of social entrepreneurs, with a case study of Bolivian universities. Thanks to her multicultural experience and international background, she has learned from different perspectives and opportunities, both from Bolivia and Europe, and this has enriched her understanding of entrepreneurship and the potential of entrepreneurs to develop valuable businesses for society. Her professional experience includes positions in the field of human resources management in Bolivia and financial positions in Luxembourg. Currently, she is working as an onboarding and client change analyst in an investment bank in Luxembourg.

Vinciane Servantie is the Vice-Dean of Academic Affairs and Associate Professor in the School of Management at the Universidad de los Andes. She currently teaches business models for sustainability, management consulting and entrepreneurship and innovation. Her research examines the processes by which organizations create value. Such processes are particularly challenging in specific entrepreneurship contexts such as international, social, sustainable or gender entrepreneurship subfields. Her research aims to understand entrepreneurial and decision-making processes for value creation.

Maria Gabriela v. B. Podcameni is Professor of Economics, Environment and Innovation of the Federal Institute of Education, Science and Technology of the State of Rio de Janeiro, researcher at the Research Network on Local Productive and Innovative Systems and Arrangements, Federal University of Rio de Janeiro, associate researcher at the Center for Environment and Sustainability and a member of the Global Network on the Economics of Learning, Innovation and Capacity Building Systems Secretariat. She holds a degree in economics from PUC-Rio and a master's degree and a PhD in economics from the Federal University of Rio de Janeiro. She worked at the Brazilian Fund for Biodiversity between 2006 and 2007 as an analyst of projects related to sustainability. Her main lines of research are eco-innovations, science, technology and innovation policy; local productive arrangements; and wind energy and sustainability.

Jon Mikel Zabala-Iturriagagoitia is Lecturer at the Department of Economics at the University of Deusto in Donostia-San Sebastian, Spain. He received his PhD in engineering and innovation projects in 2008 from the Polytechnic University of Valencia, Spain. During the PhD studies he was a visiting researcher at the Technical Research Centre of Finland. After obtaining his PhD he moved to Lund University, Sweden as a postdoc, where he also held an assistant professorship. His main research skills and interests include science, technology and innovation policy, innovation management and the use of indicators to inform policy decisions and evaluations related to innovation.

Preface

This book is about building bridges: bridges between theoretical schools of thought and bridges across continents. Keeping in mind clear but often unacknowledged theoretical linkages among different perspectives on innovation, entrepreneurship, economic growth and development, it focuses on the interactions (and the limits of such interactions) between two popular theoretical approaches within the field: entrepreneurial ecosystems and innovation systems. To take a step further, we place a special emphasis on uncommon and underrepresented regions and topics within these two established conceptual bodies of work.

The book emerged through a long-standing collaboration among alumni of the Global Network for Economics of Learning, Innovation and Competence Building Systems (Globelics) PhD Academy and is, in a sense, the result of a conversation – a conversation about what works and what does not for improving the wellbeing of places across the world. The diversity of the Globelics network in terms of the disciplines and backgrounds, but also in terms of geographies, was instrumental for seeing very clearly the existing fragmentation of scholarship that tries to better understand the role of entrepreneurship and innovation in economic development. This fragmentation is often accompanied by an exclusive (North American and European) nature of publications, conferences and networks. Both fragmentation and exclusivity, perhaps too large a topic to unpack here and now, have linguistic and economic dimensions which act, in reality, to narrow the academic conversation and exposure to new ideas and perspectives for us all. They also can make the practical policy applications of the cutting-edge research more difficult at best and misguided at worst, particularly in less developed regions.

This collection strives to contribute to the alleviation of these two drawbacks in the contemporary debates and to advance two types of conversation. One is a dialog between the entrepreneurial ecosystems and the innovation systems concepts. Despite their obvious overlap in the topics covered and approaches taken, it appears that the two frameworks mainly evolve along parallel lines. A better understanding of the promise and the boundaries of a cross-fertilization between the two can help in developing more comprehensive policy solutions workable in a variety of places, which address both phenomena of innovation and entrepreneurship for economic (and societal) development in a more harmonious manner. The second conversation is an exchange of perspectives on common topics among highly heterogeneous – including those usually underrepresented – researchers. The group of contributors to this edited book is very diverse in levels of seniority, gender, geographies, cultures, mother tongues and other characteristics. The inclusivity and the scope set this publication apart compared to other contemporary collections focused on the (eco)systemic approaches.

Acknowledgments

Editors: Jana Schmutzler is grateful for the financial support for this research received from Colciencias through grant 121577657885 as well as the financial support from Colciencias-DAAD through grant 58955.

Chapter 2: Guilherme de Oliveira Santos and Antonio Pedro da Costa e Silva Lima greatly appreciate the support of CAPES (Brazil) – financing code 001. The funding was indispensable for the continuity of the studies and research.

Chapter 4: Jana Schmutzler is grateful for the financial support for this research received from Colciencias through grant 121577657885 as well as the financial support from Colciencias-DAAD through grant 58955.

Chapter 5: The authors gratefully acknowledge the funding from the VLIR IUC program with Universidad Católica Boliviana (UCB), which made possible the visits to Bolivia to conduct field research. The authors also thank colleagues from the UCB who facilitated the links with local contacts in Bolivia during the data collection across the country. Separate thanks for the founding partners of the VUB Chair of Social Entrepreneurship in Belgium (Close the Gap, Euroclear and BNP Paribas Fortis) for their trust, support and funding of the research activities.

Chapter 6: Jon Mikel Zabala-Iturriagagoitia is indebted to the European Commission for the funding provided to develop the Advancing Knowledge-Intensive Entrepreneurship and Innovation for Economic Growth and Social Well-being in Europe (AEGIS), Grant Agreement number 225134. In particular, the author would like to thank Slavo Radosevic and Esin Yoruk for their support and commitment during the execution of the AEGIS project in general, and the development of the work package "Knowledge-intensive entrepreneurship and national innovation systems" in particular. The chapter is based on the results of this work package.

Chapter 8: The authors thank Dr. Sara Amoroso, Joint Research Centre European Commission, Sevilla, Spain and Dr. Lebene Soga at University of Reading for helpful comments and support at the earlier stage of this project.

Chapter 9: The authors are very grateful to Professors Jana Schmutzler, Alexandra Tsvetkova, Miguel Atienza and an anonymous reviewer for the constructive and helpful comments and suggestions. Félix Modrego thanks the Chilean National Commission of Scientific and Technological Research for the financial support through the Fondecyt Initiation in Research Fund 2019 (Grant: 11190112).

Chapter 11. The authors thank Economic Development Secretary Office at the Mayor of Bogotá for the financial support to this research developed between 2009 to 2014, in particular to Adriana Montenegro for her government auditor role in the administrative support process. The authors also thank to Oliver García, David Pescador, Rafael Vesga, Jorge Hernandez, Martha Hernandez, as members of the research team.

1. Introduction to Entrepreneurial Ecosystems Meet Innovation Systems: Synergies, policy lessons and overlooked dimensions

Jana Schmutzler, Rhiannon Pugh and Alexandra Tsvetkova

Systemic approaches to economic development have burgeoned recently in the wake of the emergence of a distinct research subfield that studies entrepreneurial ecosystems (EE) (for example, Mason & Brown, 2014 and Malecki, 2018). Drawing on the biological metaphor of "a biotic community, its physical environment, and all the interactions possible in the complex of living and nonliving components" (Moore, 1963, p. 249), the concept of EE is shaping understanding of entrepreneurship as an evolutionary, socially interactive and non-linear process (Colombelli, Paolucci & Ughetto, 2017).

This research area complements a long-standing interest in other "flavors" of systemic conceptualizations of the interlinked – and embedded in local context – spheres of innovation, institutions and economic development that have been popular in academic and policy practice communities (Uriona-Maldonado, dos Santos & Varvakis, 2012; Teixeira, 2014; Malecki, 2018). The idea that a place's community, and its economic and social contexts matter, however, is at least a century old. A focus on a multitude of actors, the environment and their dynamic network-like interactions in explanations of regional economic performance has given rise to concepts such as industrial districts (Marshall, 1920 [1890]), industrial clusters (Porter, 2000), innovative milieu (Camagni, 1991) and, lately, the (national/regional/technological) innovation systems (IS) (Lundvall, 1992; Asheim, Smith & Oughton, 2011; Carlsson & Stankiewitz, 1991).

Overall, these systemic frameworks prove enduringly popular, perhaps due to their ability to capture and explicate mechanisms usually assumed away in static analyses within classical economics. The rapid improvements in data, estimation techniques and computational power make it easier to account for and to track the complexity of the local and global interactions within systems.

This is likely to further expand and deepen research interest in (and policy applications of) the systems-inspired perspectives on economic processes.

This book presents current multidisciplinary research of diverse authors, which expands our knowledge about three dimensions of the systemic frameworks. The first part explores the promise but also the limits of bridging the EE and the IS concepts, particularly as applied outside of the bubbling global hubs or to the types of entrepreneurship different from the high-growth variety. Building on these insights, the second part of the book delves deeper into the links between academic knowledge and its practical applications in a variety of contexts – from a vibrant London suburb to Latin American countries – with the goal of offering place-specific policy implications. Finally, the last part of the book presents some of the overlooked dimensions of the systems perspectives, which are important for expanding the scope of the inquiry but also for a better understanding of the strengths and weaknesses of the current debates.

1.1   THE INNOVATION SYSTEM AND ENTREPRENEURIAL ECOSYSTEM: AN OVERVIEW

The systems approaches have been around for a while. Starting with the early works by Lundvall and Nelson (Lundvall 1988, 1992; Nelson, 1993), researchers used the systems logic to understand economic activity and growth at a variety of levels (e.g. localities, regions, sectors, etc.). The policy relevance of the systems approach is clear to see over time. McCann and Ortega-Argilés (2013) credit the IS thinking with shifting the predominant policy approaches to economic development away from a narrow science policy towards much broader systemic views on national and regional innovation. Systems thinking has permeated policy at regional, national and supranational levels: Lundvall (2007a) and Edquist (2005) highlight systems-premised policy advice developed by various actors such as the Organisation for Economic Co-operation and Development (OECD) (the Directorate of Science, Technology and Industry, currently the Directorate for Science, Technology and Innovation), the United Nations Conference on Trade and Development and its Industrial Development Organization and VINNOVA (the Swedish Agency for Innovation). More recently, ecosystemic perspectives are being developed at the World Bank (2010) and the Local Economic and Employment Development (LEED) Programme at the OECD Centre for Entrepreneurship, SMEs, Regions and Cities (Mason & Brown, 2014).

The IS perspective has evolved over the last three decades of work on innovation dynamics and policy from local, regional and national perspectives; it is now well established as a lens through which we can examine innovation processes and also as an influential framework for the design and delivery of innovation policy (Edquist, 2005; Lundvall, 2007a). Definitions of IS abound: summarizing these, Asheim finds that within the literature, the IS can be defined broadly, including the "wider organisations and institutions affecting and supporting learning and innovation", or narrowly, examining the "R&D [research and development] functions of universities, public and private research institutes and corporations" (2012, p. 995). According to Lundvall (2007a), it is the wide understanding that is most useful and appropriate, but policy often conceptualizes IS narrowly. From its origins in work on national IS (Lundvall, 1988, 1992; Nelson, 1993), IS approaches have since evolved into regional (Cooke, 1998; Malmberg & Maskell, 1997), technological (Carlsson & Stankiewitz, 1991) and sectoral systems of innovation (Breschi & Malerba, 1997).

The IS framework has challenged the mainstream economics view and the prevailing policy approaches (cf. Lundvall, 2007a). We can credit the IS work with shifting our understanding of innovation and economic development towards more evolutionary and interactive ways of thinking and seeing (Pugh, 2014). The IS approach is notable for its focus on learning, knowledge, networks and institutions as the central elements in enabling but also hindering innovation in different contexts (Cooke, 1998; Doloreux, 2002; Edquist, 2005; Lundvall, 1992). Most importantly, within the IS perspective, innovation is geographically, socially and historically contingent (Doloreux and Parto, 2005; Freeman, 2002; Lundvall, Johnson, Andersen & Dalum, 2002).

Because of a relatively long application of the IS concept both empirically and theoretically, we already have a critical body of work to draw on to better understand the strengths and weaknesses of the concept. A thorough review of these is provided by Edquist (2005). He identifies the strengths of the IS approach as: the holistic and interdisciplinary view; the historical and evolutionary perspectives it encompasses; the interdependence and non-linearity of the approach; and the central role of institutions in explaining the innovation process (Edquist, 2005, p. 185). On the other hand, the concept suffers from fuzziness. For example, it lacks a definition for an institution and specifications for what should be included or excluded from the system and where the system boundaries are (Edquist, 2005). Doloreux and Parto (2005) agree with this perspective, finding some definitional and conceptual stickiness around the regional variant of the IS concept. The inherent problem of a fuzzy theoretical approach is not universally derided: whilst some theorists think the IS approaches need to be rendered more "theory-like" and to strengthen their foundations in the neo-Schumpeterian and evolutionary economic thinking (e.g. Fischer, 2001; Lundvall, 2002, 2003; Lundvall et al., 2002), others see conceptual openness and flexibility as a key strength of the IS approach (Nelson and Rosenberg, 1993), allowing it to be applied in a variety of contexts (Edquist, 2005).

Recently, a newer concept within the field of entrepreneurship, innovation and economic development – entrepreneurship (or entrepreneurial) ecosystems – experienced a ballooning of interest amongst the academic as well as policy practice and advice communities. The World Bank (2018), the OECD (Mason & Brown, 2014; OECD, 2014, 2019) as well as national-level policy actors such as the German development agency GIZ (Kreuzer et al., 2018) and Scotland Can Do sponsored by the Scottish Government (2018) employ this concept in their work.

Academically, the concept of EE has gained popularity since the publication of Isenberg's (2010) piece in the *Harvard Business Review* and the mainstream book "Startup Communities" (Feld, 2012). Both authors highlight the importance of a supportive community as well as an enabling economic environment for the entrepreneur. As such, these publications embody a changing research focus in the entrepreneurship literature: away from personality-based explanations toward investigations of the entrepreneurial process in its broader social and economic environment (Spigel, 2017). The EE concept has proven particularly popular amongst scholars in entrepreneurship, management and economic geography also due to its focus on the local and regional context.

1.2   BRIDGING INNOVATION SYSTEMS WITH ENTREPRENEURIAL ECOSYSTEMS: WHAT CAN BE LEARNED?

As of today, the IS and EE perspectives have established themselves in their own right. Despite Schumpeter's (2003 [1911]) conceptualization (in his early work) of the "entrepreneur as innovator" who drives economic development, it appears that the IS and EE literatures mainly evolve along parallel lines with limited dialogue (Acs, Autio & Szerb, 2014). This is surprising given that the IS approach is often considered a predecessor of the EE framework (Stam & Spigel, 2017) and that the two perspectives often share the same methodological tools and address very closely related, if not similar, issues.

The IS and the EE concepts are rooted in the theoretical (eco)systemic foundation. This allows them to depart from the (near) linear view of economic growth by the neoclassical economic theory to try and comprehend the economic trajectory of a place from a broader perspective, which includes a multitude of actors and factors working at many levels.

Ironically, the two concepts are very similar in their received critiques. Castellacci and Natera (2013), for example, criticize the limited insights that exist regarding the drivers of change in a national IS, and the mechanisms that can explain its evolution and growth over time. In a very similar tone, Mack and Mayer (2016) highlight the little understanding regarding the interdependence of the various components of an EE and its evolutionary dynamics. This is in addition to the critiques of the IS perspective reviewed above.

The most prominent difference between the two concepts is, arguably, the frameworks' focus. While the EE puts the entrepreneur at the center of its analysis, this element has been largely overlooked by the IS literature (Metcalfe & Ramlogan, 2008). Instead, the IS tradition mainly focuses on the large, established firms and their role in generating innovations through R&D (Freeman & Soete, 1997; Autio & Levie, 2014). Thus, the individual agency so prominent in the EE works has been generally missing in the IS literature (Autio, Kenney, Mustar, Siegel & Wright, 2014). As a result, while the IS concept mainly envisions a top-down policy approach (Arocena & Sutz, 2000), the EE is characterized by bottom-up dynamics, i.e. an emerging, self-organizing and self-sustaining system (Autio & Levie, 2014).

The concern, however, is that when we have a multiplicity of similar concepts with little dialogue among them, we miss the connections, contradictions and overlaps that could help us build up better theory and policy practice regarding economic development. Much can be learned, we believe, if the two literatures feed into each other. Part I, entitled "The promise and the limits of bridging the entrepreneurial ecosystems and innovation systems approaches", therefore documents the similarities and differences between these two concepts, as well as their interlinkages and how the IS and the EE perspectives complement or contradict each other in their ability to explain specific dimensions of regional economic growth. In doing so, we build a first bridge – one that connects the two literature streams.

There are clearly multiple overlaps and areas for cross-fertilization. Chapter 2, "Bridging the literature on innovation systems and entrepreneurial ecosystems: Cross-fertilizations for understanding knowledge-intensive, social and environmental entrepreneurship" by Renata Lèbre La Rovere, Marcelo Gerson Pessoa de Matos, Guilherme de Oliveira Santos and Antonio Pedro da Costa e Silva Lima, offers an overview of the EE and the IS concepts, focusing on the similarities and differences along three dimensions, the individual, the firm and the institutional context. The authors show that while the unit of analysis in the two approaches is different, both concepts are important for a more comprehensive understanding of innovative behavior by firms. The chapter describes how both theoretical and practice-oriented work on three specific types of entrepreneurship – knowledge-intensive, social and green – can not only benefit from but rather require the integration of the two literatures.

An understanding of the similarities and differences between the two approaches is an important first step for a more comprehensive view of economic development. The applicability of this knowledge on the EE and IS, however, may be limited to the "classical" (rooted in the realities of the most developed countries in North America and Europe) context. Whether the systems approaches can and should be "exported" to other regions where the need for growth may be even more pressing is a question that receives increasing – but still insufficient – attention (Tsvetkova, Pugh & Schmutzler, 2019). Intuitively, the systems frameworks would need to be modified to be useful outside of the Global North.

Chapter 3, "Entrepreneurial ecosystems meet innovation systems: Building bridges from Latin America to the Global South" by Hugo Kantis, Manuel Gonzalo, Juan Federico and Sabrina Ibarra Garcia, provides an example of bridging the (eco)systems literature from the Latin American perspective. After summarizing the IS and the EE debate including the contribution by Latin American scholars, the authors explore how the two frameworks converge and diverge when applied in a less developed setting. They find that very specific business and social structures, limited access to finance, as well as weak demand conditions and institutions are important elements that need to be taken into consideration in order to understand Latin American (eco) systems. Another important element is the significant role that the government and policy (which are absent from the Schumpeterian view of innovation and entrepreneurship) tend to play in the efforts to promote innovation and entrepreneurship in Latin America. The (eco)systemic thinking in the region was strongly influenced by various local schools of thought and institutions, which provide a solid basis for adapting the EE and IS concepts for local applications. The other parts of the Global South seem to still lack such a thorough foundation for the reconceptualization of the (eco)systems approaches to the local conditions.

As highlighted by many chapters in this book, the EE and IS dynamics work at different levels. This difference is among the major limits to the integration and bridging of the frameworks. This point is well illustrated by the last chapter of the first part of the book, "The role of diaspora in entrepreneurial ecosystems and national innovation systems" by Veneta Andonova, Jonathan A. Perez-Lopez and Jana Schmutzler. In a particular case of the Balkan countries, a strong diaspora was instrumental in the development of a vibrant entrepreneurial community and the ecosystemic aspects surrounding and supporting it. However, the innovative performance of the region – especially that driven by larger, established firms – was not affected by the diaspora links. The careful explication of the processes that led to such divergent outcomes in the chapter highlights the potential of personal linkages among individuals to give rise to the systems-like entrepreneurial dynamics. For the systems-like innovative dynamics, at least in the classical sense of the national IS view, linkages among more institutionalized actors are more important. This observation also echoes the top-down versus bottom-up distinction between the EE and IS already stressed by the literature.

1.3 POLICY LESSONS FROM THE SYSTEMS PERSPECTIVES

Both the EE and IS frameworks have heavily influenced public policy agendas. Before policy applications of the (eco)systemic logic become the mainstream, however, we need a better understanding of the lessons from the current research and practice. More critical reflections (and more empirical and theoretical explorations) are needed to ensure that countries and regions relying on the IS and EE approaches to improve their economic fortunes do indeed move in the desired direction. Our cautiousness stems from several important limitations of the current debates and practice. These limitations include underdeveloped tools to assess and to measure the EE and (to a lesser extent) the IS; a lack of knowledge on the transferability of the (eco)systems approaches to the underdeveloped settings with weak institutions, lagging preconditions and very different cultures; and the overemphasis of the current "classical" systems concepts on patented innovation and high-growth firms, which are not necessarily the best correlates with wellbeing and can, in fact, be destructive.

In the past, industrial policy interventions – often based at least in part on some (eco)systemic logic – have been heavily criticized, as is the case, for example, of Porter's clusters. A lacking consent regarding the definition of clusters has led Martin and Sunley (2003) to affirm that "we know what they're called, but defining precisely what they are is much more difficult" (p.10). A lacking theoretical underpinning, the lack of clear boundaries and no clear measurement approach to clusters were further critiques. It seems that history repeats itself with the newly emerging frameworks of EE and IS. For example, there is no commonly agreed upon definition of what an EE is (Stam, 2015). Instead, there is a collection of different definitions (e.g. Malecki, 2018). And while this might not be the case for IS, both concepts have been criticized for being undertheorized, offering plenty of description but little analysis (Lorentzen, 2009; Edquist, 2010).

The vagueness was perhaps a reason for the wide proliferation of the (eco)systemic approaches across the world. The practical applications rarely involved a critical assessment of applicability in general or concerning specific elements of the applied concepts. The fact that the published and widely cited research is quite narrow geographically (e.g. Spigel, 2018; Texeira, 2013) only exacerbates the gap in our understanding of how the systems logic works in various contexts. As noted by Spigel (2018), the commonly accepted lists of ecosystem attributes are mainly based on case studies in an increasing number of regions of the United States (US) and Western Europe and, as such, are embedded in the Anglo-American economic and social systems.

This geographical myopia is dangerous; it implicitly assumes a well-functioning institutional context (Spigel, 2018), which for a developing or even a transition country is usually not the case (Tsvetkova, Schmutzler & Suarez, 2017). Research has shown that context matters both for innovation (Freeman, 2002; Tsvetkova, Schmutzler, Suarez & Faggian, 2017) and entrepreneurship (Welter, 2011). As such, it is not clear whether EE and IS in different contexts – peripheral regions in the Global North or regions in the Global South – have the same or similar attributes (Spigel & Harrison, 2018). Similarly, the insufficient variety of the case studies focused on systemic aspects of regional economic performance limits the design of appropriate tools to measure or develop public policies to foster systemic dynamics (Godin, 2009).

In terms of the (eco)systems' outcomes, the current research appears to be excessively focused on high-growth entrepreneurship and patenting. The EE are usually defined as those that generate high-growth entrepreneurship and, in fact, some scientific contributions have linked the success of an EE to unicorns[1] (Acs, Stam, Audretzch & O'Connor, 2017). Yet, where successful entrepreneurship is apparent, there must be a strong EE. The literature's focus on successful case studies might be misleading for public policy-makers, as it limits our insights into what triggers the emergence and what drives the development of an EE or an IS in regions with lagging preconditions (Mack and Mayer, 2016; Albuquerque, 2007). Additionally, not only have the recent cases of unicorns, such as WeWork, failed to fulfill expectations, they call into question this exaggerated focus on high growth (see also Shearmur, 2019). Empirically, the evidence is not as convincing either. Grillitsch and Nilsson (2017), for example, showed that there is "no evidence [...] that knowledge-intensive firms grow faster in knowledge-rich regions" (p.1228).

Similarly, the implicit assumption exists that innovation – often equated with R&D or patents – usually takes place in firms located in large, urban Northern agglomerations. Yet, the recent upsurge in frugal innovation (e.g. Bhatti, 2012; Weyrauch & Herstatt, 2017) or reverse innovation (von Zedtwitz, Corsi, Søberg & Frega, 2015) has shown that innovation – when understood in the Schumpeterian tradition as "creative destruction" – can be found in diverse settings, including the bottom-of-the-pyramid or the informal economy. These results uncover yet another bias inherent in innovation studies; with the over-emphasis on patents or product innovation, different kinds of innovations such as the organizational or process varieties remain undetected or understudied (Metcalfe & Ramlogan, 2008). In other words, "We often assume that these frontiers of science will benefit only the richer nations of the world [... But] in fact resource-poor settings can actually drive innovation, demanding ingenious product designs that are less expensive, and easier to use, and require less infrastructure. It is also easier to disrupt the technological status quo in the

absence of entrenched commercial interests organised around existing products" (Elias, 2006, p. 540). Along these lines, Shearmur (2017) emphasizes the
existing pro-urban bias regarding innovation and creativity. Generally, studies
on innovation and its geography seem to assume that innovation activities
occur – due to easier access to interactions and information exchange – primarily in cities. Yet, only because one does not observe something doesn't mean
that it does not exist; it may as well be caused by the data biased towards cities
(Shearmur, 2017). Governments and international organizations increasingly
realize this drawback of the innovation perception. The OECD Centre for
Entrepreneurship, SMEs, Regions and Cities is initiating a stream of work
on rural innovation. In 2015, the US Department of Agriculture's Rural
Establishment Innovation Survey was released.

Additionally, when considering the broad definition of an IS as opposed to
a narrow one, the scope of an IS analysis goes beyond R&D and science and
technology, taking into consideration cultural, geographical and historical
processes which account for differences in development trajectories and institutional evolution (Cassiolato & Lastres, 2008; Lundvall, Joseph, Chaminade
& Vang, 2011). Yet, the frameworks' insights into the factors which may break
down a certain lock-in in contexts with lagging preconditions is still limited,
lacking a clear guidance for testable propositions and policy recommendations
especially for the developing world (Lundvall, 2007b; Albuquerque, 2007;
Lorentzen, 2009).

As a result, there is a clear need for diverse contributions that explore the
relevance and applicability of the systemic concepts in a range of settings
with the goal of learning policy lessons. The second part of the book includes
several contributions with immediate policy implications.

Given the centrality of knowledge and learning to all systemic perspectives,
Part II starts with a thorough analysis of the role that universities play in supporting social entrepreneurship, particularly in the less developed contexts.
In their chapter "Beyond intellectual property and rich infrastructure: A community service learning perspective on universities' supportive role towards
social entrepreneurs", Abel Diaz Gonzalez, Nikolay A. Dentchev and Maria
del Carmen Roman Roig use the community service learning perspective
within the context of social entrepreneurship to demonstrate that universities
in less prosperous environments can support EE by leveraging the critical mass
of their students, faculty and staff members. They can be highly successful in
doing so even in the absence of a rich infrastructure or intellectual property.
The chapter is the result of a qualitative research in Bolivia. It puts together
an immediately useful list of 18 basic activities for students, faculty, staff
members and the community that promote social entrepreneurs in this country.

Chapter 6, "The entrepreneurial propensity of the Swedish national
innovation system: New challenges for policy-makers" by Jon Mikel

Zabala-Iturriagagoitia, zooms in on a more common topic within the (eco) systems literature, knowledge-intensive entrepreneurship. Using the example of Sweden, a country where very high investments in science and technology did not translate into a comparable surge in innovative entrepreneurship (the so-called Swedish paradox), the author studies the entrepreneurial propensity of IS. He argues for a holistic approach to knowledge-intensive entrepreneurship and emphasizes the importance of both the supply and demand conditions for this type of entrepreneurship to thrive. Public procurement of innovation is named as an efficient tool to ensure that the demand is sufficiently strong to drive growth in knowledge-intensive entrepreneurship.

The chapter by José Eduardo Cassiolato, Maria Gabriela v. B. Podcameni, Helena Maria Martins Lastres and Maria Cecília Junqueira Lustosa, "Territory, development and systemic innovation: A Southern perspective", moves away from learning and innovation and focuses on the industrial dimension instead. The chapter presents the Local Innovation and Production System (LIPS) framework specifically developed to adapt the systemic approaches of the Global North to Latin American conditions. As such, this chapter complements the theoretical considerations developed in Chapter 3.

LIPS is highly influential in the region and was a successful tool for regional revitalization in some parts of Brazil (Podcameni, Cassiolato, Lustosa, Marcelino & Rocha, 2019). The experience of developing the LIPS approach offers a prime example of how popular approaches that originated in the Global North can be modified for local applications elsewhere. Specifically, the LIPS adopts the broad notion of IS with an explicit focus on the territorial context, including society and nature, as crucial elements of innovation and local development and establishes a bridge between the micro, meso and macro levels and integrates social, economic and political dimensions as well as hierarchies and power elements. Such a comprehensive approach appears the most fitting for the realities of the less developed economies (Schmutzler, Suarez, Tsvetkova & Faggian, 2017).

The last chapter of Part II, "The complementarity approach to understanding entrepreneurship and innovation ecosystems taxonomy" by Maksim Belitski and Andrew Godley proposes a synergy framework for understanding (eco) systemic concepts by focusing on EE. The authors show how four components – entrepreneurial actors, resource providers, entrepreneurial networks and connectivity and entrepreneurial culture – complement each other in driving economic development through entrepreneurship. The power of this approach is in its universal applicability – the local assessments of the existing preconditions for the development of EE, for example, can rely on these components in both developed and underdeveloped contexts. Most importantly, however, the authors demonstrate that the components work in a synergy and in some cases can substitute for each other, which is of particular relevance for the territories that lack in resources and may have underdeveloped one or more components.

1.4 THE OVERLOOKED DIMENSIONS OF SYSTEMS PERSPECTIVES

The unintended consequences of the overfascination with high-growth entrepreneurship and patent-based innovation within the EE and IS literature can be the omission of a range of important topics and considerations from both the public policy and practice attention and the academic discourse.

For example, equating the idea of high growth with productive entrepreneurs might be unjustified. William Baumol (1990) differentiated the productive, the unproductive and the destructive entrepreneur. Particularly, he stated that "unproductive entrepreneurship takes many forms. Rent seeking, often via activities such as litigation and takeovers, and tax evasion and avoidance efforts seem now to constitute the prime threat to productive entrepreneurship" (p.915). The potential bias that stems from equating the high-growth entrepreneurship or patent-based innovation with success limits our understanding of where innovation and entrepreneurship take place, as aptly illustrated by Shearmur (2019). In fact, the accumulating evidence suggests that there are many other (often overlooked) sources of success in regional wellbeing. For example, even in the US, one of the most developed and growth-oriented economies, the net effects of self-employment on job creation is considerably larger than the effects of paid employment (Tsvetkova, Partridge & Betz, 2019). Likewise, also in the US, small and medium-sized cities are outperforming large urban areas in terms of population and employment growth (Partridge, 2010). This phenomenon of "large is not necessarily beautiful" applies perhaps even more outside of the Global North. In the developing countries, secondary cities and rural non-agricultural sectors offer better prospects for poverty reduction and inclusive growth (Christiaensen & Todo, 2013; Christiaensen, Weerdt & Todo, 2013). Despite this growing evidence, economic development policies and the academic debate are often driven by the considerations of the "traditional" measures of productivity and economic growth.

But the policy roles and goals, as well as the academic and policy practice discussion, can go beyond that (Fagerberg, 2017; Shearmur, 2019), as, for instance, in the case of the so-called mission-oriented policies with specific aims that target solutions for societal problems (Mowery, 2011). Additionally, against the backdrop of the Sustainable Development Goals, the need for a transition towards a more sustainable economic system is becoming more evident and urgent (Nill & Kemp, 2009). The limitation and bias generated through an excessive emphasis on high growth or patents as a way to measure the success of EE and IS become evident.

The omission of an array of important topics and dimensions from the (eco) systems-focused debates is prevalent both in the developed and the developing contexts. In the Global South, high-growth entrepreneurship and patenting are not meaningful indicators of economic performance. They are not meaningful goals either (Tsvetkova et al., 2019). More pressing challenges, such as informal entrepreneurship, inclusivity and broad-based and incremental innovations, are more relevant.

In the industrialized developed countries, in a similar vein, not enough attention is paid to inclusive entrepreneurship, the innovation-inclusiveness nexus and related topics. Research has acknowledged for some time already that both entrepreneurship and innovation are gendered (Minniti, 2009; Kirkup & Keller, 1992; Agnete Alsos, Ljunggren & Hytti, 2013; Thébaut, 2015). In fact, Morris, Neumeyer, Jang and Kuratko (2018) show that EE consist of different social clusters, which impose boundaries along various types of entrepreneurship potentially excluding minorities or women altogether or depriving them from necessary (institutional) support that the EE should be generating. While this point had been made earlier (Thébaut, 2015), and despite the attention paid to the issues of the missing entrepreneurs by international organizations (for example, OECD & EU, 2019), the efforts to remove barriers to entrepreneurship for underrepresented groups are still insufficient.

The omitted topics within the (eco)systems research are not limited to the focus of the inquiry. The complexities of the involved phenomena clearly call for a wider methodological variety. Not only quantitative but also qualitative approaches, particularly grounded in disciplines different from evolutionary economics or economic geography, can generate indispensable insights for the enhanced understanding of the ways EE and IS function and can be steered to generate greater welfare for all people.

Part III presents a few examples of work that expands the boundaries of the (eco)systemic literature by considering the main processes, such as entrepreneurship, from the unorthodox perspectives and by looking at the underexplored topics – at least in the "mainstream" research. Chapter 9, "Beyond entrepreneurial culture in the entrepreneurial ecosystems framework: Contributions from economic anthropology" by Maria Giulia Pezzi and Félix Modrego, is an example of the former. Drawing the attention of the reader to the fact that an EE cannot exist without entrepreneurial culture, the authors unpack this often overlooked dimension of an EE. Particularly in the case of high-growth entrepreneurship, which is often considered – for better or for worse – the cornerstone of EE at least in the developed countries, the societally accepted and encouraged cultural norms, such as risk taking, experimentation and innovation, are central to EE success. The chapter makes a case for an extended, anthropology-sensitive systemic approach to EE, which incorporates the view of entrepreneurship as a dynamic agency-based process of social change and is based on the view of culture as an enduring set of shared values and beliefs that molds a worldview welcoming entrepreneurial behavior.

The remainder of Part III sheds light on some of the overlooked topics. "Typifying latecomer social enterprises by ownership structure: Learning and building knowledge from innovation systems" by Jahan Ara Peerally and Claudia De Fuentes examines the performance of social enterprises in the emerging, less developed and developing so called latecomer economies. In particular, the authors explore how the ownership structure of the late-comer social entrepreneurs and their links to actors within and outside their IS determine their knowledge stock, technological capabilities and impacts on development. This chapter is a great example of cross-fertilization across research fields that feeds into a better comprehension of certain elements of the (eco)systemic dynamics, in this case, using a toolkit from the management disciplines.

Based on empirical observations of urban labor markets in Africa, the term informal economy was born (Portes & Haller, 2010). It is now widely accepted that the informal sector is not only a persistent phenomenon but also a growing one in many parts of the world. However, despite the recognition that informal innovations and informal entrepreneurship are a part of economic reality in many developing countries (Arocena & Sutz, 2000), little attention has been paid to these aspects in both the IS and EE literature. Chapter 11, "Entrepreneurial ecosystems as a mechanism to promote economic formality in emerging economies: The case of Bogota" by Andres Guerrero Alvarado and Vinciane Servantie contributes to filling this gap. The authors focus on the EE in Bogota, Colombia's capital. Using network analysis, the chapter offers practical insights into the ways EE can contribute to transforming informal entrepreneurship into a formal one, which is among the biggest challenges for Latin America. Specifically, the authors argue that an explicit focus of support institutions and actors during the later stages of the entrepreneurial process on opportunity-based entrepreneurship poses a great barrier to the process of transformation.

1.5   CONCLUDING REMARKS

The aim of this book is two-fold. On the one hand, we want to show how a conversation between the two intimately linked, yet (so far mostly) inde-pendently studied, frameworks of EE and IS can advance the field of economic development studies. The chapters in the first part of the book demonstrate that not only is such a conversation fruitful, but in many ways necessary. Both frameworks are rooted in systemic thinking and learn from the insights and critiques that often stem from and are targeted at the systemic character of the concepts. At the same time, the clear differences between the two frameworks (demonstrated by various chapters in this book) can complement and feed into each other. For example, the individual agency of entrepreneurs, which is at the core of the EE approach, may under certain circumstances substitute for the institutional void that hinders development of an IS.

On the other hand, we aim to diversify research that analyses and applies these two frameworks both in terms of geography and topics. We believe that the book offers abundant material for researchers to understand that stepping outside of the already well-studied prosperous contexts of the Global North enables a better understanding of what is able (or not) to trigger the emergence of a supportive environment for entrepreneurship and innovation. The book also calls upon practitioners and policy-makers working to build such environments to go beyond the often applied copy-and-paste approach and instead use the regional culture and institutional context as a starting point. Similarly, such a diversification allows for the inclusion of overlooked dimensions, such as the Sustainable Development Goals or the informal economy. We hope that this book offers new insights that will give way to new research and discussions that promote a better-informed dialogue on innovation and entrepreneurship.

NOTE

1.   Start-ups valued at more than 1 billion US dollars.

REFERENCES

Acs, Z. J., Autio, E., & Szerb, L. (2014). National systems of entrepreneurship: Measurement issues and policy implications. *Research Policy*, *43*(3), 476–94.

Acs, Z. J., Stam, E., Audretsch, D. B., & O'Connor, A. (2017). The lineages of the entrepreneurial ecosystem approach. *Small Business Economics*, *49*(1), 1–10.

Agnete Alsos, G., Ljunggren, E., & Hytti, U. (2013). Gender and innovation: State of the art and a research agenda. *International Journal of Gender and Entrepreneurship*, *5*(3), 236–56.

Albuquerque, E. D. M. E. (2007). Inadequacy of technology and innovation systems at the periphery. *Cambridge Journal of Economics*, *31*(5), 669–90.

Arocena, R., & Sutz, J. (2000). Looking at national systems of innovation from the South. *Industry and Innovation*, *7*(1), 55–75.

Asheim, B. T. (2012). The changing role of learning regions in the globalising knowledge economy: A theoretical re-examination. *Regional Studies*, *46*(8), 993–1004.

Asheim, B. T., Smith, H. L., & Oughton, C. (2011). Regional innovation systems: Theory, empirics and policy. *Regional Studies*, *45*(7), 875–91.

Autio, E., Kenney, M., Mustar, P., Siegel, D., & Wright, M. (2014). Entrepreneurial innovation: The importance of context. *Research Policy*, *43*(7), 1097–108.

Autio, E. & Levie, J. (2014). Hard facts or soft insights? Fact-based and participative approaches to entrepreneurship ecosystems policy and management. In: *Entrepreneurial Ecosystems, Innovation and Regional Competitiveness*, Henley Business School, University of Reading. https://strathprints.strath.ac.uk/58813/1/

Autio_Levie_2014_Hard_facts_or_soft_insights_fact_based_and_participative _approaches.pdf

Baumol, W. J. (1990). Entrepreneurship: Productive, unproductive, and destructive. *Journal of Political Economy*, *98*(5), 893–921.

Bhatti, Y. A. (2012). What is frugal, what is innovation? Towards a theory of frugal innovation. SSRN. http://dx.doi.org/10.2139/ssrn.2005910

Breschi, S., & Malerba, F. (1997). Sectoral innovation systems: Technological regimes, Schumpeterian dynamics, and spatial boundaries. In: C. Edquist (Ed.), *Systems of Innovation: Technologies, institutions and organisations* (pp. 130–56). London: Pinter.

Camagni, R. (1991). Local "milieu", uncertainty and innovation networks: Towards a new dynamic theory of economic space. In: *Innovation Networks: Spatial Perspectives* (pp. 121–44). London: Belhaven.

Carlsson, B., & Stankiewitz, R. (1991). On the nature, function and composition of technological systems. *Journal of Evolutionary Economics*, *1*, 93–118.

Cassiolato, J. E., & Lastres, H. M. (2008). *Discussing innovation and development: Converging points between the Latin American school and the innovation systems perspective?* Georgia Institute of Technology.

Castellacci, F., & Natera, J. M. (2013). The dynamics of national innovation systems: A panel cointegration analysis of the coevolution between innovative capability and absorptive capacity. *Research Policy*, *42*(3), 579–94.

Christiaensen, L., De Weerdt, J., & Todo, Y. (2013). *Urbanization and Poverty Reduction: The role of rural diversification and secondary towns*. Washington, DC: World Bank.

Christiaensen, L., & Todo, Y. (2013). *Poverty Reduction during the Rural-Urban Transformation: The role of the missing middle*. Washington, DC: World Bank.

Colombelli, A., Paolucci, E., & Ughetto, E. (2017). Hierarchical and relational governance and the life cycle of entrepreneurial ecosystems. *Small Business Economics*,1–17. https://doi.org/10.1007/s11187-017-9957-4

Cooke, P. (1998). Introduction: Origins of the concept. SSRN. https://ssrn.com/abstract =1497770

Doloreux, D. (2002). What we should know about regional systems of innovation. *Technology in Society, 24*, 243–63.

Doloreux, D., & Parto, S. (2005). Regional innovation systems: Current discourse and unresolved issues. *Technology in Society*, *27*, 133–53.

Edquist, C. (2005). Systems of innovation: Perspectives and challenges. In: J. Fagerberg, D. Mowery & R. Nelson (Eds), *Oxford Handbook of Innovation* (pp. 181–208). Oxford: Oxford University Press.

Edquist, C. (2010). Systems of innovation perspectives and challenges. *African Journal of Science, Technology, Innovation and Development*, *2*(3), 14–45.

Elias, C. J. (2006). Can we ensure health is within reach for everyone? *Lancet*, *368*, S40–S41.

Fagerberg, J. (2017). Innovation policy: Rationales, lessons and challenges. *Journal of Economic Surveys*, *31*(2), 497–512.

Feld, B. (2012). *Startup Communities: Building an entrepreneurial ecosystem in your city*. Chichester: John Wiley & Sons.

Fischer, M. (2001). Innovation, knowledge creation and systems of innovation. *Annals of Regional Science*, *35*, 199–216.

Freeman, C. (2002). Continental, national, and sub national innovation systems: Complementarity and economic growth. *Research Policy*, *31*, 191–211.

Freeman, C., & Soete, L. (1997). *The Economics of Industrial Innovation*. Cambridge, MA: MIT Press.

Godin, B. (2009). National innovation system: The system approach in historical perspective. *Science, Technology, and Human Values*, *34*(4), 476–501.

Grillitsch, M., & Nilsson, M. (2017). Firm performance in the periphery: On the relation between firm-internal knowledge and local knowledge spillovers. *Regional Studies*, *51*(8), 1219–31.

Isenberg, D. J. (2010). How to start an entrepreneurial revolution. *Harvard Business Review*, *88*(6), 40–50.

Kirkup, G., & Keller, L. S. (1992). *Inventing Women: Science, technology, and gender*. Cambridge: Polity Press.

Kreuzer, A., Mengede, K., Oppermann, A., & Regh, M. (2018). *Guide for Mapping the Entrepreneurial Ecosystem*. Bonn: Deutsche Gesellschaft für Internationale Zusammenarbeit.

Lorentzen, J. (2009). Learning by firms: The black box of South Africa's innovation system. *Science and Public Policy*, *36*(1), 33–45.

Lundvall, B.-Å. (1988). Innovation as an interactive process: From user-producer interaction to the national innovation systems. In: G. Dosi, C. Freeman, R. Nelson, G. Silverberg & L. Soete (Eds), *Technology and Economic Theory*. London: Pinter.

Lundvall, B.-Å. (1992). *National Innovation Systems: Towards a theory of innovation and interactive learning*. London: Pinter.

Lundvall, B.-Å. (2002). *Innovation, Growth and Social Cohesion: The Danish model*. Cheltenham, UK and Northampton, MA, USA: Edward Elgar Publishing.

Lundvall, B.-Å. (2003). National innovation systems: History and theory. In: H. Hanusch & A. Pyka (Eds), *Elgar Companion to Neo-Schumpeterian Economics* (pp. 872–81). Cheltenham, UK and Northampton, MA, USA: Edward Elgar Publishing.

Lundvall, B.-Å. (2007a). *Innovation System Research: Where it came from and where it might go*. Globelics Working Paper 2007-01.

Lundvall, B. Å. (2007b). National innovation systems: Analytical concept and development tool. *Industry and Innovation*, *14*(1), 95–119.

Lundvall, B.-Å., Johnson, B., Andersen, E. S., & Dalum, B. (2002). National systems of production, innovation and competence building. *Research Policy*, *31*, 213–31.

Lundvall, B. Å., Joseph, K. J., Chaminade, C., & Vang, J. (Eds) (2011). *Handbook of Innovation Systems and Developing Countries: Building domestic capabilities in a global setting*. Cheltenham, UK and Northampton, MA, USA: Edward Elgar Publishing.

Mack, E., & Mayer, H. (2016). The evolutionary dynamics of entrepreneurial ecosystems. *Urban Studies*, *53*(10), 2118–33.

Malecki, E. J. (2018). Entrepreneurship and entrepreneurial ecosystems. *Geography Compass*, *12*(3), e12359.

Malmberg, A., & Maskell, P. (1997). Towards an explanation of regional specialization and industry agglomeration. *European Planning Studies*, *5*(1), 25–41.

Marshall, A. (1920 [1890]). *Principles of Economics*. London: Macmillan & Co.

Martin, R., & Sunley, P. (2003). Deconstructing clusters: Chaotic concept or policy panacea? *Journal of Economic Geography*, *3*(1), 5–35.

Mason, C., & Brown, R. (2014). Entrepreneurial ecosystems and growth oriented entrepreneurship. Background paper prepared for the workshop organised by the OECD LEED Programme and the Dutch Ministry of Economic Affairs on Entrepreneurial Ecosystems and Growth Oriented Entrepreneurship, The Hague.

McCann, P., & Ortega-Argilés, R. (2013). Modern regional innovation policy. *Cambridge Journal of Regions, Economy and Society*, *6*(1),1–30.

Metcalfe, S., & Ramlogan, R. (2008). Innovation systems and the competitive process in developing economies. *Quarterly Review of Economics and Finance*, *48*(2), 433–46.

Minniti, M. (2009). Gender issues in entrepreneurship. *Foundations and Trends in Entrepreneurship*, *5*(7–8), 497–621.

Moore, T. (1963). Ecosystems. *American Biology Teacher*, *25*(4), 249–52. doi:10 .2307/4440335

Morris, M. H., Neumeyer, X., Jang, Y., & Kuratko, D. F. (2018). Distinguishing types of entrepreneurial ventures: An identity-based perspective. *Journal of Small Business Management*, *56*(3), 453–74.

Mowery, D. C. (2011). Federal policy and the development of semiconductors, computer hardware and computer software: A policy model for climate change R&D? In: R. M. Henderson and R. G. Newell (Eds), *Accelerating Energy Innovation: Insights from multiple sectors* (pp. 159–88). Chicago, IL: University of Chicago Press.

Nelson, R. (Ed.) (1993). *National Innovation Systems: A comparative analysis*. Oxford: Oxford University Press.

Nelson, R., & Rosenberg, N. (1993). Technical innovation and national systems. In: *National Innovation Systems: A comparative analysis*. Oxford: Oxford University Press.

Nill, J., & Kemp, R. (2009). Evolutionary approaches for sustainable innovation policies: From niche to paradigm? *Research Policy*, *38*(4), 668–80.

OECD (2014). *Job Creation and Local Economic Development*. Paris: OECD Publishing. https://doi.org/10.1787/9789264215009-en

OECD (2019). *Local Entrepreneurship Ecosystems and Emerging Industries: Case study of Malopolskie, Poland*. OECD Local Economic and Employment Development (LEED) Working Papers, No. 2019/03. Paris: OECD Publishing. https://doi.org/10.1787/d99ba985-en

OECD & European Union (2019). *The Missing Entrepreneurs 2019: Policies for inclusive entrepreneurship*. Paris: OECD Publishing. https://doi.org/10.1787/3ed84801 -en

Partridge, M. D. (2010). The duelling models: NEG vs amenity migration in explaining US engines of growth. *Papers in Regional Science*, *89*(3), 513–36.

Podcameni, M. G., Cassiolato, J. E., Lustosa, M. C., Marcelino, I., & Rocha, P. (2019). Exploring the convergence between sustainability and local innovation systems from a Southern perspective: What Brazilian empirical evidence has to offer. *Local Economy*, *34*(8), 825–37.

Porter, M. E. (2000). Location, competition, and economic development: Local clusters in a global economy. *Economic Development Quarterly*, *14*(1), 15–34.

Portes, A., & Haller, W. (2010). The informal economy. In: N. Smelser & R. Swedberg (Eds), *The Handbook of Economic Sociology*. Princeton, NJ: Princeton University Press.

Pugh, R. (2014). *Regional Innovation Policy and Economic Development: The case of Wales*. Doctoral dissertation, Cardiff University.

Schmutzler, J., Suarez, M., Tsvetkova, A., & Faggian, A. (2017). Introduction: A context-specific two-way approach to the study of innovation systems in developing and transition countries. In: A. Tsvetkova, J. Schmutzler, M. Suarez & A. Faggian (Eds), *Innovation in Developing and Transition Countries*. Cheltenham, UK and Northampton, MA, USA: Edward Elgar Publishing.

Schumpeter, J. (2003 [1911]). *Theorie der wirtschaftlichen Entwicklung*. In: *Joseph Alois Schumpeter* (pp. 5–59). Boston, MA: Springer.

Scotland Can Do (2018). Scottish Entrepreneurial Ecosystem Guide. http://cando.scot/wp-content/uploads/2019/02/V3-Scottish-Entrepreneurial-Ecosystem-Guide-Feb-2019.pdf

Shearmur, R. (2017). Urban bias in innovation studies. In: H. Bathelt, P. Cohendet, S. Henn & L. Simon (Eds), *The Elgar Companion to Innovation and Knowledge Creation* (pp. 440–56). Cheltenham, UK and Northampton, MA, USA: Edward Elgar Publishing.

Shearmur, R. (2019). Why we should stop conflating cities with innovation and creativity. www.citylab.com/perspective/2019/12/smart-city-innovation-clusters-rural-creativity-research/602626/

Spigel, B. (2017). The relational organization of entrepreneurial ecosystems. *Entrepreneurship Theory and Practice*, *41*(1), 49–72.

Spigel, B. (2018). Envisioning a new research agenda for entrepreneurial ecosystems: Top-down and bottom-up approaches. In: J. A. Katz & A. Corbett, A. (Eds), *Reflections and Extensions on Key Papers of the First Twenty-Five Years of Advances* (pp. 127–47). Emerald Publishing.

Spigel, B., & Harrison, R. (2018). Toward a process theory of entrepreneurial ecosystems. *Strategic Entrepreneurship Journal*, *12*(1), 151–68.

Stam, E. (2015). Entrepreneurial ecosystems and regional policy: A sympathetic critique. *European Planning Studies*, *23*(9), 1759–69.

Stam, E., & Spigel, B. (2017). Entrepreneurial ecosystems. In: R. Blackburn, D. de Clercq & J. Heinonen (Eds), *The SAGE Handbook of Small Business and Entrepreneurship*. London: SAGE.

Teixeira, A. A. (2014). Evolution, roots and influence of the literature on national systems of innovation: A bibliometric account. *Cambridge Journal of Economics*, *38*(1), 181–214.

Thébaud, S. (2015). Status beliefs and the spirit of capitalism: Accounting for gender biases in entrepreneurship and innovation. *Social Forces*, *94*(1), 61–86.

Tsvetkova, A., Partridge, M., & Betz, M. (2019). Self-employment effects on regional growth: A bigger bang for a buck? *Small Business Economics*, *52*(1), 27–45.

Tsvetkova, A., Pugh, R., & Schmutzler, J. (2019). Beyond global hubs: Broadening application of systems approaches. *Local Economy*, *34*(8), 755–66.

Tsvetkova, A., Schmutzler, J., & Suarez, M. (2017). Epilogue: Innovation systems in developing and transition countries: What is different, what is missing and what are the implications? In: A. Tsvetkova, J. Schmutzler, M. Suarez & A. Faggian (Eds), *Innovation in Developing and Transition Countries* (pp. 236–44). Cheltenham, UK and Northampton, MA, USA: Edward Elgar Publishing.

Tsvetkova, A., Schmutzler, J., Suarez, M., & Faggian, A. (Eds) (2017). *Innovation in Developing and Transition Countries*. Cheltenham, UK and Northampton, MA, USA: Edward Elgar Publishing.

Uriona-Maldonado, M., dos Santos, R. N., & Varvakis, G. (2012). State of the art on the systems of innovation research: A bibliometrics study up to 2009. *Scientometrics*, *91*(3), 977–96.

von Zedtwitz, M., Corsi, S., Søberg, P. V., & Frega, R. (2015). A typology of reverse innovation. *Journal of Product Innovation Management*, *32*(1), 12–28.

Welter, F. (2011). Contextualizing entrepreneurship: Conceptual challenges and ways forward. *Entrepreneurship Theory and Practice*, *35*(1), 165–84.

Weyrauch, T., & Herstatt, C. (2017). What is frugal innovation? Three defining criteria. *Journal of Frugal Innovation, 2*(1), 1.

World Bank (2010). *Innovation Policy: A guide for developing countries.* Washington, DC: World Bank.

World Bank (2018). *Tech Startup Ecosystem in West Bank and Gaza: Findings and recommendations.* Washington, DC: World Bank.

PART I

The promise and the limits of bridging the
entrepreneurial ecosystems and innovation
systems approaches

2. Bridging the literature on innovation systems and entrepreneurial ecosystems: Cross-fertilizations for understanding knowledge-intensive, social and environmental entrepreneurship

Renata Lèbre La Rovere, Marcelo Gerson Pessoa de Matos, Guilherme de Oliveira Santos and Antonio Pedro da Costa e Silva Lima

2.1 INTRODUCTION

Since the 1980s the literature on the innovation systems (IS) and the literature on entrepreneurial ecosystems (EE) seem to take separate and parallel paths. The literature on IS explains how several actors interact on capacity building and innovation and how institutions contribute to this process (Freeman, 1987; Lundvall, 1992; Nelson, 1993). This literature focuses on the firm as a unit of analysis and aims to challenge the mainstream literature in economics that states that technical progress depends on resources of the firm only. As it assumes bounded rationality of agents, decisions on innovation are seen as the result of interactions among the elements of the IS.

In contrast with the literature on IS, the literature on entrepreneurship focuses on the entrepreneur as the unit of analysis. As observed by Casson (2003), the entrepreneur is the agent who is capable to assess opportunities, to use the resources of a firm in a different way and, therefore, enhance the firm's conditions of competitiveness. Following Casson's argument, several authors evaluate entrepreneurship by analyzing individual or organizational capabilities to recognize opportunities and to create new businesses. Most of these studies assume that the entrepreneur is a rational agent that maximizes gains obtained through allocation of resources, in line with the assumptions of the neoclassical economic theory.

However, as observed by Hwang and Powell (2005), it is necessary to take into consideration the institutional environment of the entrepreneurs, as individuals and interest groups seek to mold this environment to obtain gains. These authors discuss "how shifts in the institutional environment create opportunities for individuals and organizations to seize upon recombined tools or constructs to subvert existing ways and bring about new forms of organizing" (Hwang & Powell, 2005, p. 180). The growth of professional knowledge, the establishment of new standards and the creation of laws concerning applications of this knowledge are examples of institutional changes that create new opportunities. Hwang and Powell (2005) also observe that the establishment of standards depends frequently on the social and political capacities of organizations that wish to impose the standard; and social movements can create institutional changes as well.

If institutions affect both individuals and organizations, we should expect that those effects would be treated by the IS literature (Nelson, 2007; Bosma, Content, Sanders & Stam, 2018). However, as the firm is the unit of analysis in this literature, it considers individual action only when related to learning processes of the firm (Nooteboom, 2009). Addressing this issue led authors to work with the concept of EE, defined as a set of actors, institutions, social structures and cultural values that produce entrepreneurial activity (Isenberg, 2010; Mason & Brown, 2014; Stam, 2015; Roundy, 2016). There is a gap in the literature as IS and EE frameworks have developed separately. Nevertheless, we believe that there are synergies between them, especially concerning the analysis of emerging forms of entrepreneurship.

This chapter has two main objectives. First, we analyze the main similarities and differences between the EE and the IS approaches in respect to three critical dimensions of each literature: the individual, the firm/organization and the institutional context (Lundvall, 2007; Hodgson, 2009; Cassiolato, Matos & Lastres, 2014; Sotarauta, 2016). Next, we highlight three types of entrepreneurship, knowledge-intensive entrepreneurship (KIE) (Malerba & McKelvey, 2018); social entrepreneurship (Rahdari, Sepasi & Moradi, 2016; Puri, Tavoletti & Cerruti, 2013) and green entrepreneurship (Demirel, Li, Rentocchini & Pawan Tamvada, 2017), whose analysis can be enriched by integrating the EE and IS approaches.

To assess current discussions, we did a search in international scientific databases that include 45,000 international journals, considering only peer-reviewed journals. These databases are available at Periódicos CAPES, a Brazilian government-funded database that includes major scientific databases such as EBSCO, JSTOR, SCIELO and Web of Science. We considered papers published in the period 2014–18 and searched for the following keywords:

"innovation systems"; "entrepreneurial ecosystems"; "knowledge-intensive entrepreneurship"; "social entrepreneurship" and "green entrepreneurship".

This chapter is structured as follows. We start with a review of the IS and the EE literature. Next, we explore similarities and differences of the two theories in respect to the three dimensions (the individual, the firm/organization and the institutional context). In the fourth section we briefly present the three types of entrepreneurship mentioned above and discuss the contributions of the EE and the IS approaches to the analysis of each of them. The fifth section presents conclusions and suggestions for future research.

2.2   INNOVATION SYSTEMS AND ENTREPRENEURIAL ECOSYSTEMS

2.2.1   The Innovation Systems Literature

Different approaches in the micro- and the meso-level economics build upon the following main building blocks: the main actors and their logic and pattern of interaction; the nature of the economic agent; and the environmental conditions under which economic agents act. The IS literature incorporates many converging perspectives. But in broad terms, we can identify that it builds upon specific strands of research in respect to these three dimensions.

First, in respect to the logic and the patterns of interaction we find Schumpeter's basic insight, inspired by Marx and other classical economists, that innovation is the main driver of capitalist change (Schumpeter, 1934). The concept of creative destruction summarizes the phenomenon through which new structures (firms, markets and institutions) replace other structures as a part of the dynamic change of capitalism (Schumpeter, 1942).

In terms of who is the protagonist of innovation, we find Schumpeter's early references to the pioneering role of the entrepreneur, who brings innovations to the market and creates new firms (Schumpeter, 1934). As observed by Lundvall (2007), Schumpeter's entrepreneurs are activists who bring new combinations of resources to the market but how they do this is not explained. In *Capitalism, Socialism and Democracy* (Schumpeter, 1942) the big enterprise comes in with its capacity to mobilize scattered resources and to invest in uncertain long-run search initiatives (especially formal research and development (R&D)). Rather than establishing oppositions of the Schumpeter Mark I and II types, which are rather fallacious (Langlois, 1998), we might interpret these contributions as two parts of the same complex puzzle.

The second main building block comprises an understanding of the nature of the economic agent. The evolutionary theory in general – and, by extension, the IS framework – breaks up with the neoclassical foundations such as substantive rationality and perfect information. Evolutionary theorizing adopts a perspective of bounded rationality (Simon, 1996). The implications for the firm are well explored by Edith Penrose (1959) and others who contributed to a view of the firm based on a specific set of resources and competences. Nelson and Winter (1982) show how knowledge is located in the memory of organizations and how they mobilize it through routines, constituting relatively efficient patterns of action in an uncertain environment. This stresses the central importance of cumulative learning processes for expanding and reshaping the critical knowledge set of organizations.

This view is at the basis of the concept of dynamic capabilities (Teece & Pisano, 1994), which highlights the continuously changing environmental conditions and the challenges that this poses for the firm to mobilize, to combine and reshape resources and competences for adapting and efficiently exploring opportunities (Teece, Pisano & Shuen, 1997). The mobilization of these capabilities gives the firm an essentially entrepreneurial touch as it manages to mold opportunities and perceive threats; make use of opportunities; and strengthen a competitive edge through enhancement, combination, protection and eventually reconfiguration of business assets (Teece, 2014; Zollo & Winter, 2002).

As shown by Lundvall and Johnson (1994) and Lundvall (2000), the learning process for building these new competences is of an essentially social and interactive nature. Through different types of channels and mobilizing different networks, firms constantly mobilize other firms and individuals, universities, research institutes, researchers, etc. for screening and connecting to complementary technological and managerial competences, sharing costs and risks of innovation and utilizing critical business assets.

Not by chance, the early formulations of the IS framework come accompanied by the term "national" (Freeman, 1982, 1995; Lundvall, 1988, 1992; Nelson, 1993). Learning and innovation are strongly influenced by the institutional context that is very specific from country to country. Thus, the third main building block for the IS framework is strongly influenced by institutionalists and by many scholars whose contributions can be associated with a structuralist perspective (Johnson, 1992; Hodgson, 1993; Edquist & Johnson, 1997; Cassiolato & Lastres, 2008). But more than just formal legal and regulatory structures, the IS framework specifically refers to informal institutions. Important contributions within the IS literature have shown the importance of the regional and local context, given local institutional (formal and informal institutions), social, cultural and environmental specificities, as well as the central relevance of tacit knowledge transmission through face-to-face interaction (Cassiolato et al., 2014).

In sum, the IS approach puts emphasis on historical processes that account for differences in socio-economic capabilities and different development trajectories (Freeman, 1987, 1999; Cassiolato & Lastres, 2008). But the IS framework does not equate an institutional context to a static environment. Rather, it recognizes that economic structures co-evolve with and reshape existing institutions. This co-evolution is shaped by history and the social, political and cultural dimensions that are specific to each reality (Nelson, 1994; Saviotti & Pyka, 2012).

2.2.2 The Entrepreneurial Ecosystems Literature

Although authors who study entrepreneurship have emphasized the importance of context to entrepreneurial action since the 1980s, the EE approach has become popular among scholars and policymakers since 2010 (Borissenko & Boschma, 2016; Spigel & Harrison, 2017; Yun, Cooke & Park, 2017; Neumeyer & Santos, 2018; O'Connor, Stam, Sussan & Audretsch, 2018). The term "entrepreneurial ecosystems" is indeed increasingly popular.[1] Recently, authors from different academic fields such as entrepreneurship studies, economic geography and urban economics have contributed to this literature as they analyzed the importance of context to entrepreneurship promotion (Welter, 2011; Zahra, Wright & Abdelgawad, 2014). Also, there is a growing perception among authors that not all types of entrepreneurship are important for economic growth (Stam, 2015), and there is a growing interest in the role of the entrepreneur in urban and regional economies (Acs & Armington, 2004; Feldman, 2001; Glaeser, Rosenthal & Strange, 2010). This body of research led to the emergence of the EE approach, whose objective is to understand how urban and regional contexts affect ambitious entrepreneurship (Stam & Spigel, 2016).

Acs, Stam, Audretsch and O'Connor (2017) suggest that the EE approach has its roots in two different bodies of literature: regional development and strategic management. The former emphasizes the role of agglomeration economies, their dynamics and the economic benefits that they provide, specifically studies on industrial districts (Saxenian, 1994), clusters (Porter, 1990), regional IS (Cooke, Gomez Uranga & Etxebarria, 1997) and local buzz (Bathelt, Malmberg & Maskell, 2004). The latter comprises entrepreneurship studies that went through a shift in focus in the 1980s and 1990s, from individual and personal traits of entrepreneurs to the role of economic, cultural and social forces in the entrepreneurship process (Dodd & Anderson, 2007).

This shift is inserted in a wider movement that has replaced the vision of the Schumpeterian hero-entrepreneur with a vision of entrepreneurship as an embedded social process (Steyaert & Katz, 2004). In this context, Van de Ven (1993), Bahrami and Evans (1995) and others developed the concept of entrepreneurial environment or ecosystem with the goal to explain the influence of regional, social and economic elements on the entrepreneurial process. This new perspective underlines how economic, political, social and cultural structures influence all dimensions of the entrepreneurial process. To sum up, context matters. Reckoning that context matters led authors to introduce the prefix "Eco" in the discussion of entrepreneurial systems (Xu & Maas, 2019).

Despite the recent rise in popularity, which was initiated by the studies of Feld (2012) and Isenberg (2010), a definition of the EE that is widely accepted among academics and practitioners still does not exist. Isenberg (2010, p. 3) describes an EE as "a set of individual elements – such as leadership, culture, capital markets, and open-minded customers – that combine in complex ways". Mason and Brown (2014, p. 5) suggest that an EE is a "set of interconnected entrepreneurial actors, entrepreneurial organizations, institutions and entrepreneurial processes whose interactions build a local entrepreneurial environment". Complementarily, Spigel (2015, p. 2) argues that an EE is a result of the "combinations of social, political, economic, and cultural elements within a region that support the development and growth of innovative startups and encourage nascent entrepreneurs and other actors to take the risks of starting, funding, and otherwise assisting high-risk ventures".

Roundy (2016, p. 233) defines an EE as a "set of actors, institutions, social structures and cultural values that produce entrepreneurial activity". Isenberg (2011) extends the definition by identifying six different domains within an EE: a favorable culture, support policies, appropriate availability of credit, qualified human capital, open markets and support institutions. These domains link what he calls a set of networked institutions to support entrepreneurs, and in his view the entrepreneur is both the focus of action and the measure of progress.

Stam and Spigel (2016) propose that the elements of an EE should be divided in two categories: framework conditions and systemic conditions. Framework conditions include social conditions (formal and informal institutions) and physical conditions that stimulate and restrain human interactions. Systemic conditions are elements whose interaction is crucial to the success of the ecosystem, such as entrepreneur networks, leadership, financing, talent, knowledge and support services. Acs et al. (2017) endorse Stam and Spigel's (2016, p. 3) definition of EE, which is "a set of interdependent actors and factors coordinated in such a way that they enable productive entrepreneurship within a particular territory".

These different definitions all have in common the focus on social structures and connections among the participants of the ecosystems (Roundy, 2016). They also have in common the elements considered critical to the ecosystem that are: "a supportive culture, (venture) capital, active networks of entrepreneurs, local government officials and investors, the presence of universities and support services" (Neumeyer & Santos, 2018, p. 457).

Multidirectional causality and high interactivity are the main features of an EE (Stam, 2015). Successful ecosystems provoke not only growth of entrepreneurial activity: they create feedbacks that make possible for other entrepreneurs to be successful by the valorization of success through personal networks or social norms. Social networks, published cases of success as well as university programs that promote entrepreneurial activities may stimulate entrepreneurship directly by influencing aspirations, or indirectly by reinforcing social norms focused on the valorization of financial success. The more profitable entrepreneurship is, the more resources will be allocated to it. EE normally appear in places with specific assets and non-tradable interdependencies as defined by Storper (1997), therefore some regions are more prone to entrepreneurship than others.

2.3 SIMILARITIES AND DIFFERENCES BETWEEN INNOVATION SYSTEMS AND ENTREPRENEURIAL ECOSYSTEMS APPROACHES

The IS approach is more established in the literature.[2] In contrast, the EE approach is more recent and as such still suffers from many inconsistencies. The EE approach has attracted criticism as its systemic definition leads to lack of clarity on which elements of an EE are more important to promote entrepreneurship, on what type of entrepreneurs EE analysis is considering (high-growth versus startups in general), how an EE evolves, what is the role of institutions in this process and how promoting EE can foster regional development as the concept itself lacks demarcation (Audretsch, Cunningham, Kuratko, Lehmann & Menter, 2018; Borissenko & Boschma, 2016; Daniel et al., 2018; Mack & Mayer, 2015; Stam, 2015). As the EE analysis identifies the elements that enhance entrepreneurship but fails to explain how interactions between these elements account for specific characteristics of a given EE, many EE papers tend to have a static approach (Alvedalen & Boschma, 2017). As observed by O'Connor et al. (2018, p. 1): "defining the entrepreneurial ecosystem remains difficult and the methods used to analyze them are inconsistent".

Daniel et al. (2018, p. 35) addressed these criticisms by analyzing a set of papers that were presented in a symposium on EE. They found consistencies in a variety of issues as well as tensions. Consistencies relate to the fact that there are several possible ways to create, sustain and analyze an EE. By this same reason, there are also tensions "in considering the multiple academic perspectives, temporal dynamics, nebulous boundaries, and definitional variance across levels of analysis and nomenclature".

The EE literature differs from the IS literature because it focuses its analysis on entrepreneurs and entrepreneurial activity and not on the firm. Overall, the EE approach is strongly based on the entrepreneur and startups analysis and does not consider larger and established firms nor low-growth small and medium-sized enterprises. It also gives far greater emphasis to the knowledge on entrepreneurial processes such as understanding of the challenges to entrepreneurs while they develop their businesses; how to devise business plans and pitches to angel investors and venture capitalists; and how to overcome a lack of experience to deal with clients and suppliers. This understanding of the useful knowledge is in contrast to the IS approach, which considers knowledge as technical know-how to develop new technologies, products and new markets.

2.3.1 The Individual Dimension

The EE approach reckons that entrepreneurs are part of a system and, as such, they will be affected by the characteristics of the system, but it also takes into consideration the individual capabilities of the entrepreneurs. Although it is not clear whether individual capabilities are intrinsic to the individual or emerge within the system, this literature focuses on entrepreneurial agency and human-made context (O'Connor et al., 2018).

In contrast, scholars of the IS approach consider the individual dimension when focusing on learning (Foray & Lundvall, 1996) and on cognitive distance (Nooteboom, 2009). They do not account for capabilities intrinsic to the individual. As stated in the previous section, the IS is rooted in a resource-based perspective of the firm, which stresses that firms are made up of a complex mix of individuals, their knowledge and skills. In this sense, individual learning is of critical importance, but the central dimension of capability is at the firm level.

2.3.2 The Firm Dimension

Within the EE perspective, the entrepreneurial ventures are drivers of economic growth (Fuerlinger, Fandl & Funke, 2015). By focusing on interactions, EE scholars consider networks among firms and institutions (Daniel et al., 2018); however, how networks are treated in this literature varies depending on the author (Alvedalen & Boschma, 2017). Firms considered by the EE approach are innovative firms and startups; those firms frequently are spin-offs of a larger firm or benefit from knowledge spillovers. The motivations of firms are not just pursuing profits: the enterprise has not only individual but social motivations as well (Yun et al., 2017).

In contrast, the IS literature considers all types of firms. This difference may derive from the aim or ambition of the two frameworks. While the EE approach seems to focus on a subset of actors and factors that are relevant for the overall economic dynamic, the IS framework emerges from the attempts of evolutionary scholars to provide a holistic explanation for the long-run economic dynamics of nations (and regions, localities, sectors, etc.). Innovative firms and startups are among the relevant actors and some studies explore their specific role as a part of a larger system (Jansma, Gosselt & Jong, 2018; Sharif, 2003; Edquist & Johnson, 1997). The firm is the main unit of analysis once it is seen as the main driver of innovation. In practical terms, the subsystem of production and innovation (Cassiolato & Lastres, 2008) – which is at the core of the IS approach – is made up by firms, together with other organizational forms of the production processes.

2.3.3 Institutional Context and the Role of the State

A common element of the EE and the IS approaches is the focus on context. Both approaches assume the existence of external (to the individuals and firms) forces capable of enhancing innovation and competitiveness within the boundaries of a particular region (Stam & Spigel, 2016). More specifically, the IS literature and the EE literature have in common the systemic perspective. As observed by Simon (1996), a system is not restricted to the sum of its parts because it also includes their interactions. However, these approaches differ when it comes to a more detailed examination of the relevant environmental conditions and, specifically, the relevant institutions and the ways they influence and are influenced by economic dynamics.

Although Isenberg (2011) lists institutions as one of the domains within an EE, how institutions evolve together with other domains of a given EE is an issue to be addressed. The work of Fuentelsaz, Maícas and Mata (2018) is a first step towards this issue, as they not only identify which institutions are important for an EE (as previous EE papers have done) but also state that "the role of institutions within an entrepreneurial ecosystem is contingent on what stage of the business life cycle the venture is in" (Fuentelsaz et al., 2018, p. 46). In the view of these authors, the formal institutions within an EE include institutions related to the creation of new ideas, innovations and innovative projects, such as nurseries, incubators, accelerators, coworking centers and networking areas. They also include financial institutions such as angel investors, venture capital and private equity funds, crowdfunding, private banks and government-owned financial institutions; support agencies such as universities, development agencies, technological parks, clusters, R&D centers, technological and professional associations, industry and trade chambers; and other institutions that provide entrepreneurship infrastructure such as local government agencies. Informal institutions include human resources, culture, informal networks and talent base. The importance of these institutions varies depending on whether a firm is at an intentional, conceptual, seed, startup, growth or maturity stage. For instance, during the startup phase, clusters and technological parks are more relevant than universities, which are essential, in contrast, for the intentional and conceptual phases.

It is important to stress the distinct use of the concept of institutions within the two literatures we are focusing on. Even if no clear difference can be identified, the EE literature tends to stress the role of formal organizations. On the other side, as mentioned above, the bulk of the IS literature gravitates around an understanding of institutions as "the rules of the game", giving equal weight to the set of formal (laws, regulations, etc.) and informal (social codes, cultural patterns, etc.) norms and rules (Johnson, 1992). The IS literature has been inspired by "old" institutionalists, enhancing the importance of historical and political contexts that explain how conventions are established and how these conventions influence decisions of the firms.

In fact, both systemic approaches fit within a broad definition of institutions as "systems of established and prevalent social rules that structure social interactions" (Hodgson, 2006, p. 2). Institutions structure and shape social interactions. But, in practical terms, both for analytical and for normative purposes it is important to be clear if one is talking about organizations with coordination and support functions or about immaterial rules, norms and codes.

Some authors claim that the EE focus is not limited to institutions as organizations. It also encompasses immaterial elements as systemic conditions: human resources, culture, informal networks and talent base (Fuentelsaz et al., 2018). But these immaterial elements hardly fit into the broad definition of institutions as "established and prevalent social rules". On the other hand, although the work based on the IS framework considers these factors relevant, they are rather understood as a part of organizations' capabilities, which together translate into specific features of a given IS.

The nuances in the understanding of institutions and their roles as contextual determinants lead to specificities in terms of the role of the state. In the EE framework, the external environment and the institutional set-up function as the background conditions that ideally should unleash individual creativity and initiative. Free initiative under conducive market forces does the bulk of the job. This consequence leads to a diminished role of the state that is seen more as a feeder of the ecosystem than as a leader (Feld, 2012).

This is also partially true for the IS literature. To a great extent, normative implications deriving from the IS framework have a somewhat soft touch and relate to an enabling environment. However, this literature also recognizes the complexity of knowledge bases and the high uncertainty that is inherent to innovation. Investments in basic research with uncertain potential for practical use, the high-risk, high-cost and long-term innovative efforts hardly result from individual initiative of economic actors. And these elements are even more pressing in periods of transition of techno-economic paradigms (Freeman & Perez, 1988; Pérez, 2010). This puts the state in a more com-

Table 2.1   *Main similarities and differences between IS and EE approaches*

	Entrepreneurial ecosystems	Innovation systems
Main unit of analysis	Entrepreneur (individual level) – focus on individual agency and on the human-made context	Organization (firm level) – focus on dynamic capabilities of firms as the main determinants of capitalist change
Institutional context	Both approaches use a systemic perspective, emphasize the importance of the institutional context and highlight the external forces that influence economic actors	
	EE gives more emphasis to formal institutions	IS presents a balanced perspective between formal institutions (laws, regulations) and informal institutions (social codes, cultural patterns) and puts more emphasis on historical trajectories and political context
Role of state	Has a marginal role as feeder of the ecosystem that helps to set the best structure of incentives	Has a complementary but also active role, taking a leading role in the context of high-risk activities and major technological change

Source: Own elaboration.

plementary and active role. Furthermore, if a historical account of countries' development trajectories is considered, the IS literature points to a rather active leading role of the state, taking up major risks, facing and helping to overcome strategic, political and institutional hurdles and orienting individual initiatives towards specific strategic objectives (Freeman, 1987; Nelson, 1993; Reinart, 1996; Lundvall & Borrás, 1997; Mazzucato, 2011). Table 2.1 summarizes the main similarities and differences between (the) two approaches.

Given the differences mentioned above, we may ask whether it is worthwhile to bridge the two approaches for public policy purposes. Xu and Maas (2019) extract from the IS and EE literatures a list of common principles on how to build a sound ecosystem. These principles are: listen to local needs, as each context is unique; a long-term vision, as ecosystems take time to develop; work collectively, involving public and private sectors; act responsively, that is, take into account the fact that ecosystems evolve over time; and share motivational stories to give confidence to stakeholders. Therefore, in their vision, the state may act both as feeder of the ecosystem and as a stakeholder of the efforts in building an ecosystem.

Combining the insights from the two literatures not only leads to more focused innovation and entrepreneurship policies but also helps to understand some types of entrepreneurship, as is demonstrated in the next section.

2.4   CONCEPTS THAT REQUIRE AN INTEGRATION OF THE INNOVATION SYSTEMS AND THE ENTREPRENEURIAL ECOSYSTEMS APPROACHES

In our literature review, we identified three concepts that fit well in the proposition of considering both the IS approach and the EE approach: knowledge-intensive entrepreneurship, social entrepreneurship and green entrepreneurship. In general, while the concept of knowledge-intensive entrepreneurship and green entrepreneurship seem to derive from the IS literature, the concept of social entrepreneurship seems more adherent to the EE approach. Nevertheless, we try to show that the analysis of these concepts based only on one of these literatures provides an incomplete picture.

2.4.1   Knowledge-Intensive Entrepreneurship

According to Malerba and McKelvey (2018, p. 6), "knowledge-intensive innovative entrepreneurial firms are new learning organizations that use and transform existing knowledge and generate new knowledge in order to innovate within innovation systems". Regarding the individual dimension, the Schumpeterian theory allows us to analyze conditions under which an entrepreneur acts, as well as the role of entrepreneurship in the transformation of the economy. The entrepreneur is, thus, defined as a risk-taking individual who disruptively acts through exploration and exploitation of scientific and technological opportunities. However, entrepreneurs do not act in an isolated manner; instead, they interact with a range of other actors inside specific institutional contexts. In this sense, organizations and institutions not only mold cognition and action of entrepreneurs but also affect their interactions with other actors. Knowledge-intensive entrepreneurship is also influenced by national, sectoral and regional systems of innovation, through national policies, regulations, institutions and specific sectoral characteristics acting within knowledge networks (Malerba & McKelvey, 2018).

Although the KIE concept focuses mainly on the innovative firm and its interactions with the actors of the IS in general, the role of the entrepreneur cannot be neglected. Individual agency becomes important as this entrepreneur must have the ability to exploit scientific and technological opportunities.

2.4.2   Social Entrepreneurship

The concept of social entrepreneurship is recent and open to different interpretations, even if it deals with "old" social issues like poverty, pollution and corruption. Crisan and Borza (2012, p. 107) define social entrepreneurship as "the way of using resources to create benefits for the society" and the social entrepreneur as "the person who seeks to benefit society through innovation and risk taking". Rahdari et al. (2016, p. 350), consider social entrepreneurship as "a process of creating value by combining resources, which are intended initially to explore opportunities to create social value by stimulating social change, in new ways".

This concept enhances the individual level as it defines entrepreneurs as individuals who are concerned about society, future generations and with disadvantaged communities (Rahdari et al., 2016), acting frequently to fulfill institutional voids (Puri et al., 2013). In the same line, Germak and Robinson (2014) observe five reasons that mold social entrepreneurship in the early stages: personal fulfilment, helping society, non-monetary focus, achievement orientation and closeness to social problems. On the firm level, social enterprises are the result of social innovation. These enterprises use their profits to expand their social impact, "deal with social needs and try to gratify them directly through their products and services rather than indirectly through corporate philanthropy or enlightened self-interest" (Rahdari et al., 2016). Finally, social entrepreneurship deals with a great complexity resulting from the interaction of formal and informal institutions at different levels (local, national and sometimes even global); therefore, it requires collaboration among entrepreneurs, social organizations and governments.

With regards to social entrepreneurship, the role of the entrepreneur is prominent, as it has clear personal motivations and often finds opportunities in institutional gaps, i.e. in contexts where formal institutions are absent or do not fully meet the needs of society. On the other hand, the analysis of this type of entrepreneurship can benefit from the IS approach by considering the influence of informal institutions, as well as the historical and political context of the country or region in the construction of opportunities and in incentives and barriers for social entrepreneurs.

2.4.3   Green Entrepreneurship

Green entrepreneurship is the most recent type of entrepreneurship proposed by the literature, which has gained prominence based on the perception that the new techno-economic paradigm is based on a green economy (Mazzucato, 2015). Firms that are born green are those that offer innovative products and services whose aim is to solve environmental issues while reducing pollution.

At the individual level, green entrepreneurs exploit opportunities that are inherent to relevant market failures concerning the environment. However, green entrepreneurship has to deal with a paradox because the increase in welfare produced by born-green firms is a public good and as such it is not

Table 2.2   Possibilities of convergence

Type of entrepreneurship	Convergence potential between innovation systems and entrepreneurship ecosystem approaches
Knowledge-intensive entrepreneurship	To incorporate the role of individual agency (entrepreneurial) in the analysis of the creation and evolution of knowledge-intensive firms
Social entrepreneurship	To consider the influence of informal institutions and the historical and political contexts in the construction of opportunities, incentives and obstacles to the performance of social entrepreneurs
Green entrepreneurship	To deepen the analysis of the performance of green entrepreneurs in the perception of opportunities and their relation with established rules and institutions

Source: Own elaboration.

excludable (Demirel et al., 2017). This limits the competitive advantage of born-green firms when compared with non-green firms. At the firm level, most born-green firms emerge as small and medium-sized enterprises founded by individual entrepreneurs or as spin-offs (academic or not). These enterprises take relatively more time to achieve economic viability and sustainability, as green technologies are still not mature. O'Neil and Ucbasaran (2016) remark that the process of legitimizing the green organizational identity passes through the expectations of a diverse set of actors, in addition to the beliefs of the entrepreneur herself. Being environmentally friendly is crucial to green firms, as they must present value to stakeholders such as investors (Demirel et al., 2017). Understanding the institutional structure is, therefore, crucial in order to analyze what drives green entrepreneurship (O'Neil & Ucbasaran, 2016). At the institutional level, governments may have an important role through regulatory pressures, inducing firms to be environmentally friendly and financing green technologies that are not mature enough to be developed by private firms (Mazzucato, 2015). External knowledge and collaboration among different stakeholders – green firms, industries, governments, universities and non-governmental organizations – are important assets of green firms, as green technologies are frequently complex and interdisciplinary.

Green entrepreneurship, which is still incipient, demands an active role from the state to develop. In addition, because the issues of climate change and environment are global and span many disciplines, this type of entrepreneurship needs to establish networks on various scales – both formal and informal. Nevertheless, the role of the born-green entrepreneur is still poorly understood. In the context of a shift in the techno-economic paradigm towards a green economy, the entrepreneur's roles are of great relevance, as they are able to foresee opportunities and, in some cases, act in opposition to established rules and institutions. Table 2.2 summarizes possibilities of convergence of both literatures in the analysis of the three types of entrepreneurship.

2.5 CONCLUSIONS AND SUGGESTIONS FOR FUTURE RESEARCH

This chapter aims to understand similarities and differences between the IS literature and the EE approach. While those bodies of research may be seen as complementary, there are challenges to bridge them related to the inconsistencies reported in Section 2.2 and differences found in the conceptualization of institutions.

The similarities and differences mentioned in Section 2.3 are important to understand why the recent literature on entrepreneurship sometimes seems to be based on the IS literature and sometimes seems to be based on the EE approach. However, each individual approach may be insufficient to analyze the various types of entrepreneurship in depth.

A second aim of this chapter is to discuss whether bridging the two approaches helps to improve the understanding of the interactions between entrepreneurs (individuals) and context (institutions) in the analysis of knowledge-intensive entrepreneurship, social entrepreneurship and green entrepreneurship. In Section 2.4 we briefly discuss this issue and conclude that bridging the two approaches is a promising field for future research, especially when discussing these types of entrepreneurship.

A common characteristic of both approaches relates to the risk of benchmarking rationales. Some authors from the EE framework implicitly or explicitly suggest that there might be some sort of ideal set-up of environmental conditions and suggest principles to build ecosystems (Xu & Maas, 2019). A similar perspective can be found in the "system failure" approaches. However, the recognition that countries have historically determined specificities and the impossibility to replicate institutional set-ups or to replicate development experiences is leading the IS literature to increasingly dismiss benchmark efforts and catch-up discourses (Dutrénit & Sutz, 2014; Cassiolato et al., 2014; Mason & Brown, 2014).

Despite those differences, there is a potential convergence between the IS and the EE approaches that may be explored in future research. More generally, a combination of the two literatures can help in understanding the relationship between individual agency and the institutional context (Hodgson, 2009; Sotarauta, 2016). Specifically, a combination of the two literatures can help in discussing challenges and opportunities related to the definition of public policies to support innovation and entrepreneurship.

NOTES

1.   In our search, out of 7,093 titles with the keywords "entrepreneurial ecosystems", 4,079 have been published in peer-reviewed journals since the 1970s. Out of these 4,079, 2,098 (51 percent) were published between 2014 and 2018. Therefore it seems that interest in EE is growing.
2.   Our search in peer-reviewed journals with the keywords "innovation systems" found 585,165 papers published; of those, 237,720 (40.6 percent) were published between 2014 and 2018.

REFERENCES

Acs, Z. J., & Armington, C. (2004). The impact of geographic differences in human capital on service firm formation rates. *Journal of Urban Economics*, *56*(2), 244–78.
Acs, Z. J., Stam, E., Audretsch, D. B., & O'Connor, A. (2017). The lineages of the entrepreneurial ecosystem approach. *Small Business Economics*, *49*, 1–10.
Alvedalen, J., & Boschma, R. (2017). A critical review of entrepreneurial ecosystems research: Towards a future research agenda. *European Planning Studies*, *25*(6), 887–903.
Audretsch, D. B., Cunningham, J. A., Kuratko, D. F., Lehmann, E. E., & Menter, M. (2018). Entrepreneurial ecosystems: Economic, technological, and societal impacts. *Journal of Technology Transfe*r, *44*(4), 1–13.
Bahrami, H., & Evans, S. (1995). Flexible re-cycling and high-technology entrepreneurship. *California Management Review*, *37*, 62–89.
Bathelt, H., Malmberg, A., & Maskell, P. (2004). Clusters and knowledge, local buzz, global pipelines and the process of knowledge creation. *Progress in Human Geography*, *28*(1), 31–56.
Borissenko, Y., & Boschma, R. (2016). A critical review of entrepreneurial ecosystems research: Towards a future research agenda. *Paper in Evolutionary Economic Geography*, *16*(30), 1–20.
Bosma, N., Content, J., Sanders, M., & Stam, E. (2018). Institutions, entrepreneurship, and economic growth in Europe. *Small Business Economics*, *51*(2), 483–99.
Cassiolato, J. E., & Lastres, H. M. M. (2008). *Discussing Innovation and Development: Converging points between the Latin American school and the innovation systems perspective?* Globelics Working Papers Series, Working Paper No. 08-02. https://smartech.gatech.edu/bitstream/handle/1853/44144/GA2008%20Lecture%2017.pdf?sequence=1&isAllowed=y
Cassiolato, J. E., Matos, M. P., & Lastres, H. M. M. (2014). Innovation systems and development. In: B. Currie-Alder, R. Kanbur, D. M. Malone & R. Medhora (Eds), *International Development Ideas, Experience, and Prospects* (pp. 566–81). Oxford: Oxford University Press.
Casson, M. (2003). *The Entrepreneur: An economic theory*. Cheltenham, UK and Northampton, MA, USA: Edward Elgar Publishing.
Cooke, P., Gomez Uranga, M., & Etxebarria, G. (1997). Regional innovation systems: Institutional and organizational dimensions. *Research Policy*, *26*, 475–91.
Crisan, C. M., & Borza, A. (2012). Social entrepreneurship and corporate social responsibilities. *International Business Research*, *5*(2), 106–13.
Daniel, L., Christopher, J., Medlin, C. J., O'Connor, A., Statsenko, L., Vnuk, R., & Hancock, G. (2018). Deconstructing the entrepreneurial ecosystem concept.

In: S. O'Connor, E. Stam, F. Sussan & D. B. Audretsch (Eds), *Entrepreneurial Ecosystems: Place-based transformations and transitions.* doi:10.1007/978-3-319 -63531-6

Demirel, P., Li, Q. C., Rentocchini, F., & Pawan Tamvada, J. (2017). Born to be green: New insights into the economics and management of green entrepreneurship. *Small Business Economics*, *52*(4), 1–13.

Dodd, S. D., & Anderson, A. R. (2007). Mumpsimus and the mything of the individualistic entrepreneur. *International Small Business Journal, 25*(4), 341–60.

Dutrénit, G., & Sutz, J. (2014). *National Innovation Systems, Social Inclusion and Development: The Latin American experience.* Cheltenham, UK and Northampton, MA, USA: Edward Elgar Publishing.

Edquist, C., & Johnson, B. (1997). Institutions and organizations in systems of innovation. In: C. Edquist (Ed.), *Systems of Innovation: Technologies, institutions and organizations* (pp. 165–87). London: Routledge.

Feld, B. (2012). *Startup Communities: Building an entrepreneurial ecosystem in your city.* Hoboken, NJ: Wiley.

Feldman, M. P. (2001). The entrepreneurial event revisited: Firm formation in a regional context. *Industrial and Corporate Change*, *10*(4), 861–91.

Foray, D., & Lundvall, B. A. (1996). The knowledge-based economy: From the economics of knowledge to the learning economy. In: OECD, *Employment and Growth in the Knowledge-Based Economy.* Paris: OECD Publishing.

Freeman, C. (1982). *Technological Infrastructure and International Competitiveness.* Draft paper submitted to the OECD ad hoc group on science, technology and competitiveness. http://mail.redesist.ie.ufrj.br/globelics/pdfs/GLOBELICS_0079 _Freeman.pdf

Freeman, C. (1987). *Technology Policy and Economic Performance: Lessons from Japan.* London: Pinter.

Freeman, C. (1995). The "national system of innovation" in historical perspective. *Cambridge Journal of Economics*, *19*(1), 5–24.

Freeman, C., & Perez, C. (1988). Structural crisis of adjustment, business cycles and investment behaviour. In: G. Dosi, C. Freeman, R. Nelson, G. Silverberg & L. Soete (Eds), *Technical Change and Economic Theory* (pp. 38–66). London: Pinter.

Fuentelsaz, L., Maícas, J. P., & Mata, P. (2018). Institutional dynamism in entrepreneurial ecosystems. In: S. O'Connor, E. Stam, F. Sussan & D. B. Audretsch (Eds), *Entrepreneurial Ecosystems: Place-based transformations and transitions* (pp. 23–44). New York: Springer.

Fuerlinger, G., Fandl, U., & Funke, T. (2015). The role of the state in the entrepreneurship ecosystem: Insights from Germany. *Triple Helix*, *2*(3), 1–26.

Germak, A. J., & Robinson, J. (2014). Exploring the motivation of nascent social entrepreneurs. *Journal of Social Entrepreneurship*, *5*(1), 5–21.

Glaeser, E. L., Rosenthal, S. S., & Strange, W. C. (2010). Urban economics and entrepreneurship. *Journal of Urban Economics*, *67*(1), 1–14.

Hodgson, G. M. (1993). *Economics and Evolution: Bringing life back into economics.* Ann Arbor, MI: University of Michigan Press.

Hodgson, G. M. (2006). What are institutions? *Journal of Economic Issues*, *40*(1), 1–25.

Hodgson, G. M. (2009). Agency, institutions and Darwinism in evolutionary economic geography. *Economic Geography*, *85*(2), 167–73.

Hwang, H., & Powell, W. W. (2005). Institutions and entrepreneurship. In: S. Alvarez, R. Agarwal & O. Sorenson (Eds), *Handbook of Entrepreneurship Research: Disciplinary perspectives* (pp. 201–32). New York: Springer.

Isenberg, D. J. (2010). The big idea: How to start an entrepreneurial revolution. *Harvard Business Review*, *88*(6), 41–50.

Jansma, S. R., Gosselt, J. F., & Jong, M. (2018). Technological start-ups in the innovation system: An actor-oriented perspective. *Technology Analysis and Strategic Management*, *30*(3), 282–94.

Johnson, B. (1992). Institutional learning. In: B.-Å. Lundvall (Ed.), *National Innovation Systems: Towards a theory of innovation and interactive learning*. London: Pinter.

Langlois, R. N. (1998). Schumpeter and personal capitalism. In: G. Eliasson & C. Green (Eds), *Microfoundations of Economic Growth: A Schumpeterian perspective* (pp. 57–82). Ann Arbor, MI: University of Michigan Press.

Lundvall, B.-Å. (1988). Innovation as an interactive process: From user-producer interaction to the national innovation systems. In: G. Dosi, C. Freeman, R. Nelson, G. Silverberg & L. Soete (Eds), *Technology and Economic Theory*. London: Pinter.

Lundvall, B.-Å. (1992). *National Systems of Innovation: Towards a theory of innovation and interactive learning*. London: Pinter.

Lundvall, B.-Å. (2000). Introduction. In: C. Edquist & M. McKelvey (Eds), *Systems of Innovation: Growth, competitiveness and employment*. Cheltenham, UK and Northampton, MA, USA: Edward Elgar Publishing.

Lundvall, B.-Å. (2007). *Innovation System Research: Where it came from and where it might go*. CAS Seminar, Oslo, December 4. www.redesist.ie.ufrj.br/ga2012/textos/Lundvall/Lecture%201_Postscript%20final.pdf

Lundvall, B.-Å., & Borrás, S. (1997). *The Globalising Learning Economy: Implications for innovation policy*. Brussels: Commission of the European Union.

Lundvall, B.-Å., & Johnson, B. (1994). The learning economy. *Journal of Industry Studies*, *1*(2), 23–42.

Mack, E., & Mayer, H. (2015). The evolutionary dynamics of entrepreneurial ecosystems. *Urban Studies*, *53*(10), 2118–33.

Malerba, F., & McKelvey, M. (2018). Knowledge-intensive innovative entrepreneurship integrating Schumpeter, evolutionary economics, and innovation systems. *Small Business Economics*, 1–20. doi: 10.1007/s11187-018-0060-2

Mason, C., & Brown, R. (2014). *Entrepreneurial Ecosystems and Growth-Oriented Entrepreneurship*. Background paper prepared for the workshop organised by the OECD LEED Programme and the Dutch Ministry of Economic Affairs on entrepreneurial ecosystems and growth oriented entrepreneurship. www.oecd.org/cfe/leed/Entrepreneurial-ecosystems.pdf

Mazzucato, M. (2011). *The Entrepreneurial State*. London: Demos.

Mazzucato, M. (2015). *The Green Entrepreneurial State*. Working Paper Series, SWPS 2015-28, SPRU, University of Sussex. https://papers.ssrn.com/sol3/papers.cfm?abstract_id=2744602

Nelson, R. R. (Ed.) (1993). *National Innovation Systems: A comparative analysis*. Oxford: Oxford University Press.

Nelson, R. R. (1994). The co-evolution of technology, industrial structure, and supporting institutions. *Industrial and Corporate Change*, *3*(1), 47–63.

Nelson, R. R. (2007). *Institutions, "Social Technologies", and Economic Progress*. Globelics Working Paper Series 2007-03. https://ideas.repec.org/p/aal/glowps/2007-03.html

Nelson, R., & Winter, S. (1982). *An Evolutionary Theory of Economic Change.* Cambridge, MA: Belknap Press.

Neumeyer, X., & Santos, S. C. (2018). Sustainable business models, venture typologies, and entrepreneurial ecosystems: A social network perspective. *Journal of Cleaner Production, 170*(20), 4565–79.

Nooteboom, B. (2009). *A Cognitive Theory of the Firm: Learning, governance and dynamic capabilities.* Cheltenham, UK and Northampton, MA, USA: Edward Elgar Publishing.

O'Connor, S., Stam, E., Sussan, F., & Audretsch, D. B. (2018). Entrepreneurial ecosystems: The foundations of place-based renewal. In: S. O'Connor, E. Stam, F. Sussan & D. B. Audretsch (Eds), *Entrepreneurial Ecosystems: Place-based transformations and transitions* (pp. 1–21). New York: Springer.

O'Neil, I., & Ucbasaran, D. (2016). Balancing "what matters to me" with "what matters to them": Exploring the legitimation process of environmental entrepreneurs. *Journal of Business Venturing, 31*(2), 133–52.

Penrose, E. T. (1959). *The Theory of the Growth of the Firm.* New York: John Wiley.

Pérez, C. (2010). Technological revolutions and techno-economic paradigms. *Cambridge Journal of Economics, 34*(1), 185–202.

Porter, M. E. (1990). *The Competitive Advantage of Nations.* London: Macmillan.

Puri, M., Tavoletti, E., & Cerruti, C. (2013). Business model innovation in emerging economies: Leveraging institutional voids. In: R. L. La Rovere, M. Ozorio & L. J. Melo (Eds), *Entrepreneurship in BRICS: Policy and research to support entrepreneurs.* Heildeberg: Springer International.

Rahdari, A., Sepasi, S., & Moradi, M. (2016). Achieving sustainability through Schumpeterian social entrepreneurship: The role of social enterprises. *Journal of Cleaner Production, 137*(20), 347–60.

Reinart, E. S. (1996). The role of technology in the creation of rich and poor nations: Underdevelopment in a Schumpeterian system. In: H. D. Aldcroft & R. E. Catterall (Eds), *Rich Nations and Poor Nations: The long-run perspective.* Cheltenham, UK and Northampton, MA, USA: Edward Elgar Publishing.

Roundy, P. T. (2016). Start-up community narratives: The discursive construction of entrepreneurial ecosystems. *Journal of Entrepreneurship, 25*(2), 232–48.

Saviotti, P., & Pyka, A. (2012). On the co-evolution of innovation and demand: Some policy implications. In: J. Gaffard & M. Napoletano (Eds), *Agent-Based Models and Economic Policy* (pp. 347–88). Paris: OFCE.

Saxenian, A. (1994). *Regional Advantage: Culture and Competition in Silicon Valley and Route 128.* Cambridge, MA: Harvard University Press.

Schumpeter, J. A. (1934). *Theory of Economic Development.* Cambridge, MA: Harvard University Press.

Schumpeter, J. A. (1942). *Capitalism, Socialism, and Democracy.* New York: Harper and Brothers.

Sharif, N. (2003). The role of firms in national system of innovation (NSI) framework: Examples from Hong Kong. *Innovation: Management, Policy and Practice, 5*(2), 189–99.

Simon, H. (1996). *The Sciences of the Artificial.* Boston, MA: MIT Press.

Sotarauta, M. (2016). An actor-centric bottom-up view of institutions: Combinatorial knowledge dynamics through the eyes of institutional entrepreneurs and institutional navigators. *Environment and Planning C: Government and Policy, 35*(4), 584–99.

Spigel, B. (2015). The relational organization of entrepreneurial ecosystems. *Entrepreneurship Theory and Practice, 41*(1), 1–23.

Spigel, B., & Harrison, R. (2017). Toward a process theory of entrepreneurial ecosystems. *Strategic Entrepreneurship Journal*, *12*(1), 151–68.

Stam, E. (2015). Entrepreneurial ecosystems and regional policy: A sympathetic critique. *European Planning Studies*, *23*(9), 1759–69.

Stam, E., & Spigel, B. (2016). *Entrepreneurial Ecosystems*. Utrecht University: School of Economics, Discussion Paper Series 16-13.

Steyaert, C., & Katz, J. (2004). Reclaiming the space of entrepreneurship in society: Geographical, discursive and social dimensions. *Entrepreneurship and Regional Development*, *16*(3), 179–96.

Storper, M. (1997). Regional economies as relational assets. In: R. Lee & J. Wills (Eds), *Geographies of Economies*. New York: Arnold.

Teece, D. J. (2014). A dynamic capabilities-based entrepreneurial theory of the multinational enterprise. *Journal of International Business Studies*, *45*(1), 8–37.

Teece, D. J., & Pisano, G. (1994). The dynamic capabilities of firms: An introduction. *Industrial and Corporate Change*, *3*(3), 537–56.

Teece, D. J., Pisano, G., & Shuen, A. (1997). Dynamic capabilities and strategic management. *Strategic Management Journal*, *18*(7), 509–33.

Van de Ven, A. (1993). The development of an infrastructure for entrepreneurship. *Journal of Business Venturing*, *8*(3), 211–30.

Welter, F. (2011). Contextualizing entrepreneurship: Conceptual challenges and ways forward. *Entrepreneurship Theory and Practice*, *35*(1), 165–84.

Xu, Z., & Maas, G. (2019). Innovation and entrepreneurial ecosystems as important building blocks. In: G. Maas & P. Jones (Eds), *Transformational Entrepreneurship Practices* (pp. 15–32). London: Palgrave Pivot.

Yun, J. J., Cooke, P., & Park, J. Y. (2017). Evolution and variety in complex geographies and enterprise policies. *European Planning Studies*, *25*(5), 729–38.

Zahra, S. A., Wright, M., & Abdelgawad, S. G. (2014). Contextualization and the advancement of entrepreneurship research. *International Small Business Journal*, *32*(5), 479–500.

Zollo, M., & Winter, S. G. (2002). Deliberate learning and the evolution of dynamic capabilities. *Organization Science*, *13*(3), 339–51.

3. Entrepreneurial ecosystems meet innovation systems: Building bridges from Latin America to the Global South

Hugo Kantis, Manuel Gonzalo, Juan Federico and Sabrina Ibarra Garcia

3.1 INTRODUCTION

Entrepreneurial ecosystems (EE) and national systems of innovation (NSI) are central to the study of entrepreneurship and innovation from the geographical angle. Recent bibliometric analyses show that the number of NSI citations has boomed since 2000 (Jurowetzki et al., 2015) whereas that of the EE has increased since 2010 (Alvedalen & Boschma, 2017). Although both the EE and NSI can be considered as closely related concepts, so far, the attempts to bridge the two are scarce (Acs, Stam, Audretsch & O'Connor, 2017). The task of bridging the EE and NIS concepts involves recognizing their main commonalities and differences (Alvedalen & Boschma, 2017; Stam and Spigel, 2017) but also a discussion of their antecedents and evolution as well as the existing contextual differences between the Global North and the Global South.

The main objective of this chapter is to build a bridge between the EE and NSI within the context of the Latin American Countries (LAC). To achieve this, we review the main contributions to both fields from the scholars based in this region and make first steps towards a common research agenda considering the LAC realities. We address the following research questions: What are the origins, paths and main commonalities and differences between the EE and the NSI? What are the central contributions made by Latin American scholars to both fields? What are the most important issues in the research agenda that bridges the EE and the NSI perspectives in the Global South?

In the following section, we review the contextual origin and evolution of each concept and the main commonalities and differences between them.

Then, we discuss the Latin American contributions. Finally, we suggest common lines of research for the Global South.

3.2 THE ORIGIN AND EVOLUTION OF ENTREPRENEURIAL ECOSYSTEMS AND NATIONAL SYSTEMS OF INNOVATION: COMMONALITIES AND DIFFERENCES

3.2.1 The Entrepreneurial Ecosystems Concept

The role of entrepreneurship as a driver of innovation and economic growth lies at the heart of EE research. The diffusion of the EE concept, however, is more common among policy makers than among scholars who became particularly interested in it only recently (e.g. Brown & Mason, 2017; Alvedalen & Boschma, 2017; Spigel, 2017; Kantis, 2018; Stam & Van de Ven, 2018; Acs et al., 2017).

The rapid growth of the interest in the EE concept during the last few years, particularly among policy makers, is largely explained by the shared concern about the new stage of globalization characterized by the acceleration of technological change, the industrial revolution 4.0 and the economic stagnation of most Western countries. In particular, the EE concept gained its momentum after the publication of Isenberg's article in the *Harvard Business Review* "How to start an entrepreneurial revolution" where the ecosystem metaphor was introduced to denote "a set of individual elements that combine in complex ways" (Isenberg, 2010: p. 3).[1]

The roots of the systemic perspective on entrepreneurship, nevertheless, could be traced back to a set of antecedents such as the business ecosystem (Moore, 1993), Marshallian industrial districts (Piore & Sabel, 1984; Pyke, Becattini & Sengenberger, 1990), regional innovation systems (Cooke, 1996), the innovative milieu (Maillat, 1995) and the widely diffused cluster approach (Porter, 1998). All these concepts shared a systemic understanding of competitiveness, but entrepreneurship *per se* was not central to these contributions, except for very few pioneering studies (Saxenian, 1996; Bahrami & Evans, 1995).

Within the specific field of entrepreneurship, some authors have introduced a systemic approach to understand the emergence of new firms in terms of "infrastructure" (Van de Ven, 1993) or "environment" for entrepreneurship (Bruno and Tybjee, 1982). More recently, a number of contributions proposed a more developed systemic approach, which considers a broader set of dimensions and interactions (Kantis, Ishida & Moori Koenig, 2002; Kantis, Angelelli & Moori Koenig, 2004; Neck, Meyer, Cohen & Corbett, 2004; Cohen, 2006; Qian, Acs & Stough, 2013; Acs, Autio & Szerb, 2014).

As any novel concept, the EE approach lacks a deeper theory-based discussion and no widely accepted definition of the EE nature and scope was proposed so far (Stam & Spigel, 2017). We suggest the following synthetic definition based on the examination of the current EE literature: "the set of actors, factors, relationships and processes that act and interact shaping the conditions for the creation, development and expansion of firms in a specific geographical space" (Federico, Ibarra Garcia & Kantis, 2018, p. 11). According to this definition, different sets of variables are relevant to the EE approach. The EE actors are the central component. They include the entrepreneurs but also governments, incumbent companies (especially the larger ones), universities and research and development (R&D) institutions as well as a myriad of support organizations (incubators, accelerators, mentors, co-working spaces, etc.). The funding bodies relevant to EE, besides the governments and banks, are the venture capital funds, early-stage funds, business angels and crowd-funding platforms, among others. Finally, dealmakers, i.e. individuals who – by leveraging their experiences, positions and acquaintances – successfully connect people within the EE also play an important role.

Another set of variables includes contextual factors like the entrepreneurial culture, production factor and product markets as well as the general infrastructure and social capital (Audretsch & Belitski, 2017; Neck et al., 2004; Spigel, 2017). This set of variables is related to a range of processes such as business creation and business growth. Also important is the existence of spin-offs (Brown & Mason, 2017) and entrepreneurial recycling (Mason & Harrison, 2006), i.e. successful entrepreneurs that after a business exit decide to stay in EE playing a different role.

Summing up, EE is a rather new concept. Although there are some pioneering contributions that encompass a systemic perspective, the "eco" version of it emerged only in the last decade and has been growing in a highly fragmented way since then, given its diverse antecedents and user audiences.

3.2.2   The National Systems of Innovation Concept

NSI, as a conceptual device, is mainly rooted in two main conceptual antecedents: Serra's and List's works on the relevance of the domestic market and local knowledge for development, and Schumpeter's emphasis on innovation and economic change (Shariff, 2006; Freeman, 1995; Lundvall, 2010). The current version of NSI emerged as a conceptual category in the 1980s in the context of the Organisation for Economic Co-operation and Development expert group on science, technology and competitiveness. Freeman's work (1982) reintroduced List's ideas supporting a history- and context-specific approach to competitiveness, stressing the "non-price" factors of trade dynamics (Lundvall, 2015).

As explained by Lundvall (cited in Shariff, 2006), determining who was the first scholar who spoke of NSI is, to some extent, a "chicken-and-egg" exercise. Lundvall (1985) in his work on Danish user-producer relations and interactions used the "innovation systems" concept, while Freeman (1987), in his writings on Japanese institutional and policy set-up to support competitiveness used the NSI expression. The NSI approach received much attention, mainly because both academics and policy makers were trying to understand the extraordinary competitive performance of Japan. Subsequent publications by Lundvall (1992) and Nelson (1993) were among the first works on NSI.

In this context, the NSI approach emerged to bring an alternative understanding to the mainstream neoclassical treatment of technology, institutions and agent rationality. From then on, the two main perspectives on NSI have been adopted – the narrow one and the broad one (Lundvall, Chaminade & Vang, 2009; Cassiolato & Lastres, 2005). The narrow perspective mainly focuses on innovation, science and technology development, analyzing the relationships between science and technology actors and institutions with a special emphasis on R&D (Niosi, Saviotti, Bellon & Crow, 1993). The broad perspective criticizes the linear model of innovation, understanding innovation as a systemic, contextual and cumulative process (Cassiolato & Lastres, 2005). Lundvall et al. (2009, p. 6) define the broad concept of NSI as "an open, evolving and complex system that encompasses relationships within and between organizations, institutions and socio-economic structures which determine the rate and direction of innovation and competence-building emanating from processes of science-based and experience-based learning".

Lundvall (2010) points out that the differences across the historical experiences, languages and cultures are reflected in national idiosyncrasies. These differences permeate the production system and the institutional set-up, particularly the main elements of an NSI such as: a) the firms' internal organization; b) the interfirm relationships; c) the role of the public sector; d) the institutional set-up of the financial sector; and e) the R&D intensity and organization. Firms are at the center of the NSI structure because they are considered the organizations that lead the innovation process. Then, the main role of the public sector and of the institutional setting, including R&D organizations, is the creation and transfer of new knowledge to the productive sector. Furthermore, universities contribute to the preparation of new scholars and human resources. The financial sectors, both public and private, play a significant role in financing the new projects, ideas and innovations. In the broad understanding of NSI, this set of actors is influenced by the macroeconomic context, the international context and trade policy, the labor market conditions, different national and regional regulations and so on. The main aspects of an NSI are the interactions among all these elements, actors and conditions that constitute the main process and source of innovation.

NSI was developed by researchers but in the policy-making sphere. This hybrid origin allowed NSI to become a strong conceptual tool, but, at the same time, it led to the overutilization of the concept in some instances. In fact, since the 1990s, the NSI literature has been enriched with contributions stemming from different backgrounds, theoretical perspectives and focuses such as regional systems of innovation (Cooke, 1996), technological systems (Carlsson & Stanklewicz, 1991), sectoral systems (Breschi & Malerba, 1997), institutional learning (Edquist & Johnson, 1997) and their relationship with the competition process (Metcalfe & Ramlogan, 2008).

3.2.3 Commonalities and Differences between Entrepreneurial Ecosystems and National Systems of Innovation

The NSI approach has a longer and much more consolidated academic path which boomed in the 1990s, whereas EE is a much younger concept. Nevertheless, both approaches share important conceptual aspects: a) the issue of competitiveness, which was central in the NSI origin and in some EE antecedents; b) an emphasis on a contextualized and systemic view to grasp the processes under scrutiny; c) relevance to regional or territorial characteristics and influences; and d) an emphasis on the critical role of networks and interactions among the actors and contextual factors.

Even more, since the emergence of the neo-Schumpeterian approach, Winter (1984) emphasizes the relevance of new firms for the dynamism of technological regimes. More recently, Lundvall et al. (2009, p. 382) called upon the innovation systems researchers to develop an institutionally grounded theory of entrepreneurship, stating that "bringing in the perspective of 'collective entrepreneurship' might open up more fruitful directions for research". In this vein, several authors have pointed out the relevance of new firms as a vehicle for knowledge and technology transfer from universities, R&D labs and established firms (Acs, Audretsch & Lehmann, 2013). The knowledge-based firms (Quince & Whittaker, 2002) and academic entrepreneurship (Shane, 2004) are other relevant areas of common interest. Furthermore, in their recent study, Malerba and McKelvey (2018) recognize the relevance of knowledge-intensive entrepreneurship analyzing it by combining the Schumpeterian, evolutionary economics and innovation systems perspectives. Finally, the contemporary open-innovation trend focused on the interaction between the large and new firms is another potential area of convergence between both approaches (Chesbrough, Vanhaverbeke & West, 2006).

Nevertheless, there are also differences between the two. The first is related to the output. For the broad NSI approach, the main outputs are innovation and competence building, which are related to the science-based and experience-based learning processes. Meanwhile, for EE, the main outputs are new firm creation, their subsequent growth and the exploitation of new business opportunities by existing and new firms. Consequently, the role of the entrepreneur and the entrepreneurial process are the key within the EE approach, something that is not much present in the NSI literature. For NSI, the main actor is an established firm, but without an in-depth analysis of how these firms are created and what are the founders' characteristics in terms of knowledge and networks.

This lack of a "problematization" of the new firms' origins by the NSI field is also evident when referring to financing opportunities and support institutions. Although the current NSI approach tends to consider the seed and venture capital funds, the whole financial cycle is not explored in detail.[2] In contrast, in EE, entrepreneurial finance is crucial. Consequently, angels, accelerators, venture capital lenders and other sources of funding are thoroughly analyzed (Brown & Mason, 2017). In addition, the institutional setting of the support organizations and actors (e.g. incubators, mentors, company builders and co-working spaces) receives a broader attention in EE (Brown & Mason, 2017; Alvedalen & Boschma, 2017).

Furthermore, the key role of entrepreneurs and a more individual-led approach in EE make similar actors play different roles in NSI and EE. For instance, for NSI, universities are central to the generation of new knowledge and human capital; while for EE, universities are also central in the creation of entrepreneurial capabilities and culture (Mason & Brown, 2014). For NSI, the routines of the incumbent firms are the epicenter of the innovation process, but for EE, the incumbents are relevant mostly for the development of networks and tacit knowledge, which enable the emergence of new entrepreneurial ventures.

Also, there is a different focus regarding the type of networks and interactions analyzed by each approach. NSI focuses mainly on the relations among firms, organizations and institutions, whereas EE prioritizes the study of informal networks of the entrepreneurs and their personal contacts. Only the EE perspective considers the role of dealmakers. In a similar vein, the type of relevant tacit knowledge in the two approaches is different. NSI focuses on scientific and technological knowledge while EE, without ignoring technological knowledge, considers mainly the knowledge that helps in business creation (Stam & Van de Ven, 2018). Here, the role of mentors as carriers of such tacit experienced-based knowledge is crucial.

In sum, in this section we have identified the origins and paths of the literature on the two approaches. Our review shows strong commonalities between the EE and NSI concepts, despite some differences in terms of their sources, outputs, processes and the actors involved. This allows thinking in terms of building bridges between the two approaches. In the next section, we concentrate our attention on Latin American contributions to EE and NSI and identify the common features that enable us to connect the two.

3.3   LATIN AMERICAN CONTRIBUTIONS

3.3.1   The Systemic Approach to Entrepreneurship

Since the 1990s, researchers in the fields of innovation and small and medium-sized enterprises (SMEs) have focused on new firms with specific attention given to incubators, innovative entrepreneurs and venture capital. The main bodies engaged in this research were the American Association of Technological Management, the Red Pymes Mercado Común del Sur (MERCOSUR) and the Brazilian Association of Entrepreneurship and SME Management Studies.

The pioneering Latin American contributions to the systemic approach were made in the early 2000s within an initiative of the Inter-American Development Bank aimed at understanding the reasons for the success of East Asian SMEs compared to their Latin American counterparts. To address this research question, Prodem – a research team based at the National University of General Sarmiento, Argentina – initiated a long-term project that looked at the main differences between the entrepreneurial processes in the two regions (Kantis et al., 2002).[3] Later, the research expanded to include comparisons to Italy and Spain and the specific analyses of the knowledge-based versus manufacturing new ventures and the local versus metropolitan areas (Kantis et al., 2004; Kantis & Angelelli, 2006).

The Latin American reality called for a more contextualized approach than the one prevalent in the literature, although an evolution from the individualistic focus to a process-oriented and socially embedded perspective (e.g. Gartner, 1988) was an appropriate point of departure. The following two strategic definitions were adopted at the time: a focus on the dynamic entrepreneurship and the systemic approach.

The dynamic new firms were defined as those able to overcome the first years of the highest failure rates to become new, competitive and growth-oriented SMEs (Kantis et al., 2002). Despite the seeming similarities with the "gazelles", the concept is more related to the concern with competitiveness inherited from earlier studies on SMEs by the Economic Commission for Latin America and the Caribbean (ECLAC). The subsequent elaborations on the concept made it clear that the dynamism embraces a broader variety of growth trajectories (Kantis, Federico & Ibarra Garcia, 2016; Gonzalo, Federico & Kantis, 2014), including the case of technology-based firms (Kantis & Angelelli, 2006; Gonzalo, 2012).

The dynamic new firms often result from the interactions among different factors (social, economic, cultural, political and institutional) and actors (Kantis et al., 2004; Kantis & Angelelli, 2006), which points to the need of a systemic approach in order to understand their emergence and the trajectories. The need for a context-specific perspective made it necessary to understand how structural factors affect entrepreneurship. The previous debate about NSI in Latin America and ECLAC's ideas about structural heterogeneity were inspiring for the conceptual development where the emergence of new entrepreneurs was conceptualized as the product of a long-term competence development process. For instance, the social structure is central to understanding access to education opportunities and to job skills development. In the more fragmented societies, with a lower concentration of the middle class, the emergence of dynamic entrepreneurs is less likely compared to more developed contexts. The fragmentation is also linked to the prevalence of social capital barriers, which makes building networks more challenging.

The industry and business structures are also very important. The organizational profiles of incumbent firms affect the development of employees' skills, the emergence of corporate spinoffs and the generation of opportunities for new firms.

A third structural factor, which in fact is somewhat similar to the NIS approach, is the science, technology and innovation (STI) platforms comprised of R&D institutions and their linkages with existing firms. Particularly, the extent to which the actors and their innovation activities are conducive to the emergence of new technology-based startups is important (Kantis et al., 2004). The Latin American studies also highlighted the role of the institutional subsystems, i.e. public, private and other organizations fostering entrepreneurship, such as educational institutions and support organizations (incubators, business angel networks, venture capital funds and banks) (Kantis, 2003; Kantis & Angelelli, 2006).

The context-specific differences can also be found in the rest of the systemic factors. For instance, demand-side conditions are influenced by the social structure; risk aversion and power distance are affected by macroeconomic incentives and culture. Necessity is a more common motivation for entrepreneurs compared to innovation and growth. Finally, the depth of the financial markets, the existence of "smart capital" and the relative returns of long-term productive investments (versus short-term speculative ones) are lower in the Latin American context, which affects the supply of finance. As a result, Latin American contributions have shown that the dynamic entrepreneurship is less developed in the region compared to East Asian countries, calling for a systemic and integral approach to policy, which covers the different stages of the entrepreneurial process (Kantis et al., 2004). The role of government and public–private partnerships is also stressed.

All these contributions to the systemic perspective from Latin America, made by Prodem, preceded ideas about the ecosystem coming from the developed world and gave a conceptual platform for the elaboration of the Index of Systemic Conditions for Dynamic Entrepreneurship – a tool for diagnosis and policy design available for 60 countries, 36 of which are developing and emergent countries (Kantis, Federico & Ibarra Garcia, 2014, 2015, 2018). A systemic index at the city level was also developed, considering relevant issues such as the existence of the critical mass of key factors, actors and relations; and the openness and integration of the ecosystem (Kantis, Federico, Menendez & Ibarra Garcia, 2017).

In addition, in the last few years, a number of Latin American studies adopting a systemic approach have focused on various cities (Hernández & González, 2016; Álvarez, Ibarra García, Menéndez, Federico & Kantis, 2016; Cherubini Alvez, Fisher, Vonortas & Queiroz, 2018) or countries (Júnior et al., 2016). Furthermore, a recent contribution, which takes advantage of the recent discussions in the ecosystem literature, is one of the first efforts to conceptualize a dynamic model of the EE evolution, capturing the differences among the ecosystems in developed and developing contexts (Kantis, 2018).

Overall, the Latin American contributions to the field of entrepreneurship have brought a critical perspective to the already existing literature and have provided relevant concepts and tools that could be applied not only to research but also in the policy field in Latin America and in the broader context of the Global South.

There are also common aspects between the contributions of Latin American scholars to the EE and NIS discussion. The next section offers an overview of the latter.

3.3.2 Latin American Perspectives on National Systems of Innovation

The conceptual antecedents of the Latin American perspective on the field of NSI include Prebisch's pioneering contributions to the Latin American insertion of global capitalism (the so-called core-periphery scheme) and debates on science, technology and society, especially the contributions related to Sábato's triangle (state, the universities and the scientific sector and firms; 1979), Herrera's (1995) emphasis on the relevance and differences of implicit and explicit STI policies and national projects and Varsavsky's (1974) technological development styles.[4] The former was at the root of the discussions and implications in terms of the technical progress diffusion between the center and the periphery and ECLAC's subsequent line of research on structural heterogeneity, mainly promoted by Pinto (Prebisch, 1949; Pinto, 1970).

Freeman's historical approach to the NSI and STI policy debates around the Science Policy Research Unit at the University of Sussex have influenced Latin American scholars in the adoption of the NSI framework. For instance, Lastres' (1994) PhD thesis continued Freeman's line of research on Japan, focusing on the advanced materials revolution in Japanese systems of innovation. Clearly under the influence of Freeman's approach to innovation systems, Lastres and Cassiolato later set up the research group Rede de Pesquisa em Arranjos e Sistemas Produtivos e Inovativos Locais (Redesist) at the Universidade Federal de Rio de Janeiro, Brazil. In this context, a key event in this evolution was the Redesist Project financed by the Organization of American States "Globalization and local innovation: Experiences and S&T policy recommendations in the context of Local Systems in the MERCOSUR". During this project, several scholars from MERCOSUR presented their research framed by the innovation systems approach. For example, Chudnosky (1998) delivered the first version of a paper about Argentinean NSI; Yoguel was developing the innovation systems approach at the local level (Boscherini, Lopez & Yoguel, 1998), López and Lugones (1999) studied local innovation systems and globalization while Arocena and Sutz (1999) investigated the features of Uruguayan NSI. A number of contributions from Brazilian scholars linked to Redesist were a part of this project and Freeman (1999) contributed a paper.[5] Many of these scholars and their teams would later play a major role in discussions of NSI in the Red Latinoamericana para el estudio de los Sistemas de Aprendizaje, Innovación y Construcción de Competencias (Lalics) and the Global Network for Economics of Learning, Innovation and Competence Building Systems (Globelics) research communities.

Since the 2000s, the use of the NSI approach has increased and was redefined by Latin American scholars and policy-oriented institutions such as ECLAC, the International Development Bank and others. Several issues prominently featuring in the NSI discourse in developed countries were adapted to better reflect Latin American realities.

Latin American scholars took a broader view of NSI with explicit attempts to historically contextualize it. For instance, the colonial past, the naive techno-globalism of the Latin American elites, the institutional void, weak infrastructure, volatile growth paths, the relevance of geopolitical structures, brain drain, financial exposure and some other issues are innate to the Latin American context and influence the innovation process, actors and output (Lastres & Cassiolato, 2019; Cassiolato & Lastres, 2005; Cassiolato, 2008; Arocena & Sutz, 1999; Dutrénit & Sutz, 2013; Katz, 2007).[6]

Another feature is the presence of the deepening asymmetries related to technology diffusion and appropriation, income distribution, regional development and external insertion of Latin American NSI (Cassiolato, Lastres & Soares, 2014; Yoguel, Borello & Erbes, 2009). The subordinate inclusion in global value chains has been pointed out, including discussions on the role of transnational enterprises and conceptual problems with the "catch up" and "upgrading" frameworks (Szapiro, Vargas, Brito & Cassiolato, 2015; Lavarello et al., 2017; Soares, Hausmann Tavares, Gonzalo, Tomassini & Cassiolato, 2015).

In the last decade, several contributions have focused on the potential and limitations of Latin American natural resource-based NSI. Given the Latin American endowments and increasing trade in response to the growing demand for food and natural resources from Asian countries, the discussion on how natural resources are transformed in capability has gained prominence on the research agenda of NSI scholars. In parallel, a number of environmental risks and opportunities related to the biodiversity of the region have been discussed in relation to Latin American NSI (Arza, Marín, López & Stubrin, 2018; Katz, 2016; Cassiolato et al., 2014). For instance, Brazilian NSI can leverage the Amazonas biodiversity to develop phytotherapy production.

Given the weakness of Latin American institutions and market arrangements in the economy, several scholars emphasized the more important role of the state in Latin American NSI compared to developed countries. The state should be involved more broadly in financial support, public procurement policies and other mechanisms (Cassiolato & Lastres, 2005). Besides, in the last years, some scholars have started to adapt the framework of the entrepreneurial state (Mazzucato, 2013) to the Latin American context (Dutrénit & Sutz, 2013; Cassiolato & Gonzalo, 2015).

In general terms, Latin American scholars moved away from the narrow focus on R&D. This is driven in part by the relatively low expenditure on R&D in the LAC and by a weaker connection between R&D and innovation. A range of phenomena, modernization, learning by copying, adapting and others are well documented by Latin American scholars as features of their NSI (Katz, 2007). In this context, the relevance of the STI policy design and implementation tailored to regional needs and specificities has been highlighted (Cassiolato & Lastres, 1999). In the last decade, many researchers argued in favor of relying on NSI policy efforts to solve national problems and challenges (Dutrénit & Vera-Cruz, 2016; Suárez & Erbes, 2014).

Overall, the Latin American view of NSI, which incorporates the specific contexts and challenges of the region, has enhanced the relevance of NSI both conceptually and in practical policy making. For sure, these contributions could be cross-fertilized with their counterparts in other parts of the Global South. In the next section, we explore how the Global South reality calls for more bridges and cross-fertilization based on the features characteristic of this specific context.

3.4   FINAL REMARKS: TOWARDS A RESEARCH AGENDA FOR ENTREPRENEURIAL ECOSYSTEMS AND NATIONAL SYSTEMS OF INNOVATION FROM LATIN AMERICA TO THE GLOBAL SOUTH

In this chapter, we presented and discussed the EE and NSI concepts focusing on their roots, evolution and main elements. We briefly overviewed Latin American contributions to both concepts. In doing so, we established relevant intersections, common features and origins of the two approaches such as the role of business and social structures, access to finance, demand conditions and institutional platforms for STI among others. We also found that the role of government and policy – which is missing in Schumpeter's approach of innovation and entrepreneurship – is shared by the EE and NIS concepts. This is not surprising since these two perspectives are oriented to common goals. In Latin America, ECLAC's structuralism, with its ideas of duality and structural heterogeneity, had a strong influence on both approaches.

This discussion sets a good platform for further developments and reflections on the confluence of systemic approaches to understanding innovation and entrepreneurship. On the one hand, in the Global North, there is an increasing trend towards closer links among large firms and startups in open innovation settings, encouraged by a new wave of technological change. The old debate between the Schumpeter I and Schumpeter II paradigms is giving room to a new debate focused on the emergence of a Schumpeter III paradigm, which combines the relative strengths of both types of agents. This trend has already started in the Global South, as documented by Kantis (2018). Both approaches could clearly contribute to this field; NSI with its stronger focus on large corporations' strategies and behavior, and on science and technology institutions, and EE with its better comprehension of startup dynamics, incubators and accelerators, while issues of financing are of common interest to both approaches.

On the other hand, in the Global South, two main types of challenges remain. First, there are unsolved issues related to the innovation process and entrepreneurship itself, including aspects such as how to improve the systemic conditions for the increased prevalence of innovation and more dynamic innovative startups. This leads to questions about the role of government and policies, and its possibly varying importance along the different stages of innovation and entrepreneurship system development. The role of public strategies/investments vis-à-vis private incentives/behavior in different contexts also deserves to be explored. This clearly demands an evolutionary and context-oriented model able to guide strategic policy making in different contexts. Typology building and case studies could be a route to address this theoretical and empirical challenge. For instance, to what extent is it possible to identify different types of systems and paths of development (without assuming a deterministic and linear approach)? A non-trivial issue is the existence of minimum thresholds, which different factors and actors need to achieve in order to "play the systemic game". What happens when these thresholds are not in place?

Another relevant issue is how to leverage the development of the entrepreneurship and innovation systems with external resources and alliances from other ecosystems and actors, both private and public. In this case, the effect of foreign investors, for instance, is a very important matter that deserves to be discussed with further empirical evidence. On the one hand, foreign investors could compensate for the lack of domestic resources and capabilities, i.e. risk-oriented local investors and well-trained managers of risk funds to name a few, accelerating the growth of indigenous startups and scale-ups. On the other hand, there is a high risk of an "entrepreneurial drain" associated with the "foreignization" process, i.e. intellectual property, organizational capabilities and strategic decision making transferred abroad (Gonzalo, Federico, Drucaroff & Kantis, 2013; Gonzalo, 2015; Pires-Alves, Gonzalo and Puccioni de Oliveira, 2019). Consequently, it is necessary to better understand the conditions under which this positive leverage of external resources produces more favorable effects to ecosystem development than the alternatives.

The second type of challenge is associated with the link between innovation/entrepreneurship and development in a context of structural heterogeneity, as characterized by ECLAC scholars (Pinto, 1970). Different regional and social demands, income asymmetries and a fragmented business structure demographically dominated by micro and small enterprises are a part of this heterogeneity. Thus, the existence of different domains of policy must be recognized as the point of departure. It would be a mistake to lump everything together with the illusion of "killing two birds with one stone". The contribution of entrepreneurship and innovation to achieve a more inclusive society and a more articulated productive structure is a part of the debate as well. The direct answer is that innovation and entrepreneurship contribute to building a more diversified economy with better jobs and incomes for those who participate directly and indirectly. The bridge to the rest of society is still a broader challenge.

Some hints could be explored, for instance, by considering the role and impact of the new technology diffusion on productivity growth in the context of the more traditional micro and small firms' world. In this case, NSI insights on technology diffusion and absorption could be useful, being the capabilities needed to diffuse and absorb an issue in itself. The role of innovative entrepreneurship to address some social challenges or impact investment, on the other hand, is more related to EE as it is possible to connect them through entrepreneurship public programs organized to address social challenges through public procurement. The entrepreneurial state approach could also help since it suggests organizing the promotion and financing of innovation by recognizing the entrepreneurial role of the state in fostering innovation and entrepreneurship systems, suggesting mission-oriented policies.

The route ahead is as exciting as it is challenging. The following years should let us see how researchers from both fields collaborate among themselves and with policy makers to produce new contributions aimed at addressing these relevant issues for the development of innovation and entrepreneurial systems in the Global South.

NOTES

1. Other similar contributions that were published at that time propose EE as a rainforest (Hwang and Horowitt, 2012) or emphasize the role of the community (Feld, 2012).
2. In contrast, the role of development banks in financing innovation is a key issue for NSI scholars (Mazzucato, 2013).
3. Prodem is the acronym of the Entrepreneurial Development Program (Progama de Desarrollo Emprendedor in Spanish). Prodem is a think and do tank about entrepreneurship in Latin America. Based at the National University of General Sarmiento in Argentina, this research team is known for its contributions to the systemic perspective in the Latin American context. Part of this recognition came after its members received the Award for Groundbreaking Policy Thinking given by the Global Entrepreneurship Network.
4. Other main exponents of the Latin American School on Science, Technology and Society are, among others, José Leite Lopes from Brasil, Miguel Wionczek from Mexico, Francisco Sagasti from Peru, Máximo Halty Carrere from Uruguay and Marcel Roche from Venezuela.
5. Most of these contributions were later compiled in a book which could be considered a catalyst in the Latin American thinking on NSI (Cassiolato & Lastres, 1999).
6. Cassiolato and Lastres (2005) define the broad perspective including different connecting subsystems: production and innovation, capacity building, research and technological services policy, representation and financing subsystems and the role of demand.

REFERENCES

Acs, Z. J., Audretsch, D. B., & Lehmann, E. E. (2013). The knowledge spillover theory of entrepreneurship. *Small Business Economics*, *41*(4), 757–74.

Acs, Z. J., Autio, E., & Szerb L. (2014). National systems of entrepreneurship: Measurement issues and policy implications. *Research Policy*, *43*(3), 476–94.

Acs, Z. J., Stam, E., Audretsch, D. B., & O'Connor, A. (2017). The lineages of the entrepreneurial ecosystem approach. *Small Business Economics*, *49*(1), 1–10.

Álvarez, P., Ibarra García, S., Menéndez, C. E., Federico, J., & Kantis, H. (2016). El ecosistema emprendedor de la Ciudad Autónoma de Buenos Aires. Una mirada exploratoria. *Pymes, Innovación y Desarrollo*, *4*(1), 145–73.

Alvedalen, J., & Boschma, R. (2017). A critical review of entrepreneurial ecosystems research: Towards a future research agenda. *European Planning Studies*, *25*(6), 887–903.

Arocena, R., & Sutz, J. (1999). Looking at national systems of innovation from the South. *Industry and Innovation*, *7*(1), 55–75.

Arza, V., Marín, A., López, E., & Stubrin, L. (2018). Redes de conocimiento asociadas a la producción de recursos naturales en América Latina: análisis comparativo. *Revista CEPAL*, *125*, 99–126.

Audretsch, D. B., & Belitski, M. (2017). Entrepreneurial ecosystems in cities: Establishing the framework conditions. *Journal of Technology Transfer*, *42*(5), 1030–51.

Bahrami, H., & Evans, S. (1995). Flexible re-cycling and high-technology entrepreneurship. *California Management Review*, *37*(3), 62–89.

Boscherini, F., Lopez, M., & Yoguel, G. (1998). *Sistemas locales de innovación y el desarrollo de la capacidad innovativa de las firmas: un instrumento de captación aplicado al caso de Rafaela*, Nota Técnica 17/98. Rio de Janeiro: Redesist.

Breschi, S., & Malerba, F. (1997). Sectoral systems of innovation: technological regimes, Schumpeterian dynamics and spatial boundaries. In: C. Edquist (Ed.), *Systems of Innovation: Technologies, institutions and organizations* (pp. 130–52). London: Pinter/Cassell Academic.

Brown, R., & Mason, C. (2017). Looking inside the spiky bits: A critical review and conceptualisation of entrepreneurial ecosystems. *Small Business Economics*, *49*(1), 11–30.

Bruno, A., & Tybjee, T. (1982). The environment for entrepreneurship. In: C. Kent, D. Sexton, & K. Vesper (Eds), *Encyclopedia of Entrepreneurship* (pp. 288–315). Englewood Cliffs, NJ: Prentice-Hall.

Carlsson, B., & Stankiewicz, R. (1991). On the nature, function and composition of technological systems. *Journal of Evolutionary Economics*, *1*(2), 93–118.

Cassiolato, J. (2008). As vantagens e desafios da visão sistêmica como instrumento analítico e político normativo. Nota técnica 04-2008. RedeSist.

Cassiolato, J. E., & Gonzalo, M. (2015). *O papel do Estado no desenvolvimento dos sistemas de inovação dos BRICS*, TD DIT-Nº 01/2015. Rio de Janeiro: RedeSist, Desenvolvimento, Inovação e Território.

Cassiolato, J. E., & Lastres, H. M. (1999). *Globalização e inovação localizada: experiências de sistemas locais no Mercosul*, Nota Técnica. Brasilia: Instituto Brasileiro de Informação em Ciência e Tecnologia.

Cassiolato, J. E., & Lastres, H. M. (2005). Sistemas de Inovação e Desenvolvimento: as implicações de política. *São Paulo em Perspectiva*, *19*(1), 34–45.

Cassiolato, J. E., Lastres, H. M., & Soares, M. C. (2014). The Brazilian national system of innovation: Challenges to sustainability and inclusive development. In: G. Dutrénit & J. Sutz (Eds), *National Innovation Systems, Social Inclusion and Development: The Latin American experience* (pp. 68–101). Cheltenham, UK and Northampton, MA, USA: Edward Elgar Publishing.

Cherubini Alvez, A., Fisher, B., Vonortas, N., & Queiroz, S. (2018). *Configurations of Knowledge-Intensive Entrepreneurial Ecosystems: An assessment of the state of Sao Paulo, Brazil*. Sao Pablo: X Encontro de Estudios sobre Empreendedorismo y Gestao de Pequenas Empresas.

Chesbrough, H., Vanhaverbeke, W., & West, J. (Eds) (2006). *Open Innovation: Researching a new paradigm*. Boston, MA: Harvard Business School Press.

Chudnovsky, D. (1998). *El Enfoque del Sistema Nacional de Innovación y las Nuevas Políticas de Ciencia y Tecnología en la Argentina*, Nota Técnica, 14/98. Rio de Janeiro: Instituto de Economia da Universidade Federal do Rio de Janeiro.

Cohen, B. (2006). Sustainable valley entrepreneurial ecosystems. *Business Strategy and the Environment*, *15*(1), 1–14.

Cooke, P. (1996). *Regional Innovation Systems: An evolutionary approach*. London: London University Press.

Dutrénit, G., & Sutz, J. (2013). *Sistemas de innovación para un desarrollo inclusivo*. México, DF: Lalics.

Dutrénit, G., & Vera-Cruz, A. (2016). Políticas públicas de CTI, problemas nacionales y desarrollo. In: A. Erbes & D. Suarez (Eds), *Repensando el desarrollo latinoamericano. Una discusión desde los sistemas de innovación* (pp. 350–83). Buenos Aires: Universidad Nacional de General Sarmiento.

Edquist, C., & Johnson, B. (1997). *Systems of Innovation: Technologies, institutions and organisations*. London; Washington, DC: Pinter.

Federico, J., Ibarra Garcia, S., & Kantis, H. (2018). Enfoque sistémico del emprendimiento: estado del arte y desafíos conceptuales. In: D. Suarez, A. Erbes & F. Barletta (Eds), *Teoría de la innovación: evolución, tendencias y desafíos. Herramientas conceptuales para la enseñanza y el aprendizaje*. Buenos Aires, Madrid: Universidad Nacional de General Sarmiento-Universidad Complutense de Madrid.

Feld, B. (2012). *Startup Communities: Building an entrepreneurial ecosystem in your city*. Hoboken, NJ: John Wiley & Sons.

Freeman, C. (1982). *Technological Infrastructure and International Competitiveness*. Working Paper. OECD Ad Hoc Group on Science, Technology and Competitiveness.

Freeman, C. (1987). *Technology Policy and Economic Performance: Lessons from Japan*. London: Pinter.

Freeman, C. (1995). The national innovation systems in historical perspective. *Cambridge Journal of Economics*, *19*(1), 5–24.

Freeman, C. (1999). Innovation systems: City-state, national, continental and sub-national. In: J. Cassiolato & H. Lastres (Eds), *Globalização & Inovação Localizada. Experiências de Sistemas Locais no Mercosul*. Edição: IBIC.

Gartner, W. B. (1988). Who is an entrepreneur? Is the wrong question. *American Journal of Small Business*, *12*(4), 11–32.

Gonzalo, M. (2012). *El proceso de crecimiento de las gacelas tecnológicas en Argentina: cuatro casos de estudio*. Master Thesis, Universidad Nacional de General Sarmiento, Buenos Aires.

Gonzalo, M. (2015). Creación, desarrollo y extranjerización "temprana" de capacidades empresariales locales en la Argentina de inicios del siglo XXI: el caso Core Security. *H-Industri@: Revista De Historia De La Industria, Los Servicios Y Las Empresas En América Latina*, 17, 150–74. http://ojs.econ.uba.ar/index.php/H-ind/article/view/843

Gonzalo, M., Federico, J., Drucaroff, S., & Kantis, H. (2013). Post-investment trajectories of Latin American young technology-based firms: An exploratory study. *Venture Capital*, *15*(2), 115–33.

Gonzalo, M., Federico, J., & Kantis, H. (2014). Crecimiento y adaptación en un contexto de crisis internacional: el caso de tres empresas jóvenes dinámicas argentinas. Boletín Informativo Techint 343, January–April, 117–34.

Hernández, C., & González, D. (2016). Study of the start-up ecosystem in Lima, Peru: Collective case study. *Latin American Business Review, 17*(2), 115–37.

Herrera, A. (1995). Dossier: Los determinantes sociales de la política científica en América Latina. Política científica explícita y política científica implícita. *Redes: Revista de estudios sociales de la ciencia, 2*(5), 117–31. Disponible en RIDAA-UNQ Repositorio Institucional Digital de Acceso Abierto de la Universidad Nacional de Quilmes. http://ridaa.unq.edu.ar/handle/20.500.11807/438

Hwang, V. W., & Horowitt, G. (2012). *The Rainforest: The secret to building the next Silicon Valley.* Los Altos, CA: Regenwald.

Isenberg, D. J. (2010). How to start an entrepreneurial revolution. *Harvard Business Review, 88*(6), 40–50.

Júnior, E. I., Dionisio, E. A., Gimenez, F. A. P., & Morini, C. (2016). Análise do Ecosistema Empreendedor do Brasil. Paper presented at IX EGEPE–Encontro de Estudos sobre Empreendedorismo e Gestão de Empresas. Passo Fundo–RS.

Jurowetzki, R., Lundvall, B., & Lema, R. (2015). Overcoming intellectual tribalism. A bibliometric mapping of innovation systems and global value chain literatures. 13th Globelics Conference, La Havana, September 23–26.

Kantis, H. (2003). *Estudios sobre el desarrollo emprendedor en Argentina. Creación de empresas en Argentina y su entorno institucional.* Final Report. Buenos Aires: Agencia de Cooperación Internacional del Japón; Universidad Nacional de General Sarmiento.

Kantis, H. (2018). *Mature and Developing Ecosystems: A comparative analysis from an evolutionary perspective.* Working Paper. Buenos Aires: Universidad Nacional de General Sarmiento. https://prodem.ungs.edu.ar/publicaciones_prodem/mature-and -developing-ecosystems-a-comparative-analysis-from-an-evolutionary-perspective/

Kantis, H., & Angelelli, P. (2006). El proceso de creación de empresas basadas en el conocimiento en América Latina: una visión comparada. *Ekonomiaz: Revista vasca de economía, 62,* 240–63.

Kantis, H., Angelelli, P., & Moori Koenig, V. (2004). *Desarrollo emprende- dor: América Latina y la experiencia internacional.* Washington, DC: Banco Interamericano de Desarrollo. https://publications.iadb.org/en/publication/16310/ developing-entrepreneurship-experience-latin-america-and-worldwide

Kantis, H., Federico, J., & Ibarra Garcia, S. (2014). *Índice de condiciones sistémicas para el emprendimiento dinámico. Una herramienta para la acción en América Latina.* Rafaela: Asociación Civil Red Pymes Mercosur. Recuperado en: https:// prodem.ungs.edu.ar/icsed/reportes-anuales/

Kantis, H., Federico, J., & Ibarra Garcia, S. (2015). *Condiciones Sistémicas para el Emprendimiento Dinámico: América Latina en el nuevo escenario global.* Rafaela: Asociación Civil Red Pymes Mercosur. https://prodem.ungs.edu.ar/icsed/reportes -anuales/

Kantis, H., Federico, J., & Ibarra Garcia, S. (2016). *Condiciones Sistémicas e Institucionalidad para el Emprendimiento y la Innovación Hacia una Agenda de Integración de los Ecosistemas en los Países de la Alianza del Pacífico.* Rafaela: Asociación Civil Red PyMes Mercosur. https://prodem.ungs.edu.ar/icsed/reportes -anuales/

Kantis, H., Federico, J., & Ibarra Garcia, S. (2018). *Condiciones Sistémicas para el Emprendimiento Dinámico: Las brechas abiertas de América Latina: ¿Convergencia o divergencia?* Rafaela: Asociación Civil Red Pymes Mercosur. https://prodem.ungs .edu.ar/icsed/reportes-anuales/

Kantis, H., Federico, J., Menendez, C., & Ibarra Garcia, S. (2017). *Condiciones para emprender en ciudades argentinas: Síntesis de estudio de diagnóstico. Secretaria de emprendedores y PyMEs.* Buenos Aires: Ministerio de producción y Trabajo. Presidencia de la Nación.

Kantis, H., Ishida, M., & Moori Koenig, V. (2002). *Empresarialidad en economías emergentes: Creación y desarrollo de nuevas empresas en América Latina y el Este de Asia.* Washington, DC: Inter-American Development Bank.

Katz, J. (2007). Reformas estructurales orientadas al mercado, la globalización y la transformación de los sistemas de innovación en América Latina. In: G. Dutrénit, J. Jasso & D. Villavicencio (Eds), *Globalización, acumulación de capacidades e innovación. Los desafíos para las empresas, localidades y países* (pp. 27–60). México, DF: Fondo de Cultura Económica-OEI.

Katz, J. (2016). Sistemas de innovación y lo macro y micro de crecer con base en recursos naturales. In: A. Erbes & D. Suarez (Eds), *Repensando el desarrollo latino-americano. Una discusión desde los sistemas de innovación* (pp. 249–67). Buenos Aires: Universidad Nacional de General Sarmiento.

Lastres, H. M. (1994). *Advanced Materials Revolution and the Japanese System of Innovation.* London: Macmillan.

Lastres, H. M., & Cassiolato, J. (2019). Arranjos produtivos e inovativos locais: desenvolvimento e os desafios da colonialidade do saber. *Debates sobre Innovación, 2*(1), paper 61.

Lavarello, P., Robert, V., & Vázquez, D. (2017). Integrating global value chain with national innovation systems approaches: Some dimensions disregarded by the current debate. Presented at the 10th Jornadas de Economía Crítica, September 7–9, Universidad Nacional de General Sarmiento.

López, A., & Lugones, G. (1999). *Globalização e inovação localizada: Experiências de sistemas locais no Mercosul.* Rio de Janeiro: Instituto de Economia da Universidade Federal do Rio de Janeiro.

Lundvall, B. (1985). *Product Innovation and User-Producer Interaction.* Aalborg: Aalborg University Press.

Lundvall, B. (1992). *National Systems of Innovation: Towards a theory of innovation and interactive learning.* London: Pinter.

Lundvall, B. (Ed.) (2010). *National Systems of Innovation: Toward a theory of innovation and interactive learning.* London: Anthem Press. www.jstor.org/stable/j .ctt1gxp7cs

Lundvall, B. (2015). *The Origins of the National Innovation System Concept and Its Usefulness in the Era of the Globalizing Economy.* 13th Globelics Conference, Havana, Cuba.

Lundvall, B., Chaminade, C., Joseph, K. J., & Vang, J. (2009). Epilogue: which way now? In: B. Lundvall, K. J. Joseph, C. Chaminade & J. Vang (Eds), *Handbook of Innovation Systems and Developing Countries* (pp. 380–6). Cheltenham, UK and Northampton, MA, USA: Edward Elgar Publishing.

Maillat, D. (1995). Territorial dynamic, innovative milieus and regional policy. *Entrepreneurship and Regional Development, 7*(2), 157–65.

Malerba, F., & McKelvey, M. (2018). Knowledge-intensive innovative entrepreneurship integrating Schumpeter, evolutionary economics, and innovation systems. *Small Business Economics*, 1–20. doi:https://doi.org/10.1007/s11187-018-0060-2

Mason, C. M., & Brown, R. (2014). *Entrepreneurial Ecosystems and Growth Oriented Entrepreneurship.* Background paper prepared for the workshop organized by the OECD LEED Programme and the Dutch Ministry of Economic Affairs on

Entrepreneurial Ecosystems and Growth Oriented Entrepreneurship, The Hague, Netherlands.

Mason, C. M., & Harrison, R. T. (2006). After the exit: Acquisitions, entrepreneurial recycling and regional economic development. *Regional Studies, 40*(1), 55–73.

Mazzucato, M. (2013). *O estado empreendedor.* New York: Portfolio Penguin.

Metcalfe, S., & Ramlogan, R. (2008). Innovation systems and the competitive process in developing economies. *Quarterly Review of Economics and Finance, 48*(2), 433–46.

Moore, J. F. (1993). Predators and prey: A new ecology of competition. *Harvard Business Review, 71*(3), 75–86.

Neck, H., Meyer, D., Cohen, B., & Corbett, A. (2004). An entrepreneurial system view of new venture creation. *Journal of Small Business Management, 42*(2), 190–208.

Nelson, R. R. (Ed.) (1993). *National Innovation Systems: A comparative analysis.* Oxford: Oxford University Press.

Niosi, J., Saviotti, P., Bellon, B., & Crow, M. (1993). National systems of innovations: In search of a workable concept. *Technology in Society, 15*(2), 207–27.

Pinto, A. (1970). Naturaleza e implicancias de la "heterogeneidad estructural" en América Latina. *El Trimestre Económico. Fondo de cultura económica, 37*(145), 83–100.

Piore, M., & Sabel, C. (1984). *The Second Industrial Divide.* New York: Basic Books.

Pires-Alves, C. Gonzalo, M., & Puccioni de Oliveira Lyra, M. (2019). Startups and young innovative firms mergers and acquisitions: Lessons from the ICT tecno-economic paradigm. *Revista de Economia Contemporânea, 23*(2), 1–40.

Porter, M. E. (1998). Clusters and the new economics of competition. *Harvard Business Review, 76*(6), 77–90.

Prebisch, R. (1949). El desarrollo económico de América Latina y algunos de sus principales problemas. *Bolletín Económico de la Amércia Latina, 7*(1), 1–24.

Pyke, F., Becattini, G., & Sengenberger, W. (Eds) (1990). *Industrial Districts and Inter-Firm Co-operation in Italy.* Genova: International Institute for Labour Studies.

Qian, H., Acs, Z., & Stough, R. (2013). Regional systems of entrepreneurship: The nexus of human capital, knowledge and new firm formation. *Journal of Economic Geography, 13*(4), 559–87.

Quince, T., & Whittaker, H. (2002). *High Tech Businesses in the UK: Performance and niche markets.* Working Paper 234. Cambridge: Centre for Business Research, University of Cambridge. https://econpapers.repec.org/paper/cbrcbrwps/wp234.htm

Sábato, J. (1979). El triángulo nos enseña donde estamos. In: J. Sábato, *Ensayos en campera* (pp. 21–35). Buenos Aires: Universidad Nacional de Quilmes.

Saxenian, A. (1996). *Regional Advantage.* Cambridge, MA: Harvard University Press.

Shane, S. A. (2004). *Academic Entrepreneurship: University spinoffs and wealth creation.* Cheltenham, UK and Northampton, MA, USA: Edward Elgar Publishing.

Sharif, N. (2006). Emergence and development of the national innovation systems concept. *Research Policy, 35*(5), 745–66.

Soares, C., Hausmann Tavares, J., Gonzalo, M., Tomassini, C., & Cassiolato, J. (2015). *The Need of an Alternative Approach to GVC'S Literature: Transnational corporations and national systems of innovation systems in a Latin American perspective.* 13th Globelics International Conference, Havana, Cuba.

Spigel, B. (2017). The relational organization of entrepreneurial ecosystems. *Entrepreneurship Theory and Practice, 41*(1), 49–72.

Stam, E., & Spigel, B. (2017). Entrepreneurial ecosystems. In: R. Blackburn, D. De Clercq, J. Heinonen & Z. Wang (Eds), *Handbook for Entrepreneurship and Small Business* (pp. 407–22). London: SAGE.

Stam, F. C., & van de Ven, A. (2018). *Entrepreneurial Ecosystems: A systems perspective*. Working Paper series, 18-06. Utrecht: Utrecht School of Economics. https://ideas.repec.org/p/use/tkiwps/1806.html

Suárez, D., & Erbes, A. (2014). Desarrollo y Subdesarrollo Latinoamericano. Un análisis crítico del enfoque de los sistemas de innovación para el desarrollo. *REDES-Revista de Estudios Sociales de la Ciencia, 20*(38), 97–119.

Szapiro, M., Vargas, M., Brito, M., & Cassiolato, J. (2015). *Global Value Chains and National Systems of Innovation: Policy implications for developing countries*. 13th Globelics International Conference Havana, Cuba.

Van de Ven, H. (1993). The development of an infrastructure for entrepreneurship. *Journal of Business Venturing, 8*(3), 211–30.

Varsavsky, O. (1974). *Estilos tecnológicos*. Buenos Aires: Ediciones Periferia.

Winter, S. (1984). Schumpeterian competition in alternative technological regimes. *Journal of Economic Behavior and Organization, 5*(3–4), 287–320.

Yoguel, G., Borello, J., & Erbes, A. (2009). Argentina: How to study and act upon local innovation systems. *CEPAL Review, 99*, 63–80.

4. The role of diaspora in entrepreneurial ecosystems and national innovation systems

Veneta Andonova, Jonathan A. Perez-Lopez and Jana Schmutzler

4.1 INTRODUCTION

The history of Southeastern Europe and more specifically the Balkans is rich in disruptive historical events causing a spread of migrants. The post-Cold War realities of this region, characterized by the absence of economic and social progress, expelled a great number of economic migrants. The wars in former Yugoslavia produced significant numbers of political and ethnic refugees. The estimated size of the Bulgarian economic diaspora in 2019, for example, is over 2 million people, close to 30 percent of the current population of about 7 million. The Romanian diaspora is estimated to be anywhere between 5 and 6.5 million. One hundred thousand people were killed and over 2 million were displaced during the Bosnian war. These sizable movements of people have had significant and diverse effects on the local productive systems.

The end of the communist regimes triggered a huge brain drain in the Balkan countries, understood as the migration of engineers, physicians, scientists and other highly skilled professionals with university training. This brain drain has been and still is an important phenomenon for the region (Sergi, Henry, Weeks, Slinn & Dumanova, 2004). According to Gallup's Potential Net Migration Index, the share of highly skilled population that is willing to emigrate from Albania is 50 percent, Bulgaria 16 percent, Bosnia and Herzegovina 40 percent, Croatia 14 percent, Greece 11 percent, Kosovo 43 percent, Macedonia 39 percent and Romania 22 percent (Gallup, 2018). It is not hard to imagine that these realities have negative repercussions for the countries' national production system in general and national innovation systems (NIS) in particular. Highly skilled labor is a *sine-qua-non* here; its lack leads to low research and development (R&D) investments and few innovations.

This gloomy reality, however, contrasts with the vibrant entrepreneurial activities in the region: from 2010 to 2017, 15 venture capital-backed exits were reported for Central and Eastern Europe; seven of those were from the Balkans. This activity represented a €5 billion euro return to the investors. In the years after 2012, the European Union funded early-stage technological startups in the region through seed and venture capital. For example, Bulgaria received investments of about US$1.5 billion from the Joint European Resources for Micro to Medium Enterprises program. Four Bulgarian funds were selected to manage a total amount of €350 million, according to their capacity to raise additional private funds. These initial public investments produced a 2.57 multiplier effect by 2017, creating incentives for firms to locate in cities like Sofia, the most relevant growth hub for the Balkan tech sector today. According to the European Investment Fund, growth in Central and Eastern Europe has been exponential, representing in 2015 3 percent of the total venture capital in Europe (Ezekiev, 2017). In 2016, 210 startups from the Balkan region raised US$74 million (O'Brien, 2018). As of 2019, it is esti-mated that the total valuation of the unicorns from Central and Eastern Europe is around $30 billion (Draganov, 2019).

The question that inevitably arises is: How can a region with persistently weak innovation systems and worrying emigration statistics be able to build bubbling entrepreneurial ecosystems (EE)? In this chapter, we explore the idea that at least part of the answer lies in the role the regional diasporas play in turning – arguably – the brain drain into a brain gain. The diaspora in transition and developing countries is often considered a significant engine for economic development through remittances, the promotion of trade and investments as well as knowledge and technology transfers (Plaza & Ratha, 2011). However, the role of diaspora for the development of local EE remains virtually unknown in the case of massive migration. Moreover, despite the theoretical recognition that the brain drain can be turned into a brain gain through appropriate public policies (UNCTAD, 2012), the absence of the *de facto* government strategies has made this a distant possibility in most Balkan nations. We argue that the creation of local EEs might have been an unintentional yet effective brain gain strategy for the region. We hereby advance research by showing that the entre-preneurial activity in a country does not depend only on the current residents but also on the ties that keep it connected via its diaspora to global entrepre-neurial hubs. Additionally, we explore first evidence of why this influence has not been equally positive for NIS. Instead, the brain drain adversely affected NIS in the Balkan countries.

We rely on the context of the Balkans after the turn of the century. It is an interesting case study not only because large migration movements have affected it. In addition, those economic migrants maintain strong links with their homeland and are actively engaged in economic activities, including investments in their country of origin (see, for example, Vadean, 2007). We analyzed the period after the turn of the century, as this is the time when entrepreneurial activity started to take up in the Balkans. For our data analysis, we relied on detailed interviews of both diaspora members and EE's members and complemented these with secondary data.

4.2 ENTREPRENEURIAL ECOSYSTEMS AND NATIONAL INNOVATION SYSTEMS

EE and NIS emerged as influential concepts for studying entrepreneurship and innovation, the two fundamental processes for economic growth (Malecki, 1997). While these two are intimately linked since the early works of Schumpeter (1934) and have even been dubbed "allied concepts" (Stam & Spigel, 2016), "the two literatures, those of NIS and entrepreneurship, have largely developed in parallel, independent of one another" (Acs, Autio & Szerb, 2014, p. 478). Instead of a thorough review, we restrain ourselves to point out the characteristics relevant for this study.

The NIS literature challenged the long-prevailing view of innovation as a linear model; instead, a systems approach was introduced (Smits & Kuhlmann, 2004). Freeman's contribution (1995) was critical because it connected Friedrich List's (1904 [1841]) ideas to the NIS concept, since it highlighted the role of a state in catching-up processes (Lundvall, 2007b). Comparative studies on NIS revealed how national institutions affect technical change (Nelson, 1993), and how this effect is different even in neighboring countries (Edquist & Lundvall, 1993). As a result, today learning and innovation are defined as interactive and socially embedded processes, which can only be fully understood when the institutional context is taken into account (Lundvall, 2007a). Innovation systems – despite varying definitions – are generally understood as systemic arrangements including firms, institutions and socioeconomic structures and relationships (Lundvall, 1992), "which determine the rate and direction of innovation and competence-building emanating from processes of science-based and experience-based learning" (Lundvall, Vang, Joseph & Chaminade, 2009, p. 7). We subscribe to this definition, which reflects the broad rather than the narrow view of the innovation system (Cassiolato & Lastres, 2005; Lundvall et al., 2009) as a framework more apt for transition countries.

The EE is a younger concept; some authors even argue that one of its theoretical roots lies in the innovation systems literature (Spigel & Harrison, 2018). Despite various incipient initiatives to understand entrepreneurship from a systemic point of view (e.g. Van de Ven, 1993), it was the seminal work of Isenberg (2010) which boosted the concept. EE can generally be understood as "a set of interdependent actors and factors coordinated in such a way that they enable productive entrepreneurship within a particular territory" (Isenberg, 2010, p. 3). In the quest for advancing the theory, Spigel (2017) defines internal attributes of an EE, the relationship among them and how each attribute contributes to the reproduction of the EE as well as for resources to new ventures. He suggests that three attributes characterize an EE: cultural, social and material-based. We subscribe to this definition as a way to portray an EE given the emphasis on detail, the consideration of institutional actors and the use of social network perspectives, all of which are aligned with our approach to the diaspora's influence on Balkan EE.

Both concepts share a "systemic perspective" where systems are understood as a set of interacting elements.[1] That is, both the entrepreneurial as well as the learning and innovative processes are viewed in a contextualized way, recognizing that they do not take place in a vacuum. Additionally, the system perspective points towards the interactions and networks among the actors constituting the system, which enables these processes. Finally, both concepts carry a territorial boundary.

Despite these commonalities, several differences exist. First, while the EE puts the entrepreneur at the center of its analysis (Acs et al., 2014), the NIS literature emphasizes the role of the large corporation in R&D (Freeman & Soete, 1997) and focuses on the established firm (Autio & Levie, 2017). Thus, the missing individual agency and the absence of the entrepreneur (Acs et al., 2014) have characterized the NIS literature. In the EE domain, entrepreneurial finance through venture funds and seed capital (Brown & Mason, 2017) as well as incubators, mentors and other supporting institutions (Alvedalen & Boschma, 2017) not only play a significant role but are analyzed in detail. The innovation systems approach lacks such an in-depth analysis at the micro level. Instead, it focuses more on other types of industrial advantages (Spigel, 2017). Furthermore, the role that key actors play in each of the two concepts differs. Universities and research centers appear mainly as knowledge generators in the innovation system (e.g. Edquist & Johnson, 1997), whereas in the EE they take on the role of potential incubators and generators of an entrepreneurial culture (Mason & Brown, 2014). Finally, the EE is often viewed – analogous to the biological metaphor – as emergent, self-organizing and self-sustaining (Isenberg, 2016), where policymakers cannot easily address well-defined market failures through a top-down approach (Autio & Levie, 2017). And though the innovation system is characterized by the same systemic view as the EE is, the focus on established firms and knowledge production often is linked with top-down policy approaches (Arocena & Sutz, 2000). In sum, we can show that there are strong commonalities between the two concepts with marked differences mainly linked to the output at play.

4.3   DIASPORA AND ITS ROLE IN ECONOMIC DEVELOPMENT

Despite varying definitions (e.g. that of the United States State Department versus the African Union), the diaspora is generally defined as those people and their descendants who have migrated but retain a connection to their homeland/home region. For a long time, migrants were seen as a negative trend public policies should prevent; they left their country of origin, settled in the new one, integrated into that new society and were "lost" (Plaza & Ratha, 2011). However, the diaspora – today enabled through technology – often retains the connection to their country of origin. There is growing empirical evidence that diaspora plays a major role in shaping the economic development of their country of origin that goes far beyond that of transferring remittances. Diasporas may become sources of knowledge, skills and investments; they may bring into their country of origin new ideas and attitudes and enable the connection of their country of origin to global business networks (e.g. Girma & Yu, 2002; Head & Ries, 1998; Leblang, 2010).

The relationship between migrants and entrepreneurship is not new. Migrants founded trading companies centuries ago (Minoglou & Ioannides, 2004), historically engaged in small business enterprises and contributed to their host country's economic development (Waldinger, Aldrich & Ward, 1990). Today, ethnic entrepreneurship – business activities or self-employment by foreign migrants – is a rising subject of study (e.g. Dana, 2007; Masurel, Nijkamp, Tastan & Vindigni, 2002; Volery, 2007; Zhou, 2006). Additionally, migrants engage in venture creation as returnees (e.g. Kenney, Breznitz & Murphree, 2013; Pruthi, 2014) or transnational entrepreneurs (e.g. Sommer & Gamper, 2018). We shift the lens and evaluate the way diaspora shapes its home country's EE. While the EE concept demands the consideration of various stakeholders, the role of diaspora has remained outside mainstream discussions with very few exceptions (e.g. Riddle & Brinkerhoff, 2011). And even though the role of non-local linkages for innovation especially in the case of high technology has been outlined in research (Bathelt, 2005), those linkages generally are understood as linkages with non-local actors. Thus, for both the EE and innovation system concepts, an analysis of how diaspora may shape the local system has generally been lacking.

We argue that the connectedness to the diaspora is one external resource that can create competitive advantage (Spigel, 2017) beyond the physical co-location. Those ties can depict networks of knowledge sharing and spillovers, constituting social capital and gateways to investors that come from geographically distant regions. The diaspora can thus create competitive advantages that the national or regional context cannot create with the resources available within their narrow geographical limits.

4.4   CASE STUDY: METHODOLOGY AND DATA

The present study is set in the context of the Balkan region, comprising the countries Albania, Bosnia and Herzegovina, Bulgaria, Croatia, Montenegro, Republic of North Macedonia, Romania, Serbia and Slovenia. It draws on previous research meant to describe the emergence of an EE in Southeastern Europe. The extensive data-collection process included more than 70 face-to-face interviews with entrepreneurs, startup experts, public officials and researchers across countries in the region and gave rise to a book (please refer to Andonova, Nikolova & Dimitrov, 2019 for a detailed description of the interview partners). The structured interviews were recorded and subsequently analyzed. This analysis was complemented by secondary data and detailed case studies. Information was complemented through literature research and archival documents.

This research project was focused on the EE in general. However, during the data collection and analysis, the influence of the diaspora on the development of the Balkan EE was recurrently highlighted by the interviewees. Additionally, quite a few insights were generated as well regarding the NIS.

We complement the qualitative evidence through an examination of the quantitative data. We rely on the Global Entrepreneurship Monitor (GEM) and Global Entrepreneurship and Development Index (GEDI). Specifically, we take into account the GEDI subindices as proxies for the EE inputs and describe the EE outputs through the total early-stage entrepreneurial activity and entrepreneurial intentions from the GEM database. For NIS, we rely on the Global Innovation Index (GII) and focus on the NIS inputs by examining the GII input pillars and the NIS outputs through the GII output pillars. As proxies for the size of diaspora we used migration stock as a percentage of total population from the United Nations and the annual remittances in million dollars from the World Bank. Table 4.1 contains the respective indicators. The data comprise the average for the time period between 2013 and 2016. Combining qualitative with quantitative data offers a more robust understanding of the role of diaspora.

4.5   ENTREPRENEURIAL ECOSYSTEMS AND INNOVATION SYSTEMS IN THE BALKANS

In this section we describe the social, cultural and material attributes of the Balkan's EE and NIS. We provide a brief description of the quantitative indicators of the EE and NIS for each country. We then proceed to analyze the

Table 4.1 Descriptive statistics and correlations for EE inputs and outputs, NIS inputs and outputs and diaspora

Countries			ALB	BIH	BGR	HRV	MNE	ROU	SRB	SVN	MKD	Corr. with mig.	Corr. with remitt.
EE	Input	GEDI	31.07	28.40	43.23	40.47	38.70	44.93	31.80	52.07	56.60	-0.77	-0.22
		Attitudes	29.50	28.17	45.57	34.77	40.17	38.13	39.73	48.17	54.23	-0.90	-0.14
		Abilities	34.57	27.73	38.07	36.73	31.60	41.40	24.67	53.37	55.40	-0.51	-0.37
		Aspirations	29.10	29.37	46.20	49.83	44.30	55.30	31.03	54.73	40.20	-0.69	-0.10
	Output	TEA	–	0.09	0.05	0.09	–	0.11	–	0.07	0.07	0.30	0.68
		EI	–	0.24	0.09	0.24	–	0.31	–	0.13	0.27	0.42	0.44
NIS	Input	Institutions	60.03	58.74	68.50	70.39	68.68	67.70	62.52	79.36	57.56	-0.93	-0.42
		HC&R	23.83	34.31	32.83	35.71	39.79	29.12	32.78	49.12	33.98	-0.44	-0.67
		INF	36.93	30.38	43.16	45.44	38.33	43.93	41.12	48.11	33.89	-0.89	0.11
		MS	57.27	51.10	45.17	44.59	50.65	43.40	39.19	47.36	49.74	0.64	-0.59
	Output	BS	23.58	36.54	34.97	35.44	34.23	30.99	29.81	41.69	32.64	-0.23	-0.55
		K&T	18.79	25.07	34.67	31.58	24.91	35.20	30.71	37.24	26.05	-0.87	0.15
		CO	21.00	21.12	41.13	38.49	38.99	33.25	31.13	45.51	35.38	-0.94	-0.40

Countries		ALB	BIH	BGR	HRV	MNE	ROU	SRB	SVN	MKD	Corr. with mig.	Corr. with remitt.
	Mig. (% total popul.)	0.40	0.46	0.17	0.21	0.22	0.18	0.13	0.07	0.25	1	0.20
Diaspora	Remitt. (US$ million)	1,325	1,928	1,628.25	2,154.25	407.75	3,368.50	3,574.25	366.25	335.25	0.20	1
Econ. data	GDP per capita	11,665.25	11,818.92	18,548.03	23,540.98	16,759.39	22,515.45	14,334.50	31,942.11	13,991.45	−0.84	−0.08

Notes: EE inputs come from GEDI; EE outputs come from GEM; NIS inputs and outputs come from GII; migration data stock from United Nations; remittances data from World Bank. Abbreviations: TEA – Total early-stage Entrepreneurial Activity; EI – Entrepreneurial Intentions; HC&R – Human Capital and Research; INF – Infrastructure; MS – Market Sophistication; BS – Business Sophistication; K&T – Knowledge and Technology; CO – Creative Outputs. Country abbreviations: ALB – Albania; BIH – Bosnia and Herzegovina; BGR – Bulgaria; HRV – Croatia; MNE – Montenegro; ROU – Romania; SRB – Serbia; SVN – Slovenia; MKD – Republic of North Macedonia.

interviews in light of the three attributes as defined by Spigel (2017) for EE. While NIS have usually not been characterized relying on the same attributes as EE, we will make use of this taxonomy – social, cultural and material attributes – in order to address the way in which diaspora influenced in a differentiated way EE and NIS in the Balkans, accentuating similarities and highlighting the differences.

4.5.1 Analysis of Entrepreneurial Ecosystems, National Innovation Systems and Diaspora Indicators: Preliminary Quantitative Evidence

Table 4.1 gives an account of the internal heterogeneity among the Balkan countries in relation to a number of indicators. The *attitudes* toward entrepreneurship, understood as the population's general feelings about entrepreneurial activity (Acs, Szerb & Autio, 2015), are higher in Slovenia, Bulgaria and Montenegro than in the other countries. Specifically, recognizing opportunities, acquiring more social capital, relating entrepreneurial activity with high status and being more risk seeking in terms of business startups show higher scores. The entrepreneurial *abilities*, which are the skills of the entrepreneurs and characteristics of their businesses (Acs et al., 2015), are higher in Slovenia and Romania, and lower in Serbia and Bosnia and Herzegovina. This implies that there will likely be more innovation-driven entrepreneurial ventures created by educated and opportunity-guided entrepreneurs. In terms of *aspirations*, which reflect the quality and ambitions of startups and new businesses (Acs et al., 2015), Romania, Slovenia and Croatia score higher on introducing innovations in products, services and/or processes, exploring foreign markets, investing in human capital and seeking financing. On the contrary, Bosnia and Herzegovina and Albania have the lowest scores in *aspirations*. These three indicators, which we interpret as proxies for inputs of an EE, correlate negatively with migration and remittances.

The *Total early-stage Entrepreneurial Activity* (TEA) rate refers to the percentage of the population between 18 and 64 who are either a nascent entrepreneur or an owner-manager of a new business. Romania scores highest, whilst Bulgaria the lowest. However, the differences are very small with very similar TEA scores. Similarly, *Entrepreneurial Intentions* (EI) exhibit very similar behavior. In contrast to the EE inputs, the EE outputs correlate positively with migration and remittances, which we use as proxies for the role of diaspora. NIS inputs and the two output proxies vary between relatively narrow margins across the Balkan countries. The inputs are *Institutions*, representing the political, regulatory and business environment; *Human Capital and Research* (HC&R), constituted by education and R&D; *Infrastructure* (IN), conformed by information and communications technology, general infrastructure and sustainability; and *Business Sophistication* (BS), comprising knowledge workers and knowledge absorption. The outputs are *Knowledge and Technology* (K&T), referring to knowledge creation, impact and diffusion; and *Creative Outputs* (CO), such as intangible assets and creative goods and services. In all these dimensions, Slovenia and Croatia scored highest and Bosnia and Herzegovina and Albania scored the lowest. All of the above variables correlate negatively with migration and remittances.

All in all, we find preliminary evidence, which supports the validity of the general tenet that diaspora has a differential effect on EE and NIS. Diaspora proxies are positively related with entrepreneurial activity and negatively related with entrepreneurship perceptions and skills at home. This reflects a widely held belief, which goes in line with early research on diaspora. Migration is correlated with entrepreneurial output, which among others includes self-employed who start a business out of necessity to provide for income. Remittances in this case may boost this kind of entrepreneurship. The negative correlation with the EE inputs, however, can be, in a way, related with brain drain, in which case the negative correlation is expected. A similar conjecture about brain drain is consistent with the negative correlation between innovation indicators and diaspora proxies. Of course, this is a very coarse approximation. The data are aggregated and do not allow us to disentangle the mechanisms behind the reported correlations. Yet, the data suggest that more effort is needed to understand the role of diaspora for both EE and NIS. In what follows we explore qualitative evidence in order to disentangle the causal mechanisms behind the correlations.

4.5.2   Social Attributes

The EE's social attributes comprise those "resources composed of or acquired through the social networks" (Spigel, 2017, p. 53); that is actors' networks and resources, which stem from these networks such as investment capital, the advice of mentors and dealmakers as well as worker talent. In the case of the Balkans' EE, most entrepreneurial activity supported through Accelerator Venture Fund investments has been technology-driven. In these processes, diaspora members participate as investors, but usually the size of their investment participations was modest. Rather than as a source of investment, the most significant role of the diaspora in the Balkans has been its reach and connection to global hubs of entrepreneurship and to potential clients and investors. As both entrepreneurs and investors put it:

> I came back [to my home country] in 2008 and there are many people [diaspora members] abroad with whom I keep in touch. And they have been very helpful [...] the thing they have been really useful was an outsider's point of view, and contacts

with potential investors and potential customers. (Svilen Rangelov, Founder and CEO, Dronamics; included in Andonova et al., 2019)

In the case of Sensika [a Bulgarian entrepreneurial venture], they got in touch with a Bulgarian national living in Dubai and she helped them open many doors, alongside investing a small ticket in the company. So in their case the diaspora was very supportive and played a role in their launch in an unfamiliar market. (Ivaylo Simov, Investor; included in Andonova et al., 2019)

Trust – an essential prerequisite to establish collaborations (Gillespie, Riddle, Sayre & Sturges, 1999) – among the diaspora members played an important role. One of the largest startups in the region is Telerik, which was acquired by Progress in 2016 for over US$250 million. The international growth of Telerik prior to its acquisition relied heavily on the diaspora members in key foreign markets:

In some places we set up our offices through friends from Bulgaria we knew in that country or city [...] you need someone with whom you have a great level of trust. You need someone who is like a blurred copy of yourself in order to make it work, and for this person to be able to convey the company culture in this new market. So in some of the core markets for us, like the UK, USA and Australia, our offices were kick-started by Bulgarians [from the diaspora], and it wouldn't have happened without them. (Svetlozar Georgiev, Founder of Telerik; included in Andonova et al., 2019)

As a result, the EE's networking and resulting mentorships and dealmakers cannot be easily disentangled from the investment capital and worker talent. Two accelerator venture funds launched in 2012 – Eleven (www.11.me) and LAUNCHub (www.launchub.vc) – channeled a substantial share of funds from the European Union and became relevant for Balkan entrepreneurial community building. Eleven, which was selected in 2012 as a fund manager of Joint European Resources for Micro to Medium Enterprises, a European investment fund's accelerator and seed fund instrument, was one of the most important European accelerators in terms of both number and amount of investment by 2017 (Eleven, 2017). LAUNCHub started in 2012 and has increased its venture funds from €9 million to €92 million in 2017. In both cases, the attraction of substantial private capital was catalyzed by public financial resources that both accelerators were able to channel. Benefits of the private investment to the startups were the expertise, discipline and know-how. Also, as a result of the community built around these accelerators, other advantages emerged: contacts, scrutiny of strategy and keeping the ventures and their portfolios on track. Thus, many additional assets apart from financing were essential in the creation of the entrepreneurial community. Diaspora members joined the ecosystem in every possible role – investors, mentors and entrepreneurs.

Establishing a desire for belonging and giving back was possibly one of the most significant motivations among them:

> The diaspora was super helpful in what we did. We see the things here through a spyhole, while the people outside of this geography, who had more experience than us, could give us the bigger picture and are always available for advice [...] These people really want to see you succeed, not just help you with one thing or another. (Georgi Petrov, Founder and CEO, Coherent Labs; included in Andonova et al., 2019)

> I use this opportunity to tell anyone making plans to work in the Middle East that they can reach out anytime, and I will be more than happy to give back and help as I can. (Konstantin Hristov, Founder and CEO, Sensika Technologies; included in Andonova et al., 2019)

NIS in the Balkans did not go through a similar energizing experience, mainly because it is – by definition – dependent on the well-established companies rather than on young entrepreneurial ventures. According to Hellman (1998), the countries in the post-Communist Bloc entered into a "Partial-Reform Equilibrium" during the first years after the fall of communism; the most fierce opposition against market reforms should be expected from managers, bankers and corrupt officials who took the positions of rent seekers or "first-round winners". For this, they built schemes and networks in order to benefit from arbitraging state-controlled and market prices on goods that were still regulated; borrowed from the government at negative real interest rates; manipulated nascent currency markets; and took bribes to participate in all of the above. The original theory of Partial-Reform Equilibrium predicts that if the first-time losers were included in the political process of regular elections, they would eventually overturn the "first-round winners" and as a result market liberalization reforms would be completed, while the state and productive resources would be free from capture. Eventually, in the Balkans, a different equilibrium took place (Barnes, 2007). Indeed, it became evident that political confrontation and elections brought the new leaders outside the group of the rent-seeking elite, but prone to capture the state for their own interests. As a result, a persistent "Equilibrium of Competitive Capture" arises, *de facto* institutionalizing the capture of the productive resources. Arguably, under such conditions, the incentives to develop a strong NIS were rather weak. Unlike the case of EE in the Balkans, where venture capital was made available in the region and served as an anchor to connect to the diaspora and leverage its resources, such anchors have not yet been created in NIS. As a result, the diaspora did not participate in NIS to the extent it did in the local EE; the positive externalities generated through the bridge-building functions often assumed by the diaspora members were not realized.

4.5.3 Cultural Attributes

Cultural attributes refer to the "underlying beliefs and outlooks about entrepreneurship" (Spigel, 2017: 4). After the Second World War, the Balkan countries were ruled by a dictatorship relying on planned economies originating in a particular style of the collectivist ideology, resulting in the collectivization of private property. With the fall of the Communist regimes in the 1990s, the institutions protecting private property were reinstated. However, the transition from the past Communist mindset is reported to be slow and hard to encourage.

Additionally, conflict arose between the process of implementing the formal rules and institutions to modernize the productive systems and the prevalent informal rules of this region. In other words: "Let it be a lesson to all reformers of today and tomorrow [...] to all those who come to the government with pockets full of bills which get passed but are never applied, because the poor nation lives much better on its customs than on all the laws; it turns a good law into a custom, leaving aside the bad ones" (Iorga, 1992 [1927], cited in Mungiu-Pippidi, 2005).

It is thus not surprising that a very strong orientation towards employment rather than self-employment exists. The members of the Balkan EE describe a local tendency to shy away from responsibility and to overanalyze failure. The scarcity of positive outlooks towards entrepreneurship, especially among the older generations, comes in a combination with a defining element of Balkan culture: an all-pervasive pessimism ingrained through the heavy burden of the historical protagonism of the Balkans in the world's history (Andonova et al., 2019). *To Balkanize*, defined as "to break up into smaller and hostile units" by the Webster Dictionary, was coined as a result. Parallel to this, the Western-style business culture is rare and foreign experts frequently point out a lack of business and marketing skills.

Members of the diaspora community as well as returnees have brought in a significant cultural shift to the region. They are imprinting their global outlook and behavior, leading to a much-needed shift in mentality, frequently becoming entrepreneurs themselves. "The most recognizable entrepreneurial culture and skills are observed among people who have studied and lived abroad, and then have come back, or they have travelled or worked for a foreign company, or a family member has been abroad" (Mira Krusteff, Co-founder of GEM Bulgaria; included in Andonova et al., 2019).

Balkan entrepreneurs who are engaged with the EE shaped by diaspora members have become indistinguishable from their global partners regarding their work ethics and attitudes:

> I came back [...] in 2008, and there are many people abroad with whom I still keep in touch. And they have been very helpful [...] Bulgaria is the country with the

fastest declining population, but a lot of that is because alongside our population of 7 million, there are 2–3 million more Bulgarians who currently live outside of its borders. That is why the diaspora already does and will continue to play an ever-increasing role in Bulgaria's economy, and our company is an example where half of the team have already studied and worked abroad. (Svilen Rangelov, Founder and CEO, Dronamics; included in Andonova et al., 2019)

The influence of the diaspora on NIS has not been equally positive. Why is this the case? We believe the answer lies in the lacking insertion of a diaspora in the innovation systems combined with the legacy of unfinished reforms to provide incentives for competitiveness-enhancing R&D activities. Whereas EE focuses on entrepreneurs and is intimately linked with incubators and venture capital funds attracting mostly young people largely unburdened with the Communist or post-transition ideologies, NIS focuses on the established firms and important institutional linkages such as universities, research centers and government agencies. Diaspora members – at least based on our case study – tend to take part in the first, mainly by setting up business themselves, by contributing private capital to the new local ventures or by providing mentorships. However, most established firms and legacy institutions are unable to attract (highly successful) diaspora members nor do universities or research institutes. As a result, while in the EE a process of mindset change is ongoing, this process is almost absent in the NIS.

Additionally, success stories – which would inspire new entrepreneurial ventures or innovative undertakings – can be found among entrepreneurs:

Some of the first success stories, which inspired entrepreneurship in Romania, were in the tech domain and that is an important reason why this sector picked up. In the early 2000s in Romania, we saw some cases of startups that grew fast and then were acquired by Microsoft and by Adobe [...] They were very inspiring to me and to others like me. (Mircea Pasoi, Romanian Entrepreneur; included in Andonova et al., 2019)

Success stories of this kind are mainly absent for long-standing firms. Additionally, the process of early capital accumulation that took place immediately after the fall of the Communist regimes created an environment in which there was a general lack of trust and even dislike towards members of the newly emerged economic/political elites that control the most long-standing productive assets. Two arguments can help explain this outcome: first, the post-Communist years witnessed a sharp increase in inequalities perpetuated by the privatization processes by national and foreign investors (Bandelj & Mahutga, 2010), creating a sort of nostalgia for the past and a rejection of the new social order. Second, the origin of the wealth of the Balkan business leaders remain obscured in the chaos of the early years of liberalization, leading to a negative and cynical connotation of the word "businessperson" as synonymous to a thug or a thief. As Jakob Modéer put it:

> In the Balkans, there is something called the "businessman" that comes with a negative meaning. We all know these people made money easily, very quickly and in most cases through misuse of public funds [...] So, this image of easy money is still lingering on. Whether we want it or not, there are still forces that make heroes out of these people and of course they are not heroes. Where I come from, in Sweden, we have other heroes like Volvo, Scania and IKEA, and so people know them. (Jakob Modéer, Regional Entrepreneurship Program Manager for the Western Balkans, Swisscontact Worldwide; included in Andonova et al., 2019)

Additionally, most technology- or innovation-driven projects are not getting much attention from the majority of wealthy investors in the region, since the latter seem more attracted to old-fashioned extractive businesses. One additional element is the consumption patterns of local tycoons: they spend lavishly on yachts and other luxury goods but do not see themselves as investors in high-tech ventures (Andonova at el., 2019). It is not surprising either that the success stories of these businessmen and businesswomen have not turned into an inspiration, or that their companies attract little admiration.

Moreover, the business and political leaders with such a mindset generally invest little in Balkan innovation systems. The gross expenditure on R&D (GERD) in the Western Balkans, for example, has declined dramatically in the past decades. In 2013, the region was investing approximately €495 million in R&D per year, which corresponded to roughly the amount invested by the second-largest United States research university in 2011. In the same period, other emerging economies, such as China and Turkey, systematically raised investments in R&D and innovation (Correa & Zuniga, 2013). The worrisome situation with the Balkan innovation systems is not only due to the cultural specificities of the legacy businesses. The Balkan innovation system has important structural deficiencies such as top-down decision making and a high level of centralization combined with a high dependence on the political class. This type of closed centralized system with complex political rather than market-driven dynamics seems to be the antithesis of the Balkan EE, as the former is particularly ill-designed to connect, absorb and leverage the capabilities of diaspora members.

4.5.4   Material Attributes of the Balkan Entrepreneurial Ecosystems

The material attributes are tangible resources present in the region, such as universities, entrepreneurial policies and support facilities and services (Spigel, 2017). Despite lagging behind the Western European countries with respect to physical infrastructure (see for example the Infrastructure Gap Index), access to (public) physical as well as commercial infrastructure is perceived to be one of the main strengths of the Balkan EE (Andonova et al., 2019). In essence, while physical infrastructure still has a long way to go, there are various initiatives – often driven by Chinese investments (e.g. Andromidas, 2013) – which pave the way for promising improvements. For example, Bulgaria and Romania already are among the top 30 countries worldwide with respect to fastest internet connections (*Sofia Globe*, 2017).

Universities are often envisioned as the key players in the EE both in their role of developing human capital and fostering an entrepreneurial mindset (Wolfe, 2005) as well as in their role of providing technological knowledge (Lawton Smith, Chapman, Wood, Barnes & Romeo, 2014). They may provide potential entrepreneurs with opportunities to be exploited or instead be the origin of academic entrepreneurs (Shane, 2004). However, so far there has been little contribution from Balkan universities to their local EE. Most of the actors in Balkan's EE perceive knowledge and university processes as out of date and out of sync with the necessities of current economies even when occasionally some science, technology, engineering and medicine-related departments receive recognition for their ability to provide large-scale basic training.

> I have the feeling that, from a purely technical point of view, we are beginning to lag behind; because it is known that educational institutions in the region are very good at the fundamentals such as mathematics, but they do not really offer advanced tech skills. I fear that there is a risk that because of this we might lose our technological advantage. (Max Gurvits, Serial Entrepreneur; included in Andonova et al., 2019)

State-owned universities have been slow to adapt and innovate. One possible reason is that the introduction of new and innovative programs represents a threat to the established faculty members who are government employees and have no incentive to be entrepreneurial or innovative. Thus, the new programs are either kept small-scale or aborted altogether soon after the pilot launch. Additionally, entrepreneurial education so far has not played a role in public universities. The vacuum left by the short-sightedness of the educational sector in the Balkans is huge. While in the case of up-to-date and innovative programs that help develop entrepreneurial skills private initiatives can be a positive force, as the setup costs of such programs are rather low, private investments for significant R&D-related programs are absent. The latter is likely a result of the huge investments needed for such programs.

A very specific (educational) segment that thrives in the Balkans, however, juxtaposes this situation. Historically routed, the regional programming talent of the Balkans is excellent (e.g. Hallet, 1997). Stack Overflow, one of the most prominent Q&A platforms for coders, ranks the proficiency of coders. Relying on these data, most of the best coders are from the Balkans (Salkever, 2015).

Looking at the average country rankings of 14,898 Stack Overflow users with the highest reputation scores, Bulgarian coders come at the top. Forty top-performing users of this platform come from Bulgaria. Their contributions make Bulgaria the country with the highest average reputation in the world. Other Balkan countries like Croatia and Greece are in 6th and 19th place, respectively. At the same time, this top performing talent in coding and related spheres earn moderate wages. According to data from the Entrepreneurship Database Program at Emory University, on average, startups from the Balkans perform at a 50 percent discount when compared to labor costs in Latvia, Lithuania and Estonia (Andonova et al., 2019). To some extent, the proliferation of this talent alone might not have been sufficient. And even though it was not originated by the diaspora in the early moments, the connection of this talent to the global market was a tipping point for the emergence of the startup scene. Today, many of the inspirational role models of the region operate in the technology domain (Andonova et al., 2019).

> I think the big turning point [in the entrepreneurship processes], at least for Romanians, was the acquisition of the first Romanian IT company by Microsoft in 2003 [...] So this acquisition created the model for local entrepreneurs who saw how they could make money in IT. Until then they did not have that notion. (George Roth, Honorary Consul of Romania in San Francisco, included in Andonova et al., 2019).

On the other hand, innovation capabilities are highly determined by R&D and, thus, public spending is an essential part of any NIS (Hammadou, Paty & Savona, 2014). In comparison with other European countries, R&D in the Balkans is relatively low. Economies like Bulgaria, Croatia, Greece and Serbia invested in 2015 nearly 0.9 percent of their gross domestic product (GDP) on R&D. Contrary to this, European Union countries spent an average 2.05 percent in the same year. Baltic and Central European economies allocated about 1.5 to 2 percent on R&D. Meanwhile, Romania is far behind, with a public investment in R&D at 0.5 percent of their GDP in 2015. Slovenia is a positive outlier: 2.2 percent of their GDP is dedicated to R&D, placing it above average for the European Union (World Bank, 2016). Our case study shows that the key stakeholders in the Balkans believe that the root cause of the problem with NIS is the broken linkage between the academic and research entities, on the one hand, and the markets and market participants, on the other hand. Additionally, R&D expenditures not only tend to be low but they generate limited scientific and economic results.

4.6   CONCLUSIONS

In this chapter we build a case study about the Balkans. We argue that the Balkan diaspora actively contributed to the construction and evolution of EE, but did not play an equally positive role for NIS. Based on our case study, we suggest that the study of EE and NIS in countries with significant outward migration flows and sizable diaspora cannot be properly understood unless these factors are taken into consideration.

Based on this first exploration, we can conclude that the Balkan EE has managed to flourish in places where governments let a bottom-up approach unfold, allowing access through market mechanisms of multiple stakeholders, including diaspora members. The latter rapidly turned into entrepreneurs, mentors and investors energizing the link of the Balkans' EE with global entrepreneurial hubs and markets. In the case of the Balkans' NIS, however, government spending on R&D is meager; policies are too slow, overly bureaucratic and misaligned with market dynamics, leaving little opportunity for high-impact research to connect with global markets with the help of diasporas. NIS would need to undergo a change in ways similar to EE to benefit from diaspora. Yet, it is not clear that the political and economic elites have the will to undertake it.

Our results are not necessarily generalizable to every country with high migration. They are consistent across the Balkan countries as they present similarities in terms of their diasporas and migration dynamics on the one hand and in terms of institutional context on the other hand. Most economic migrants from the Balkans maintain strong links with their homeland and are actively engaged in economic activity, including investment in their country of origin, where one main motivation is the sense of giving back. These strong links to the country of origin can establish suitable characteristics of a diaspora to be relevant in the development of the local EE. Additionally, the background of the diaspora members allowed them to thrive exceptionally abroad. Such success gave way to several strategies through which diaspora could influence the construction of an EE. This needs to be seen in combination with home-country settings. All of the Balkan countries have small national markets, requesting an early internationalization strategy, which was favored by the diaspora. In addition to this, the programming talent of the region enabled technology-based startups, some of which were able to internationalize successfully. Despite these very specific characteristics of the studied region, we suggest that a diaspora engagement policy could pose a differentiator variable to the countries that would like to stimulate the relationships of the locals with expatriates in order to vitalize those networks in favor of EE. In order to evaluate this potential further, more research on the role of diaspora is needed in countries which are dissimilar to those of the Balkans.

Future research should also focus on understanding in greater detail the motivations of the diaspora to engage actively in Balkan EE. The insights of these research endeavors can have a profound impact on government policies related to the brain gain and productivity. The first evidence in this regard suggests deeply emotional, rather than economic, reasons behind the involvement of diaspora:

I haven't discussed the motivation of such people to get involved with local companies, but from what I see, I believe there is a level of nostalgia for Bulgaria, and some part of their lives which they cherish and they feel some sort of guilt not being there and not being able directly to influence and drive positive change, so when someone who is making something meaningful approaches them they try to help in any way they can. (Daniel Tomov, Investor and Partner in Eleven Ventures, included in Andonova et al., 2019)

In essence, a fine-grained comprehension of the barriers and catalyzers of diaspora involvement as well as data-rich quantitative research will most likely change our previous understanding about building vibrant EE and NIS.

NOTE

1.   This interpretation follows the definition of ecosystem as proposed in biology by Von Bertalanffy (1968).

REFERENCES

Acs, Z. J., Autio, E., & Szerb, L. (2014). National systems of entrepreneurship: Measurement issues and policy implications. *Research Policy*, *43*(3), 476–94. https://doi.org/10.1016/j.respol.2013.08.016

Acs, Z. J., Szerb, L., & Autio, E. (2015). The global entrepreneurship and development index. In: *Global Entrepreneurship and Development Index 2014* (pp. 39–64). New York: Springer. https://doi.org/10.1007/978-3-319-14932-5_4

Alvedalen, J., & Boschma, R. (2017). A critical review of entrepreneurial ecosystems research: Towards a future research agenda. *European Planning Studies*, *25*(6), 887–903. https://doi.org/10.1080/09654313.2017.1299694

Andonova, V., Nikolova, M. S., & Dimitrov, D. (2019). *Entrepreneurial Ecosystems in Unexpected Places: Examining the success factors of regional entrepreneurship.* New York: Palgrave Macmillan. https://doi.org/10.1007/978-3-319-98219-9

Andromidas, D. (2013). China develops Balkan infrastructure that the European Union won't build. *Executive Intelligence Review*, *40*, 33–9.

Arocena, R., & Sutz, J. (2000). Looking at national systems of innovation from the south. *Industry and Innovation*, *7*(1), 55–75. https://doi.org/10.1080/713670247

Autio, E., & Levie, J. (2017). Management of entrepreneurial ecosystems. In: G. Ahmetoglu, T. Chamorro-Premuzic, B. Klinger & T. Karcisky (Eds), *The Wiley*

Handbook of Entrepreneurship (pp. 423–49). Chichester: John Wiley & Sons. https://doi.org/10.1002/9781118970812.ch19

Bandelj, N., & Mahutga, M. C. (2010). How socio-economic change shapes income inequality in post-socialist Europe. *Social Forces*, *88*(5), 2133–61. https://doi.org/ 10.1353/sof.2010.0042

Barnes, A. (2007). Extricating the state: The move to competitive capture in post-communist Bulgaria. *Europe-Asia Studies*, *59*(1), 71–95. https://doi.org/10 .1080/09668130601072688

Bathelt, H. (2005). Cluster relations in the media industry: Exploring the "distanced neighbour" paradox in Leipzig. *Regional Studies*, *39*(1), 105–27. https://doi.org/10 .1080/0034340052000320860

Brown, R., & Mason, C. (2017). Looking inside the spiky bits: A critical review and conceptualization of entrepreneurial ecosystems. *Small Business Economics*, *49*(1), 11–30. https://doi.org/10.1007/s11187-017-9865-7

Cassiolato, J. E., & Lastres, H. M. M. (2005). Sistemas de inovação e desenvolvimento: As implicações de política. *São Paulo Em Perspectiva*, *19*(1), 34–45. https://doi.org/ 10.1590/S0102-88392005000100003

Correa, P., & Zuniga, P. (2013). *Western Balkans Regional R&D Strategy for Innovation: Overview of the research and innovation sector in the western Balkans*, Technical Assistance project p123211. www.worldbank.org/content/dam/ Worldbank/document/eca/Western-Balkans-Research&Innovation-Overview.pdf

Dana, L. P. (Ed.) (2007). *Handbook of Research on Ethnic Minority Entrepreneurship: A co-evolutionary view on resource management*. Cheltenham, UK and Northampton, MA, USA: Edward Elgar Publishing.

Draganov, I. (2019). The rise of Central and Eastern European tech (with Google for startups). Blog Post, March 18. Dealroom. https://blog.dealroom.co/the-rise -of-central-eastern-european-tech-with-google-for-startups/?_ga=2.79584912 .58503476.1565984088-1468312190.1565984088

Edquist, C., & Johnson, B. (1997). Institutions and organizations in systems of inno- vation. In: C. Edquist (Ed.), *Systems of Innovation: Technologies, institutions and organizations* (pp. 41–63). London: Cassell.

Edquist, C., & Lundvall, B.-Å. (1993). Comparing the Danish and Swedish systems of innovation. In: R. Nelson (Ed.), *National Innovation Systems: A comparative analysis* (pp. 265–98). Oxford: Oxford University Press.

Eleven (2007). Quarterly report. Private correspondence with the managing founders.

Ezekiev, P. (2017). The $5 billion CEE exits lead table. Blog Post. Neo Ventures, August 6. https://neoventures.net/2017/08/06/5-bn-lead-table-cee-rising-in-technology/

Freeman, C. (1995). The "national system of innovation" in historical perspec- tive. *Cambridge Journal of Economics*, *19*(1), 5–24. https://doi.org/10.1093/ oxfordjournals.cje.a035309

Freeman, C., & Soete, L. (1997). *The Economics of Industrial Innovation*, 3rd ed., Vol. 1. Cambridge, MA: MIT Press.

Gallup (2018). *Potential Net Migration Index*. http://news.gallup.com/migration/ interactive.aspx?g_source=link_newsv9&g_campaign=item_245204&g_medium= copy

Gillespie, K., Riddle, L., Sayre, E., & Sturges, D. (1999). Diaspora interest in homeland investment. *Journal of International Business Studies*, *30*(3), 623–34. https://doi .org/10.1057/palgrave.jibs.8490087

Girma, S., & Yu, Z. (2002). The link between immigration and trade: Evidence from the United Kingdom. *Weltwirtschaftliches Archiv, 138*(1), 115–30. https://doi.org/10.1007/BF02707326

Hallet, M. (1997). *National and Regional Development in Central and Eastern Europe: Implications for EU structural assistance.* European Economy – Economic Papers 2008–2015, no. 120. Directorate General Economic and Financial Affairs, European Commission. https://ideas.repec.org/p/euf/ecopap/0120.html

Hammadou, H., Paly, S., & Savona, M. (2014). Strategic interactions in public R&D across European countries: A spatial econometric analysis. *Research Policy, 43*(7), 1217–26. https://doi.org/10.1016/J.RESPOL.2014.01.011

Head, K., & Ries, J. (1998). Immigration and trade creation: Econometric evidence from Canada. *Canadian Journal of Economics, 31*(1), 47–62. https://doi.org/10.2307/136376

Hellman, J. S. (1998). Winners take all: The politics of partial reform in post-communist transitions. *World Politics, 50*(2), 203–34. https://doi.org/10.1017/S0043887100008091

Iorga, N. (1992 [1927]). Village and town. Conference at the Romanian social institute. In: I. Chimet (Ed.), *Dreptul la memorie*, 4th ed. (p. 93). Cluj: Dacia.

Isenberg, D. J. (2010). How to start an entrepreneurial revolution. *Harvard Business Review, 88*(6), 40–50.

Isenberg, D. J. (2016). Applying the ecosystem metaphor to entrepreneurship. *Antitrust Bulletin, 61*(4), 564–73. https://doi.org/10.1177/0003603X16676162

Kenney, M., Breznitz, D., & Murphree, M. (2013). Coming back home after the sun rises: Returnee entrepreneurs and growth of high tech industries. *Research Policy, 42*(2), 391–407. https://doi.org/10.1016/J.RESPOL.2012.08.001

Lawton Smith, H., Chapman, D., Wood, P., Barnes, T., & Romeo, S. (2014). Entrepreneurial academics and regional innovation systems: The case of spin-offs from London's universities. *Environment and Planning C: Government and Policy, 32*(2), 341–59. https://doi.org/10.1068/c11159b

Leblang, D. (2010). Familiarity breeds investment: Diaspora networks and international investment. *American Political Science Review, 104*(3), 584–600. https://doi.org/10.1017/S0003055410000201

List, F. (1904 [1841]). *The National System of Political Economy.* London: Longmans Green and Co.

Lundvall, B.-Å. (Ed.) (1992). *National Systems of Innovation: Towards a theory of innovation and interactive learning.* London: Pinter.

Lundvall, B.-Å. (2007a). Innovation system research: Where it came from and where it might go. *Globelics 5th Academy Working Paper No. 2007-01.* Atlanta, GA: Georgia Institute of Technology.

Lundvall, B.-Å. (2007b). National innovation systems: Analytical concept and development tool. *Industry and Innovation, 14*(1), 95–119. https://doi.org/10.1080/13662710601130863

Lundvall, B.-Å., Vang, J., Joseph, K., & Chaminade, C. (2009). Innovation system research and developing countries. In: B.-Å. Lundvall, J. Vang, K. Joseph & C. Chaminade (Eds), *Handbook of Innovation Systems and Developing Countries: Building domestic capabilities in a global setting* (pp. 1–30). Cheltenham, UK and Northampton, MA, USA: Edward Elgar Publishing.

Malecki, E. (1997). *Technology and Economic Development: The dynamics of local, regional and national competitiveness*, 2nd ed. London: Addison Wesley Longman.

Mason, C., & Brown, R. (2014). Entrepreneurial ecosystems and growth oriented entrepreneurship. Final Report to OECD, Paris, *30*(1), 77–102.

Masurel, E., Nijkamp, P., Tastan, M., & Vindigni, G. (2002). Motivations and performance conditions for ethnic entrepreneurship. *Growth and Change*, *33*(2), 238–60. https://doi.org/10.1111/0017-4815.00189

Minoglou, I. P., & Ioannides, S. (2004). Market-embedded clans in theory and history: Greek diaspora trading companies in the nineteenth century. *Business and Economic History On-Line*, *2*.

Mungiu-Pippidi, A. (2005). Deconstructing Balkan particularism: The ambiguous social capital of Southeastern Europe. *Southeast European and Black Sea Studies*, *5*(1), 49–68. https://doi.org/10.1080/1468385042000328367

Nelson, R. R. (1993). *National Innovation Systems: A comparative analysis*. Oxford: Oxford University Press.

O'Brien, C. (2018). Bulgaria rising: Can a growing startup movement reinvent the country's economy? Blog Post, March 23. VentureBeat. https://venturebeat.com/2018/03/23/bulgaria-rising-can-a-growing-startup-movement-reinvent-the-countrys-economy/

Plaza, S., & Ratha, D. (Eds) (2011). *Diaspora for Development in Africa*. https://elibrary.worldbank.org/doi/abs/10.1596/978-0-8213-8258-5

Pruthi, S. (2014). Social ties and venture creation by returnee entrepreneurs. *International Business Review*, *23*(6), 1139–52. https://doi.org/10.1016/J.IBUSREV.2014.03.012

Riddle, L., & Brinkerhoff, J. (2011). Diaspora entrepreneurs as institutional change agents: The case of Thamel.com. *International Business Review*, *20*(6), 670–80. https://doi.org/10.1016/J.IBUSREV.2011.02.013

Salkever, A. (2015). Data: Best programming talent in the world is not in California. Blog Post, April 5. VentureBeat. https://venturebeat.com/2015/04/05/data-best-programming-talent-in-the-world-is-not-in-california/

Schumpeter, J. A. (1934). *The Theory of Economic Development: An inquiry into profits, capital, credit, interest, and the business cycle*. Cambridge, MA: Harvard University Press.

Sergi, B. S., Henry, A., Weeks, G., Slinn, H., & Dumanova, Y. (2004). Four accounts on "brain drain" in the Balkans. *SEER: Journal for Labour and Social Affairs in Eastern Europe*, *6*, 13–26. https://doi.org/10.2307/43293007

Shane, S. (2004). *Academic Entrepreneurship: University spinoffs and wealth creation*. Cheltenham, UK and Northampton, MA, USA: Edward Elgar Publishing.

Smits, R., & Kuhlmann, S. (2004). The rise of systemic instruments in innovation policy. *International Journal of Foresight and Innovation Policy*, *1*(1/2), 4–32. https://doi.org/10.1504/IJFIP.2004.004621

Sofia Globe (2017). Internet connection speeds: Bulgaria among top 30 in the world.

Sommer, E., & Gamper, M. (2018). Transnational entrepreneurial activities: A qualitative network study of self-employed migrants from the former Soviet Union in Germany. *Social Networks*, *53*, 136–47. https://doi.org/10.1016/j.socnet.2017.04.007

Spigel, B. (2017). The relational organization of entrepreneurial ecosystems. *Entrepreneurship Theory and Practice*, *41*(1), 49–72. https://doi.org/10.1111/etap.12167

Spigel, B., & Harrison, R. (2018). Toward a process theory of entrepreneurial ecosystems. *Strategic Entrepreneurship Journal*, *12*(1), 151–68. https://doi.org/10.1002/sej.1268

Stam, E., & Spigel, B. (2016). Entrepreneurial ecosystems. *USE Discussion Paper Series*, *16*(13).

UNCTAD (2012). *The Least Developed Countries Report 2012: Harnessing Remittances and Diaspora Knowledge to Build Productive Capacities* (p. 192). United Nations. https://unctad.org/en/PublicationsLibrary/ldc2012_en.pdf

Vadean, F. (2007). Skills and remittances: The case of Afghan, Egyptian and Serbian immigrants in Germany. *Asia Research Institute Working Paper No. 92*. https://doi.org/10.2139/ssrn.1317135

Van De Ven, H. (1993). The development of an infrastructure for entrepreneurship. *Journal of Business Venturing*, *8*(3), 211–30. https://doi.org/10.1016/0883-9026(93)90028-4

Volery, T. (2007). Ethnic entrepreneurship: A theoretical framework. In: L. P. Dana (Ed.), *Handbook of Research on Ethnic Minority Entrepreneurship: A co-evolutionary view on resource management* (pp. 30–41). Cheltenham, UK and Northampton, MA, USA: Edward Elgar Publishing.

Von Bertalanffy, L. (1968). *General Systems Theory*. New York: George Braziller.

Waldinger, R. D., Aldrich, H., & Ward, R. (Eds) (1990). *Ethnic Entrepreneurs: Immigrant business in industrial societies*. Newbury Park, CA: SAGE.

Wolfe, D. (2005). The role of universities in regional development and cluster formation. In: G. Jones, P. McCarney & M. Skolnik (Eds), *Creating Knowledge, Strengthening Nations* (pp. 167–94). Toronto: University of Toronto Press.

World Bank (2016). Research and development expenditure (% of GDP). https://data.worldbank.org/indicator/GB.XPD.RSDV.GD.ZS?locations=EU&name_desc=false

Zhou, M. (2006). Revisiting ethnic entrepreneurship: Convergencies, controversies, and conceptual advancements. *International Migration Review*, *38*(3), 1040–74. https://doi.org/10.1111/j.1747-7379.2004.tb00228.x

PART II

Policy lessons from the systems perspectives

5. Beyond intellectual property and rich infrastructure: A community service learning perspective on universities' supportive role towards social entrepreneurs

Abel Diaz Gonzalez, Nikolay A. Dentchev and Maria del Carmen Roman Roig

5.1 INTRODUCTION

The role of universities in the supportive ecosystems of entrepreneurs is predominantly illustrated with cases from developed countries in Europe and North America. It is generally argued that universities provide support by means of their modern facilities and access to financial resources (Kirby, 2006). In addition, the generation of specialized knowledge based on scientific research is regarded as a valuable university contribution to ecosystems (Etzkowitz, 2004). This refers to the so-called Triple Helix (Etzkowitz & Leydesdorff, 2000) and Quadruple Helix (Carayannis & Campbell, 2010) of universities. However, such a Western view on the role of universities in the entrepreneurial ecosystem is difficult to adopt in many developing countries. A vast majority of the universities in these countries are focusing on teaching, with basic facilities, limited funding and underdeveloped scientific research. There are also developing countries where the knowledge of entrepreneurship is not at all established among university professors, especially in cases with an outspoken communist or authoritarian context.

Moreover, the typical focus on high-tech entrepreneurship is irrelevant in many contexts where universities have limited resources and intellectual property (IP) generation. Therefore, in this chapter we take the context of social entrepreneurship. Social entrepreneurs (SEs) are known for their contribution to resolve social and environmental issues (Smith & Woodworth, 2012), while being innovative in the use of available resources (Mair & Martí, 2006). These contributions are not easily realized. SEs are quite creative with their solutions for social and environmental issues, even though they face many challenges in their endeavors (Mair, Robinson & Hockerts, 2006). Typical challenges are the lack of financial resources, scarce human capital, and limited access to support networks, partnerships and alliances (Montgomery, Dacin & Dacin, 2012). Therefore, ecosystems supportive to SEs are helpful to improve their contribution to society due to the interconnectedness of various actors (Alvord, Brown & Letts, 2004; Benneworth & Cunha, 2015). Among these actors, universities are highlighted as playing a rather central role as hub and resource providers (Howard & Sharma, 2006; Smith & Woodworth, 2012; Malecki, 2018).

With this chapter, we will argue that universities have a role to play in the support of social entrepreneurship, even if they have limited resources and lack IP based on academic research. The need to address this knowledge gap is well expressed by Siegel and Wright (2015, p. 583):

> [T]he debate regarding universities and academic entrepreneurship has relied too much on the research – third mission nexus, with its narrow focus on university–industry links. This has arisen because of the undue narrow emphasis of academic entrepreneurship on the transfer of scientists' inventions from the laboratory to licences and start-ups, particularly in relation to formal IP, such as patents and licences.

We address the above knowledge gap by arguing that universities can always leverage their students, staff and existing networks to support social entrepreneurship, even when they have scant resources, limited fundamental research and even a certain ignorance of entrepreneurship. We use the theoretical lens of Community Service Learning (CSL) (Furco, 1996) to make this argument. To realize our objectives, we have conducted an explorative case study research in Bolivia, using data from 21 semi-structured interviews and three focus groups, complemented with secondary data and observations in the cities of Santa Cruz, San Jose de Chiquitos, Tarija, La Paz, Cochabamba and Batallas. We aim at describing the various existing activities and we illustrate new opportunities that universities could explore to contribute to the ecosystems in support of social entrepreneurship.

The remainder of this chapter is divided into six sections. Section 5.2 presents the main challenges that SEs face and how ecosystems can help to resolve these challenges, without possessing many resources or IP. Section 5.3 introduces the theoretical framework of CSL. Section 5.4 describes the methodology used for this study. Section 5.5 presents an overview of the background of Bolivia, i.e. the context of our study, while Section 5.6 is dedicated to the results, discussing the current role and future opportunities for Bolivian universities within the ecosystems in support to SEs through CSL. Section 5.7 presents the conclusions of this chapter.

Table 5.1   Challenges for social entrepreneurs

Type of challenge	Authors discussing it in the literature
Mission and strategy	
Lack of orientation; mission drift; difficulties to formulate sustainable short- and long-term strategy; inadequate legal forms	Austin, Stevenson & Wei-Skillern (2006); Certo & Miller (2008); Dees (1998); Honig (1998); Mair et al. (2006); Martin & Osber (2007)
Education and competences	
Lack of managerial and financial knowledge; difficulties when matching mission and values; strong and specific competencies needed to achieve social impact	Certo & Miller (2008); Dees (2007); Letaifa (2016); Volkmann, Tokarski & Ernst (2008); Webb, Kistruck, Ireland & Ketchen (2010); Wincent et al. (2016)
Funding and resource attraction	
Difficulties to manage and achieve financial sustainability; complex ways to access capital; challenges of attracting investment; complex efforts to access financial services	Bloom & Dees (2008); Letaifa (2016); Roundy (2017); Shaw & Carter (2007); Wincent et al. (2016)
Human resources	
Selection and engagement of people with the right profile; relying on volunteers; challenges to compete with market rates in terms of salaries	Dees (2012); Letaifa (2016); Roundy (2017); Sharir & Lerner (2006); Totterman & Sten (2005)
Evaluation and performance	
Difficulties to establish/determine performance indicators and impact on social or environmental projects; social return on investment is often subjective	Ardichvili, Cardozo & Ray (2003); Autio, Kenney, Mustar, Siegel & Wright (2014)

5.2   THE CHALLENGES FOR SOCIAL ENTREPRENEURS ADDRESSED FROM AN ECOSYSTEM PERSPECTIVE

Before elaborating on the main argument of our chapter – i.e. universities can support SEs without specific resources, research or even knowledge about entrepreneurship – one needs to first understand the main challenges of SEs, and hence grasp the potential roles of other ecosystem actors. SEs are confronted by different types of challenges depending on their context, goals and sector of activity (Mair & Martí, 2006). In Table 5.1, we summarize the main challenges faced by SEs as discussed in the relevant literature.

The first challenge is related to SEs' mission and strategy. Having a clear social mission is a central attribute for SEs (Austin et al., 2006). Drift in their social orientation is one of the most important concerns, since some SEs tend to lose the focus of their social mission upon the maturity of their organization (Wronka, 2013). This concern is also related to subsequent strategic choices related to income generation (profit) or the transitioning to hybridity (parallel profit and non-profit activities or only adopting a non-profit type of organization).

The second challenge is related to the educational background and competences of SEs, who can lack managerial and business skills (Dees, 2007) as they often have not benefited from a business-related education. Some SEs do not even have post-secondary education. Lacking business-related skills, or even formal education in some cases, represents a barrier for the daily business activities and for the strategic development of social enterprises (Mair et al., 2006).

Funding and the attraction of resources are among the main obstacles for SEs. They are constantly looking to capture the stakeholder's interest and trust to gain the support needed to scale up their social venture (Shaw & Carter, 2007). Moreover, their social missions are often seen as opposed to the creation of economic value and profitability (Mair & Martí, 2006). In addition to this, access to finances (venture capital, investment funds, banks or investors) requires competences and time effort that are often not feasible for SEs (Casson & Della Giusta, 2007).

The attraction of qualified human resources is the next challenge for SEs, presented in Table 5.1. SEs often cannot afford to pay competitive salaries to their employees (Sharir & Lerner, 2006), and hence they most likely may not attract the employees with the best profiles from the perspective of competences. In addition, it appears difficult to attract people with the right profile that share the same values, ideas, vision and are able to create social connections and alliances based on limited resources (Volkmann et al., 2008). Moreover, SEs often rely on volunteers whose commitment and availability can fluctuate over time (Sharir & Lerner, 2006).

The last challenge discussed in the literature is the performance evaluation of SEs. It is barely based on economic indicators, while social impact measurement is complex, subjective and in practice insufficiently adopted (Mair & Martí, 2006). Consequently, SEs have no clear stimuli to improve their performance and increase their social impact. It is also difficult for them to communicate the added value of their venture convincingly to their stakeholders.

Keeping in mind these five sets of challenges, it is important to mention that the success (or failure) of SEs does not only rely on their own activity, but also on the environment composed by other entrepreneurs, supportive organizations, policies, funders and other relevant stakeholders within their ecosystem (Roundy, 2017). Entrepreneurial ecosystems are based on the connection of multiple actors with complementary knowledge and assets, which all together lead to better business activity (Autio et al., 2014; Roundy, 2017).

Thanks to the variety of actors, entrepreneurial ecosystems provide (a) access to different type of resources, (b) qualified human capital, (c) linkages between organizations, (d) institutional robustness to promote adequate demand for specific goods and services, (e) political willingness and (f) collective action and high levels of social capital (Biggeri, Testi & Bellucci, 2017; Goyal, Sergi & Jaiswal, 2016; Letaifa, 2016). Universities have been highlighted as a key player in entrepreneurial ecosystems because of their knowledge and assets (Sánchez-Barrioluengo & Benneworth, 2019). Moreover, the role of universities in entrepreneurial ecosystems is noteworthy as they typically interact with stakeholders such as government organizations, public- and private-sector actors (e.g. banks, non-governmental organizations (NGOs), labor unions, industrial associations, small and medium-sized enterprises and multinational enterprises) (Spigel & Harrison, 2018). After all, neither the above-mentioned challenges of SEs nor the general networking role of universities presuppose abundant resources or fundamental research. We will further use the theoretical framework of CSL to develop our argument that universities can provide tremendous support based on the critical mass of students and faculty.

5.3   COMMUNITY SERVICE LEARNING

In higher education, CSL is a pedagogic strategy aimed at offering students the opportunity to work with local community groups in resolving their real social challenges (Jones, Warner & Kiser, 2010). In doing so, students are confronted with the needs of communities, which gives them the opportunity to reflect upon and resolve the rather challenging social issues that they face (Furco, 1996).

In the words of Ejiwale and Posey (2008, p. 3), CSL is presented as an "opportunity for students to develop their leadership skills, discover talents and gain meaningful personal insights". This is achieved by applying theoretical learning content (from courses) during a practical experience, characterized by incorporated social engagement (Bringle & Hatcher, 1996). The activities organized within CSL are based on the expertise, contacts and connections of faculty, university administration and staff, with the objective to pursue social goals (Vogelgesang & Astin, 2000).

Thus, students are assigned to work on different tasks within their community, where a task can vary depending on the content of the class and the desired learning outcome, through either direct or indirect contact with the groups within the targeted community (Bringle & Hatcher, 1996). CSL focuses on personal growth and the transformation of its participants, where values such as trust, mutual dependence, reciprocity, self-confidence and justice are placed at the core of the learning process (Vogelgesang & Astin, 2000). Depending on the approach and the strategies, CSL initiatives can be organized through curricular or extra-curricular activities or a combination of both (Brower, 2011). When the activities are organized in an extracurricular way, the engagement of the participants occurs mainly through voluntarism and is not limited to students only, but is open to the whole academic community (Furco, 1996). On the other hand, when CSL initiatives are part of the curricula, activities are credit-bearing educational experiences, i.e. mostly compulsory for the students (Bringle & Hatcher, 1996). Both, learning approaches provide meaningful learning experiences while serving the community through available university assets (Jones et al., 2010), which are mainly related to the willingness of students, faculty and staff to provide support.

For students, CSL offers the opportunity to confront real-life situations by applying theories and concepts studied in their courses and thereby achieving a higher degree of social awareness and commitment. For professors, these strategies create valuable partnerships with their communities that could potentially open up new possibilities for projects and collaborations. Furthermore, they motivate students to be more engaged and committed to the course and the further learning of the subject. For the community in general, CSL provides additional human resources that work on their own challenges, while having a continued exchange of knowledge via students and feedback from university experts (Vogelgesang & Astin, 2000). Some examples of CSL programs in developing countries are related to homeless and indigenous groups, minorities and vulnerable communities. Students contribute by proposing alternative solutions to recurrent problems related to food, health, employment, shelter and education (Jones et al., 2010). Overall, a CSL perspective makes it clear that universities do not need access to extraordinary resources and fundamental research to support the community.

5.4   METHODOLOGY

To highlight the objective of this chapter – i.e. arguing that universities can contribute within the ecosystem in support of SEs without ample resources and high-cost research – we have chosen the context of Bolivia. Bolivian universities are predominantly teaching-oriented, working with limited resources and basic infrastructure, while technology transfer between universities and entrepreneurship is still in its infancy (Gottwald, Buch & Giesecke, 2012). We have adopted a qualitative research method (Eisenhardt, 1989) to study the Bolivian context of universities, their interaction with SEs and other actors in the ecosystem. Our study is based on 21 in-depth, semi-structured interviews and three focus groups, collected and held in Bolivia during four non-consecutive weeks in different months between December 2017 and December 2018.

The following cities in Bolivia were selected for our study: Santa Cruz de la Sierra, La Paz, Cochabamba, San Jose de Chiquitos, Batallas and Tarija.

Table 5.2   *List of respondents*

No.	Code	Profile	Sector/type of organization	City
1	P1	University professor	Academia	Santa Cruz
2	P2	University professor	Academia	La Paz
3	P3	University professor	Academia	Tarija
4	P4	University professor	Academia	Santa Cruz
5	P5	University professor	Academia	Batallas
6	P6	Technical/vocational trainer	Academia	Cochabamba
7	P7	University professor	Academia	La Paz
8	P8	Manager	Consulting company	Santa Cruz
9	P9	Manager	Entrepreneur	Santa Cruz
10	P10	Manager	Entrepreneur	Cochabamba
11	P11	Head of government department	Government	San Jose de Chiquitos
12	P12	Manager	Incubator – private	Santa Cruz
13	P13	Head of network	International network	Cochabamba
14	P14	Manager	Non-governmental organization	Santa Cruz
15	P15	Manager	Non-governmental organization	Santa Cruz
16	P16	Executive member	Professional network	Santa Cruz
17	P17	Professional	Professional network	Santa Cruz
18	P18	Manager	Social enterprise	Santa Cruz
19	P19	Manager	Social enterprise	Santa Cruz
20	P20	Manager	Social enterprise	Cochabamba
21	P21	Manager	Social enterprise	Santa Cruz
22	FG1	Team – government division	Government	Tarija
23	FG2	Team – incubator	Incubator – public	Tarija
24	FG3	Team – university network/student association	Academia	La Paz

According to the local knowledge of our contacts in Bolivia, these locations were a good setting for the study because of the presence of one (or several) universities, the presence of SEs and other relevant supportive organizations of the entrepreneurial ecosystem. After discussions with various professors and university staff members from Bolivia, we aimed at interviewing respondents with various backgrounds. An overview of the interviews and focus groups can be found in Table 5.2.

Respondents in the data collection included SEs, regular entrepreneurs, representatives from public institutions, incubators, funding organizations, technical and vocational education institutions and universities. We used two different interview protocols (see Appendix) for our study: one was designed for individual entrepreneurs and the other was used for supportive organizations (viz. universities, NGOs, incubators, networks, government). Several versions of the interview protocol were discussed in advance with nine different scholars in Belgium and Bolivia in order to select the most appropriate structure and questions.

As a measure of construct validity (Brink, 1993), participants were informed about the purpose of the study and given the opportunity to ask questions during interviews. This resulted in a better understanding of the phenomenon of study and improved the trust relationship between researchers and respondents. This step was especially relevant when approaching SEs living in extreme poverty, as they are not used to participating in any type of scientific study. Interviews were recorded and further transcribed to increase the reliability of the study (Brink, 1993). During the analysis of the research, all information was coded and organized (Braun, Clarke, Hayfield & Terry, 2018).

Using a methodological triangulation (Golafshani, 2003), we combined primary data collection (i.e. interviews and focus group discussions) with more than 70 documents obtained during our visit to Bolivia in combination with participant observations (Eisenhardt & Graebner, 2007). The secondary data sources included brochures, university reports, events material, promotional material, information from companies and organizations, different types of campaigns and project materials. This triangulation method reduces the potential bias and allows the researcher to acquire in-depth knowledge of the context and enhances the reliability of the results.

Another triangulation tactic was the organization of events in which entrepreneurs and other ecosystem actors took part. In collaboration with the Catholic University of Bolivia in Cochabamba and Tarija, we co-organized (1) two open lectures with approximately 90 attendees each of students, social and conventional entrepreneurs, (2) the entrepreneurship fair "Yo Emprendo Tarija" with the participation of more than 60 local entrepreneurs and 600 attendees and (3) a group mobility with nine MSc and two PhD students from Belgium, which took place in Tarija with more than 100 local social, student and conventional entrepreneurs in December 2018. Throughout all these activities, we observed the various roles that local universities were capable of adopting and saw several opportunities for them to continue supporting these types of interventions and activities.

5.5   THE BOLIVIAN CONTEXT

In 2005, the victory of the "Movement for Socialism" lead Bolivia to adopt political, social and economic reforms (Querejazu, Zavaleta & Mendizabal, 2014), with a major impact on entrepreneurship. With the approval of the new constitution in 2009, the country was reorganized under the "plural economy model", characterized by state (state-owned companies); private (private businesses); cooperative (cooperatives and formal associations); and community economies, in which a vast majority of the country's workforce is located by means of peasant, community, artisan and indigenous organizations (Galway, Corbett & Zeng, 2012). In practice, these reforms left the country with an environment that is somewhat demotivating to entrepreneurs. An indication for this are inadequate enterprise laws, consecutive waves of nationalization and the outspoken socialist views of the country's leadership.

Bolivia is rich in natural resources, such as fertile lands, bountiful minerals, water and forest (Querejazu et al., 2014). The government actively seeks to generate profits out of the natural gas reserves, as this, along with other natural resources, has always been and is a significant part of the Bolivian economy (Mares, Hartley & Medlock, 2008). These natural resources become relevant when formulating the development strategies for the country. In spite of these rich veins of natural resources, it is argued that Bolivia suffers from poor governance and inadequate institutional policies (cf. Kaplan, 2006).

In the field of higher education, there are 15 public universities across the country grouped in the Comité Ejecutivo de la Universidad Boliviana University System, which serves the majority of the university students in the country. There are also several private universities with a teaching orientation present in the country, where the main source of funding is tuition fees from students and other activities organized through executive education. Both types of university lack fundamental research capacities and established technology transfer offices and procedures (Rodriguez Ostria & Weise Vargas, 2006).

All public universities have offices dedicated to managing social engagement or extension offices, which have as purview the developing of the strategies for engaging the university with industry, government and society at large. At the private level, the General Regulation of Private Universities requires private universities to develop extension activities, community engagement and promotion of local culture (Rodriguez Ostria & Weise Vargas, 2006). These policies force universities to establish and maintain links with their local communities, especially in a country where there is clear fragmentation and where there are many inequalities among the population (Galway et al., 2012). The disparity in ethnics, socio-economic situation and geographical location show a fractured country where the majority of the population is indigenous (Anderson, Honig & Peredo, 2006).

Overall, the Bolivian context is quite relevant to our study. The research tradition in this context is rather scant, as universities are not endowed with many resources. Moreover, the entrepreneurial climate and knowledge are not particularly stimulated due to the political context of the country. In Bolivia, SEs address the primary needs of individuals and communities, related to their survival (Gaiger, Nyssens & Wanderley, 2019). In this country, we can count SEs among the peasant, community, artisan associations and cooperatives, as they are ultimately driving social change (Querejazu et al., 2014).

5.6　　FINDINGS

Following the analysis of the collected data, we hereby present an overview of the role of universities within the entrepreneurial ecosystem in Bolivia. We will show the main challenges that universities face to support SEs, as it confirms the relevance of the setting with respect to the knowledge gap identified – universities with limited IP generation, scarce resources and even general ignorance of entrepreneurship. Further, we discuss how higher education institutions (HEIs) mobilize their critical mass (students and staff) in support of SEs through CSL.

5.6.1　　Main Challenges of Bolivian Higher Education Institutions to Support Social Entrepreneurs

Firstly, it is important to discuss the challenge Bolivian HEIs face to provide entrepreneurial training (Lekhanya, 2016). Several universities have programs in business and management sciences (both at undergraduate and graduate levels), where entrepreneurship is being taught. Yet, their current curriculum is deemed insufficient to provide students with the proper knowledge and tools to develop their entrepreneurial ventures. Different studies also mention that in developing countries, such as Bolivia, universities lack ready mentors who can coach new start-ups of staff and students (Ozgen & Baron, 2007). Our findings reveal that this lack of qualified mentorship and adequate knowledge of entrepreneurship in Bolivian universities constitutes an important challenge:

> P9:　　There is not sufficient qualified human capital to accompany nascent entrepreneurs in the launch of their businesses at universities.
> P10:　　Salaries and incentives to become an entrepreneur are low and not competitive. While this is important for some students, they also need to be motivated to take the risk of not becoming employees but entrepreneurs.

Scientific research in the field of entrepreneurship represents the second challenge that our study has revealed. Only a few universities in the country are conducting scientific research on topics related to entrepreneurship, viz. the Catholic University of Bolivia and Universidad Mayor de San Simon. This is not surprising, as we find the overall research skills in Bolivia to be limited in general, since most universities are only now starting to develop entrepreneurship programs. This challenge can be illustrated with the following quotes:

> P5:   We find only a few academics involved in research on Social Entrepreneurship in the country. I don't know if we can talk about publications, but they are doing some efforts.
> P18:   We need more innovation to address multiple issues and challenges from our city. There are several problems here such as transport, health, environmental, etc., and I think this should be the departing point from universities to collaborate with the government to develop fundamental research that could be translated into real solutions for our society. Social Entrepreneurship can become a solution for many of these problems.

The third challenge is related to the overall insufficient integration of basic entrepreneurship in the curricula. While universities within the entrepreneurial ecosystem are expected to stimulate training opportunities for SEs (Roberts & Eesley, 2011), some of our respondents voice a concern in this regard:

> P13:   Universities are immersed in their own issues, and sometimes they should think more about the importance of giving the right education and life tools for their students to succeed. This is not only coming from the inside of academia, but from the collaboration with companies or businesses.
> P2:   Universities nowadays have a very important role within the ecosystem. This is the moment to officially establish in all universities a course on entrepreneurship, not only focusing on profitability and businesses, but also on the social aspect, such as social entrepreneurship.

In general, the challenges mentioned above confirm that Bolivian universities are only just beginning to generate scientific research and entrepreneurship. Despite this shortcoming, our research of Bolivian universities indicates that HEIs have developed various activities in support of social enterprises, as SEs clearly provide creative solutions to local societal problems. Hence, it is important to support SEs and universities clearly have a role to play in that support, which we will discuss below.

5.6.2   The CSL Perspective in Support of Social Entrepreneurs

The CSL is a way in which universities can support local SEs. In this section, we present the activities that universities can deploy in support of SEs, by focusing on the three main actors in CSL: (1) students, (2) faculty and staff and (3) the community itself. In Table 5.3 and the related text below, we elaborate on how exactly universities can support SEs and what are the different support-ive roles of actors within HEIs or across the ecosystem. The various activities mentioned in Table 5.3 are based on the finding of our study, and elaborated in further detail in the subsections below. Furthermore, we make some practical recommendations as to how universities can support SEs.

5.6.3   Students

Business programs at HEIs in Bolivia (at undergraduate and graduate levels) with compulsory assignments could be used to provide specific support to SEs by means of business advice, product development, market research and/or marketing communications support. These student class assignments (compul-sory, credit bearing) are one of the more prominent opportunities for univer-sities in Bolivia to support SEs. Assignments can adopt many different forms (reports, essays, presentations) based on case studies and day-to-day business analysis of local SEs. The faculty will set the objectives of these assignments at strengthening the social entrepreneurial project and impact, by using the input of students, their knowledge and involvement, as available resources during this intervention. Some professors have also reflected on the impor-tance of using the classroom as a space where students can debate the different strategies that could address social issues, especially as they accompany SEs' initiatives in specific hands-off support. These findings are in alignment with recent studies on SE (Biggeri et al., 2017) and have been expressed as follows by our respondents:

> P7:   Our students need to see other realities beyond poverty and unemployment. They need to learn how to tackle these problems. We need to incorporate more this subject of social entrepreneurship not only in the curriculum but also on the level of research to have more impact on local policies and agenda.
> FG1:   Universities should also teach in their entrepreneurship courses about resil-ience, responsibility and social commitment. This will further lead students to think more responsibly while creating their business and becoming social entrepreneurs.

Students could contribute beyond their direct support of SEs during CSL activities: they could also advocate CSL initiatives to other students, friends and family, irrespective of their academic involvement. Students could stim-ulate the use of conventional and new technologies (i.e. conventional and social media channels) to communicate their involvement in CSL programs. Communication increases the chance that other stakeholders will recognize their needs and offer support to SEs. Finally, students could volunteer in different activities dedicated to supporting SEs and their broader ecosystem.

Table 5.3   *Community service learning lens on higher education institution activities in support of social entrepreneurs*

CSL actors	Activities
Students	• Select and attend courses in which compulsory assignments are dedicated to supporting social entrepreneurship.
	• Promote their experiences in CSL activities (advantages, outcomes) to engage fellow students.
	• Establish students' organizations to support CSL initiatives.
	• Submit their best practices to student competitions and awards, to raise more awareness on the importance of CSL projects in support of community needs.
	• Use social media and other means of communication (Facebook, Instagram, WhatsApp, student blogs) to publicize the projects in the community, attract more volunteers and promote results and experiences.
	• Volunteer in local events (university level, community level) to support all different CSL initiatives.
University staff and faculty	• Establish an internal formal committee to lead and develop a CSL framework program at university.
	• Engage faculty members to update/adapt the curriculum to include CSL activities.
	• Organize meetings with students and faculty to reflect upon the experiences of CSL existing activities.
	• Participate in conferences and other events related to CSL (national and international levels).
	• Establish networks of collaboration with local government and relevant actors of the entrepreneurial ecosystem to create or strengthen CSL initiatives.
	• Actively promote and publicize existing CSL programs and results.
	• Participate in grants or project proposals, involving all different actors (students, faculty and community) in activities related to CSL.
Community	• Identify local leaders to work with the university (faculty and students) to design intervention actions through CSL programs.
	• Participate at different workshops, meetings and events organized by the university to discuss and reflect on CSL programs and opportunities.
	• Propose their own business and social projects to be subject of intervention through CSL activities.

CSL actors	Activities
	• Be reciprocal with students; engage them as much as possible in their community life and activities (fairs, social events, talks) to create long-term commitment and trust among all different stakeholders.
	• Provide timely feedback to university members and faculty about their experience with students, CSL approach and how to further improve the intervention.

This has been observed as a practice where students are eager to participate in different fairs, events and other activities organized locally, and dedicated to promoting projects of SEs, their projects and activities.

5.6.4   University: Faculty and Staff

With the use of CSL activities in support of SEs, faculty members are encouraging students to use and apply the knowledge disseminated in their courses. Moreover, CSL can be utilized by faculty members to conduct research: by collecting relevant data from their own cases they could realize scientific publications.

Our findings suggest that universities could also leverage their own resources to offer consultancy services to the private sector and the government. Examples of university consultancy services are: consulting on business planning, tax returns and legal management by specialized academics who also understand the value of the sustainability principle and the rationale of a business model with social impact (Cohen, 2006). Our findings suggest that in all cities studied, there is a demand for such consulting services:

P15:   We need sometimes some special skills that we can only find at universities. They should exploit more their consultancy services to support the growth of our city and expand the creation of businesses in certain types of areas, for instance, tourism.

P11:   We have already requested some support from the university to offer technical assistance in projects. We benefit from external aid and, our farmers, don't have the knowledge to deal with complex applications and grants request, and this is where the university can collaborate with them. Also, to support them when we receive the resources for machinery or for raw material. We definitely need to collaborate with universities in that sense.

In the Bolivian context, especially in La Paz and in Tarija, incubators represent a strategic partner to carry out university CSL programs and activities to support local entrepreneurs. Universities could contribute to social and economic development by integrating their services and resources with local incubators (Bruneel, Ratinho, Clarysse & Groen, 2012; Roberts & Eesley, 2011). Our findings suggest that interactions between universities and incubators could be further exploited by converging students' efforts, the needs of entrepreneurs and the incubators' programs and activities:

> FG2: We are an incubator funded by the government. One of our most important key partners is the university, as they surround us with different activities (complementary) most of them being events and fairs. However, we have been in conversations to develop more structural cooperation for the technical assistance to our entrepreneurs and to strengthen our cooperation to support the innovation and knowledge transfer within our projects.
> P5: We (Universities) participate as jury members of some of the competitions for a local incubator. However, we also can participate in the coaching of entrepreneurs and other activities of the program.

Concrete ways of intensifying university–incubator interactions is to involve the faculty in the decision-making processes of these incubators (advisory boards, board of directors), but also by launching joint initiatives such as contests, hackathons, promotional events, fairs and consolidating the different programs to guide and coach social enterprises jointly.

5.6.5 The Community

The community is often seen as a beneficiary of CSL initiatives (Furco, 1996). They benefit from these interventions by gaining alternative insights into their community issues. In this sense, SEs obtain from students not only innovative ideas and reflections on their business approach but also get an opportunity to integrate solutions with the involvement of several stakeholders from academia and the broader ecosystem. Universities and the community could find new connections, open alternative spaces for discussion, connect in new and alternative ways through students and their proposals and bring in new resources through the involvement of other stakeholders in the CSL. These stakeholders are government institutions, NGOs (national and international), training centers, other entrepreneurs and financial organizations.

In the Bolivian context, local government plays an important role in dynamizing the connections between the university and the community. As discussed in the literature, governments can play a significant role in accelerating (or hindering) the development of social enterprises through their policies, political environment, incentives, subsidies and grants, among other mechanisms (Cohen, 2006). Developing countries have to deal with barriers of low income, feeble technology and exploitation of an underskilled workforce, which triggers the informal economy (Prahalad & Hart, 1999). In the case of Bolivia, more than 85 percent of businesses are said to belong to the informal sector.

To diminish this, appropriate government policies should be established to stimulate the economy, offer more incentives and develop an appropriate business environment (Galway et al., 2012). Our findings suggest that currently in Bolivia both the public and private sectors generally tend to work in isolation and/or their efforts to cooperate are not self-evident.

> P15:   There are low or inexistent incentives from the central government to support the launch of new businesses. We have learned, for example, from CAINCO, a program that is executed in Latin America oriented to support the development of entrepreneurship, with technical assistance, calls, coaching, etc. We don't have something like this in the country.
> P7:   In our ecosystem, we don't have a local policy, nor a single officer in the local government (or in the state government) that is talking or leading the conversation on entrepreneurship or innovation.

In this respect, this study emphasizes the impact that universities could have in the decision-making process of the government by adopting new policies and by implementing more practical programs to foster the entrepreneurial culture within the local ecosystem. This finding of our research is in line with the Quadruple Helix conception of linking academic entrepreneurship to business, government and society at large (Carayannis & Campbell, 2010).

We have observed that in cities such as Tarija and La Paz, the local governments have the willingness to collaborate with universities to support SEs (through workshops, training, coaching, fairs and events). These programs and initiatives could be further improved upon by involving more faculty and students. Several of the interviewees pointed out the importance of networking activities and recognized it as one of the most influential aspects of the social entrepreneurial development process. In this sense, all the participants agreed that networking creates access to new funding opportunities, business development, sales and visibility in Bolivian society. The need for networking is well illustrated in the following quotes:

> P18:   Social networking is one of the most important aspects. Without working in your network, the appearance of the society becomes really hard. If you want to work with the government, you need to know people from the government; if you want to work with the businessmen, you need to know people from private companies.
> P12:   I think networking is the most important thing. I have seen, several times, social entrepreneurs, who could, maybe, have more competences or originality than us, but if they do not have the right connections that are needed to all type of entrepreneurship, they will not get very far.

Universities are the usual suspects to coordinate and intensify such networking activities due to their contacts with various stakeholders, irrespective of resource availability and research orientation.

5.7 CONCLUSIONS

Our study shows that Bolivian universities play an important role in the supportive ecosystem of SEs, despite their limited resources, scant fundamental research and even inadequate understanding of entrepreneurship. To fulfill that role, universities can rely on their basic infrastructure and the critical mass of students, faculty and staff members.

With the involvement of these in the community, universities can create a supportive environment in the SE ecosystem. Using the theoretical lens of CSL, we have discussed 18 different activities on three levels (students, faculty and staff and the community) while indicating that no major resources nor fundamental research are required to implement them. Our findings are arguably relevant to other contexts, including Western countries, where universities could substantially increase their impact on social and conventional entrepreneurship by leveraging students, faculty and staff. We also argue that future research into entrepreneurial universities should reach beyond the traditional IP-based technology transfer.

REFERENCES

Alvord, S. H., Brown, D., & Letts, C. (2004). Social entrepreneurship and societal transformation: An exploratory study. *Journal of Applied Behavioral Science*, *40*(3), 260–82.

Anderson, R. W., Honig, B., & Peredo, A. M. (2006). Communities in the global economy: Where social and indigenous entrepreneurship meet. In: D. Hjorth & C. Steyaert (Eds), *Entrepreneurship as Social Change: A third new movements in entrepreneurship book* (pp. 56–78). Cheltenham, UK and Northampton, MA, USA: Edward Elgar Publishing.

Ardichvili, A., Cardozo, R., & Ray, S. (2003). A theory of entrepreneurial opportunity identification and development. *Journal of Business Venturing*, *18*(1), 105–23.

Austin, J., Stevenson, H., & Wei-Skillern, J. (2006). Social and commercial entrepreneurship: Same, different, or both? *Entrepreneurship: Theory and Practice*, *30*(1), 1–22.

Autio, E., Kenney, M., Mustar, P., Siegel, D., & Wright, M. (2014). Entrepreneurial innovation: The importance of context. *Research Policy*, *43*(7), 1097–108.

Benneworth, P. & Cunha, J. (2015). Universities' contributions to social innovation: Reflections in theory and practice. *European Journal of Innovation Management*, *18*(4), 508–27.

Biggeri, M., Testi, E., & Bellucci, M. (2017). Enabling ecosystems for social enterprises and social innovation: A capability approach perspective. *Journal of Human Development and Capabilities*, *18*(2), 299–306.

Bloom, P. N., & Dees, G. (2008). Cultivate your ecosystem. *Stanford Social Innovation Review, 6*(1), 47–53.

Braun, V., Clarke, V., Hayfield, N., & Terry, G. (2018). Thematic analysis. In: P. Liamputtong (Ed.), *Handbook of Research Methods in Health Social Sciences* (pp. 2–17). Singapore: Springer.

Bringle, R., & Hatcher, J. A. (1996). Implementing service learning in higher education. *Journal of Higher Education, 67*(2), 221–39.

Brink, H. (1993). Validity and reliability in qualitative research. *Curationis, 16*(2), 35–8.

Brower, H. H. (2011). Sustainable development through service learning: A pedagogical framework and case example in a third world context. *Academy of Management Learning and Education, 10*(1), 58–76.

Bruneel, J., Ratinho, T., Clarysse, B., & Groen, A. (2012). The evolution of business incubators: Comparing demand and supply of business incubation services across different incubator generations. *Technovation, 32*(2), 110–21.

Carayannis, E. G., & Campbell, D. F. J. (2010). Triple helix, quadruple helix and quintuple helix and how do knowledge, innovation and the environment relate to each other? *International Journal of Social Ecology and Sustainable Development, 1*(1), 41–69.

Casson, M., & Della Giusta, M. (2007). Entrepreneurship and social capital: Analysing the impact of social networks on entrepreneurial activity from a rational action perspective. *International Small Business Journal, 25*(3), 220–44.

Certo, S. T., & Miller, T. (2008). Social entrepreneurship: Key issues and concepts. *Business Horizons, 51*(4), 267–71.

Cohen, B. (2006). Sustainable valley entrepreneurial ecosystems. *Business Strategy and the Environment, 15*(1), 1–14.

Dees, G. (1998). The meaning of social entrepreneurship. *Stanford University Working Paper*. Stanford, CA. https://sehub.stanford.edu/sites/default/files/TheMeaning ofsocialEntrepreneurship.pdf

Dees, G. (2007). Taking social entrepreneurs seriously. *Transaction: Social Science and Modern Society, 44*(3), 24–31.

Dees, J. G. (2012). A tale of two cultures: Charity, problem solving, and the future of social entrepreneurship. *Journal of Business Ethics, 111*(3), 321–34.

Eisenhardt, K. M. (1989). Building theories from case study research. *Academy of Management Review, 14*(4), 532–50.

Eisenhardt, K. M., & Graebner, M. E. (2007). Theory building from cases: Opportunities and challenges. *Academy of Management Journal, 50*(1), 25–32.

Ejiwale, J., & Posey, D. (2008). Enhancing leadership skills through service learning. Proceedings from American Society for Engineering Education (ASEE) Conference and Exposition, Pittsburgh, PA.

Etzkowitz, H. (2004). The evolution of the entrepreneurial university. *International Journal of Technology and Globalisation, 1*(1), 64.

Etzkowitz, H., & Leydesdorff, L. (2000). The dynamics of innovation: From national systems and "mode 2" to a triple helix of university–industry–government relations. *Research Policy, 29*, 109–23.

Furco, A. (1996). Service-learning: A balanced approach to experiential education. In: B. Taylor (Ed.), *Expanding Boundaries: Serving and learning* (pp. 2–6). Washington, DC: Corporation for National Service.

Gaiger, L. I., Nyssens, M., & Wanderley, F. (2019). *Social Enterprise in Latin America: Theory, models and practice*. New York: Routledge.

Galway, L. P., Corbett, K. K., & Zeng, L. (2012). Where are the NGOs and why? The distribution of health and development NGOs in Bolivia. *Globalization and Health*, *8*(38), 1–13.

Golafshani, N. (2003). Understanding reliability and validity in qualitative research. *Qualitative Report*, *8*(4), 597–607.

Gottwald, J., Buch, F., & Giesecke, K. (2012). Understanding the role of universities in technology transfer in the renewable energy sector in Bolivia. *Management of Environmental Quality*, *23*(3), 291–9.

Goyal, S., Sergi, B. S., & Jaiswal, M. P. (2016). Understanding the challenges and strategic actions of social entrepreneurship at base of the pyramid. *Management Decision*, *54*(2), 418–40.

Honig, B. (1998). What determines success? Examining the human, financial, and social capital of Jamaican microentrepreneurs. *Journal of Business Venturing*, *13*(5), 371–94.

Howard, J., & Sharma, A. (2006). Universities' third mission: Communities engagement. *Business/Higher Education Round Table, B-Hert Position Paper No.11*.

Jones, A. L., Warner, B., & Kiser, P. M. (2010). Service-learning and social entrepreneurship: Finding the common ground. *Partnerships: A Journal of Service Learning and Civic Engagement*, *1*(2), 1–15.

Kaplan, S. (2006). Making democracy work in Bolivia. *Orbis*, *50*(3), 501–17.

Kirby, D. A. (2006). Creating entrepreneurial universities in the UK: Applying entrepreneurship theory to practice. *Journal of Technology Transfer*, *31*(5), 599–603.

Lekhanya, L. M. (2016). The role of universities in promoting social entrepreneurship in South Africa. *Journal of Governance and Regulation*, *4*(3), 67–71.

Letaifa, S. B. (2016). How social entrepreneurship emerges, develops and internationalises during political and economic transitions. *European Journal of International Management*, *10*(4), 455.

Mair, J., & Martí, I. (2006). Social entrepreneurship research: A source of explanation, prediction, and delight. *Journal of World Business*, *41*(1), 36–44.

Mair, J., Robinson, J., & Hockerts, K. (2006). Introduction. In: Mair, J., Robinson, J., & Hockerts, K. (Eds), *Social Entrepreneurship* (pp. 1–13). New York: Palgrave Macmillan.

Malecki, E. J. (2018). Entrepreneurship and entrepreneurial ecosystems. *Geography Compass*, *12*(3), 1–21.

Mares, D. R., Hartley, P. R., & Medlock, K. B. (2008). Energy security in a context of hyper-social mobilization: Insights from Bolivia. Working Paper Series: The Global Energy Market: Comprenhensive strategies to meet geopolitical and financial risk. Rice University. https://scholarship.rice.edu/bitstream/handle/1911/91430/IEEJBolivia.pdf?sequence=1

Martin, R. L., & Osberg, S. (2007). Social entrepreneurship: The case for definition. *Stanford Social Innovation Review*, *5*(2), 29–39.

Montgomery, A. W., Dacin, P. A., & Dacin, M. T. (2012). Collective social entrepreneurship: Collaboratively shaping social good. *Journal of Business Ethics*, *111*(3), 375–88.

Ozgen, E., & Baron, R. A. (2007). Social sources of information in opportunity recognition: Effects of mentors, industry networks, and professional forums. *Journal of Business Venturing*, *22*(2), 174–92.

Prahalad, C., & Hart, S. (1999). Strategies for the bottom of the pyramid: Creating sustainable development. Working Paper, University of Michigan and University of North Carolina. http://pdf.wri.org/2001summit_hartarticle.pdf

Querejazu, V., Zavaleta, D., & Mendizabal, J. (2014). Bolivia's entrepreneurship profile: The trade-off between growth and entrepreneurial activity rates. *GEM Global Entrepreneurship Monitor, Global Reports*.

Roberts, E. B., & Eesley, C. E (2011). Entrepreneurial impact: The role of MIT. *Foundations and Trends® in Entrepreneurship*, *7*(1–2), 1–149.

Rodriguez Ostria, G., & Weise Vargas, C. (2006). Educacion superior universitaria en Bolivia. *Estudio Nacional UNESCO IESALC*, 1–204.

Roundy, P. (2017). Social entrepreneurship and entrepreneurial ecosystems. *International Journal of Social Economics*, *44*(9), 1252–67.

Sánchez-Barrioluengo, M., & Benneworth, P. (2019). Is the entrepreneurial university also regionally engaged? Analysing the influence of university's structural configuration on third mission performance. *Technological Forecasting and Social Change*, *141*, 206–18.

Sharir, M., & Lerner, M. (2006). Gauging the success of social ventures initiated by individual social entrepreneurs. *Journal of World Business*, *41*(1), 6–20.

Shaw, E., & Carter, S. (2007). Social entrepreneurship: Theoretical antecedents and empirical analysis of entrepreneurial processes and outcomes. *Journal of Small Business and Enterprise Development*, *14*(3), 418–34.

Siegel, D. S., & Wright, M. (2015). Academic entrepreneurship: Time for a rethink? *British Journal of Management*, *26*(4), 582–95.

Smith, I. H., & Woodworth, W. P. (2012). Developing social entrepreneurs and social innovators: A social identity. *Academy of Management Learning and Education*, *11*(3), 390–407.

Spigel, B., & Harrison, R. (2018). Toward a process theory of entrepreneurial ecosystems. *Strategic Entrepreneurship Journal*, *12*(1), 151–68.

Totterman, H., & Sten, J. (2005). Business incubation and social capital. *International Small Business Journal*, *23*(5), 487–511.

Vogelgesang, L. J., & Astin, A. W. (2000). Comparing the effects of community service and service-learning. *Michigan Journal of Community Service Learning*, *7*(1), 25–34.

Volkmann, C., Tokarski, K. O., & Ernst, K. (2008). *Social Entrepreneurship and Social Business: An introduction and discussion with case studies*. Wiesbaden: Gabler.

Webb, J. W., Kistruck, G. M., Ireland, R. D., & Ketchen, D. J. (2010). The entrepreneurship process in base of the pyramid markets: The case of multinational enterprise/nongovernment organization alliances. *Entrepreneurship: Theory and Practice*, *34*(3), 555–81.

Wincent, J., Thorgren, S., & Anokhin, S. (2016). Costly ties: Social capital as a retardant of network-level entrepreneurial orientation. *Journal of Small Business Management*, *54*(1), 229–4.

Wronka, M. (2013). Analyzing the success of social enterprises: Critical success factors perspective. *Proceedings from Management, Knowledge and Learning International Conference*, *1*, 593–605.

APPENDIX

Interview Protocol for Entrepreneurs

Background information

1. Tell me about yourself (studies, family situation (kids, married, siblings) profession, etc.).
2. Can you describe your day-to-day routine?

Business model of the (social) entrepreneur – how does it work?

1. What product/service is being provided?
2. To whom?
3. How many customers have been served?
4. Where are you providing your products/services?
5. What are the major costs of your activity (materials, labor, etc.)?
6. How is your activity funded?
7. Do you consider yourself as an entrepreneur?
8. Is there an entrepreneurial culture in [city name]?

Supportive needs of (social) entrepreneurs

1. What are the main problems of your business activity?
2. What type of support do you need as an entrepreneur (financial, networking, legal, coaching)?
3. What are the organizations or people in Bolivia (San José, Santa Cruz, Cochabamba, Tarija, La Paz, etc.)?
4. Are you part of a network or a group? Can you describe how that works?
5. What is the role of universities in support of social entrepreneurs?

Interview Protocol for Organizations Supporting Entrepreneurship

Organization profile

1. Can you describe the mission of your organization (association, NGO, government, training, financing, education, other)?
2. Describe your organization: legal status, years of operation, founders, capital, top management, board of director (if applicable) and other relevant information about the management of the organization.

Relationship with entrepreneurship and entrepreneurial ecosystem

3. Is there a culture for entrepreneurship in [city]? What is the most relevant activity for entrepreneurs in [city]?
4. What is your relationship with entrepreneurship/entrepreneurs in your city?
5. Policy environment for social entrepreneurs:
   a. What is the role of the government in supporting entrepreneurship: programs, needs, or constraints?
   b. What is your perception of the policy environment: ease to create new businesses, taxes, incentives, regulations, grants, other programs?
   c. Are there any other institutions or organizations having an influence on the organization's environment?
6. What are the principal obstacles in the local market for your organization?
7. Do you consider there is sufficient and qualified human capital to stimulate entrepreneurship/support entrepreneurs? If not, what type of profiles are missing?
8. Infrastructure: what is your perception (electricity, telecommunications – internet, water, gas and transport)?
9. Can you please describe the business environment for your organization (competitors, supply chain, informal competition, and other relevant aspects)?
10. Support:
   a. What type of support is available to entrepreneurs in the city: networking, training, mentorship, coaching, legal, funding?
   b. Who provides this support?
11. What do you consider is further needed to stimulate entrepreneurship in this city?
12. Who are the relevant entrepreneurs/entrepreneurial organizations in this city?
13. What is the role of universities in support of social entrepreneurs?

6. The entrepreneurial propensity of the Swedish national innovation system: New challenges for policy-makers

Jon Mikel Zabala-Iturriagagoitia

6.1 INTRODUCTION

Sweden is usually ranked among the innovation leaders according to several international rankings such as the European Innovation Scoreboard (European Union, 2018) and the Global Innovation Index (Dutta, Lanvin & Wunsch-Vincent, 2017). Most of these innovation-related indices and scoreboards conclude that Sweden has a mature innovation system, with consolidated trade in global markets and high exports that allow the country to enjoy a positive macro-economic environment for innovation and a high level of technological readiness and business sophistication.[1]

However, as it has been argued for a long time (e.g. Growth Analysis, 2011; Edquist, Zabala-Iturriagagoitia, Barbero & Zofio, 2018), the outstanding levels of investment in science and technology (S&T) that led to a developed innovation system did not translate into growth and productivity for the whole economy. This discrepancy between the investment levels devoted to the system and their weak effects on the overall growth performance has been traditionally labeled as the Swedish Paradox.

The origins of the Swedish Paradox formulation go back to the 1990s when Edquist and McKelvey (1998, p. 131) argued that while a high proportion of the gross domestic product (GDP) was spent on formal research and development (R&D), the Swedish economy produced "a below average percentage of R&D-intensive products relative to total manufacturing, compared to the average for the OECD [Organisation for Economic Co-operation and Development] countries". The low productivity of the national innovation system (NIS) was interpreted as a systemic failure. The authors identified both industry-specific and national contextual factors that are needed to translate the results of the R&D activities into commercial innovative products. Since then, the notion of the Swedish Paradox has been widely spread not only in

Sweden (Granberg & Jacobsson, 2006; Edquist, 2010; Ejermo & Kander, 2011; Ejermo, Kander & Svensson Henning, 2011) but also elsewhere, particularly in Europe.[2]

More recently, lacking entrepreneurship has also been singled out as a hampering factor for growth (Braunerhjelm, Acs, Audretsch & Carlsson, 2010). Radosevic and Yoruk (2013, p. 1016) define the entrepreneurial propensity of an innovation system as "its capacity to generate and exploit entrepreneurial opportunities in order to create new knowledge-intensive enterprises, new technologies (innovations), and new knowledge". According to this concept, entrepreneurship would be regarded as a systemic property of an innovation system, which enables the transitions needed to transform new knowledge into innovations and the emergence of new enterprises that ultimately increase the overall innovation performance.

This chapter aims to explore the properties and the nature of knowledge-intensive entrepreneurship (KIE) as a systemically distributed phenomenon. In particular, by using the previous notion of the entrepreneurial propensity of innovation systems (Radosevic & Yoruk, 2013), the chapter investigates the possible interplay between NIS and KIE. This interplay is studied in the particular case of Sweden, the country where the Swedish Paradox originated. The research question that leads the current chapter can thus be formulated as follows: What are the main entrepreneurial opportunities of the Swedish innovation system, which can be exploited to improve its overall performance?

The remainder of the chapter is structured as follows. Section 6.2 presents the conceptual framework that relates NIS and KIE. In line with this, Section 6.3 introduces the methodology that allows the measuring of the entrepreneurial propensity of innovation systems, as well as the sources of information used to gather the quantitative data. The results for the Swedish case are overviewed in Section 6.4, which describes the main components of the entrepreneurial propensity of the Swedish NIS, emphasizing the strengths and areas for potential improvement. Section 6.5 provides a discussion of the main policy implications.

6.2   CONCEPTUAL FRAMEWORK: NATIONAL INNOVATION SYSTEMS AND KNOWLEDGE-INTENSIVE ENTREPRENEURSHIP

Innovation systems are composed of a complex network of interacting organizations, policies and institutions (Metcalfe, 1995; Palmberg, 2006). For decades, the literature on innovation systems has attempted to analyze the conditions under which the emergence, generation, diffusion and uptake of innovations takes place. In this systemic stream of work, entrepreneurship, and the activities derived from and related to it, are regarded as a determinant, or a property, of the evolutionary dynamics that take place within an innovation system (Edquist, 2005, 2011). Some scholars talk about the activities developed within, or the functions accomplished by, innovation systems (e.g. Hekkert, Suurs, Negro, Kuhlmann & Smits, 2007; Bergek, Jacobsson, Carlsson, Lindmark & Rickne, 2008), among which entrepreneurship plays a central role.

The dominant perspective pervading entrepreneurship research is however focused on entrepreneurship as a micro phenomenon (Jones, Coviello & Tang, 2011; Chen, Chan, Hung & Lin, 2019). While acknowledging this relevant research field in the literature, we also contend in this chapter that from a systemic perspective, entrepreneurship cannot only be derived from the behavior of enterprising individuals, but from the structure of the whole system in which entrepreneurial activities are embedded (Radosevic & Yoruk, 2013). Although it emerges as an individual "act" (Uygur, 2019), entrepreneurship takes place in a systemic context, i.e. shaped and conditioned by a variety of macro, meso and micro factors (Dopfer, Foster & Potts, 2004), and hence, it is plausible to state that there are close relations between entrepreneurship and innovation (Radosevic, 2010) that may lead to characterizing entrepreneurship as a macro-systemic phenomenon.

One of the assumptions often made in the literature is that entrepreneurial activity may lead to structural, institutional and societal changes (Landström, 2005; Radosevic, Yoruk, Edquist & Zabala, 2010, p. 9) and innovation systems are no exception for such systemic outcomes. Radosevic and Yoruk (2013) introduce a conceptual framework for studying entrepreneurship as a systemic phenomenon in the context of innovation systems (see Figure 6.1). They discuss how, from an innovation systems perspective, entrepreneurship is the outcome of the simultaneous emergence of three types of opportunities and the interactions among them (Radosevic et al., 2010, p. 21):

- Technological opportunities represent the "capabilities and skills of enterprises and the population, investments in new knowledge creation and diffusion, and knowledge linkages".
- Market opportunities represent the real and potential purchasing power of the economy, as well as the number of potential and existing users for knowledge-intensive products and services.
- Institutional opportunities represent the "legal, regulatory, policy, social and cultural factors which can operate as enablers/inducements or obstacles to the KIE".

As a result of these three types of opportunities, Radosevic and Yoruk (2013) introduce the notion of entrepreneurial propensity of innovation systems. This concept is defined as the degree to which an innovation system is conducive to entrepreneurship, creating the context for the emergence of new enterprises in knowledge-intensive sectors, which are able to grow and generate sales as a result of their innovation activities, and which also help increase the knowledge intensity of the system as a whole, creating thus a feedback loop that feeds again into the system.

Hence, in the context of this chapter, KIE is understood as a systemic phenomenon related to firms' innovativeness, the knowledge intensity of the systems, its translation into more productive processes and innovative products and the creation of new systemic opportunities. In the rest of this chapter, the concept of KIE embraces: a) new innovative firms, b) firms with a significant knowledge intensity of their activity and c) firms that perceive, capture and respond to new opportunities (see Radosevic et al., 2010, p. 9).

6.3   THE MEASUREMENT OF THE ENTREPRENEURIAL PROPENSITY OF INNOVATION SYSTEMS

Following the conceptual framework and methodology depicted by Radosevic et al. (2010) and further developed by Radosevic and Yoruk (2013), the entrepreneurial propensity of an innovation system can be measured through two indices.[3] The Index of Knowledge Intensive Entrepreneurship (IKIE), regarded as an outcome variable, represents the outcome produced as a result of the opportunities generated by the system as a whole. In turn, the Index of Knowledge Intensive Entrepreneurial Opportunities (IKIEO) aims to capture the extent to which the structural conditions of an innovation system are actually conducive to entrepreneurship.

Following the previous conceptual framework and methodology, the IKIE is composed of three components with equal weights (see Table 6.1): new enterprises (NE), new technology and innovations (NTI) and knowledge intensity (KI). Each of these three components is likewise created from a number of output indicators. Overall, the IKIE is composed of nine indicators, all of which receive equal weights.

$$IKIE = NE + NTI + KI$$

Similarly, as discussed by the previous authors, the IKIEO is also composed of three indices with equal weights: Index of Technological Opportunities (ITO), market opportunities (IMO) and institutional opportunities (IIO), embracing a total amount of 30 indicators, all of which receive equal weights.

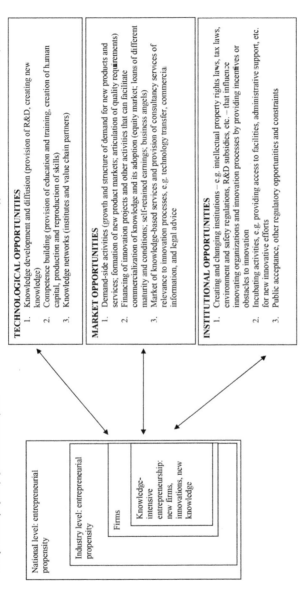

Opportunities and activities in the innovation system

Entrepreneurial propensity of the innovation system

TECHNOLOGICAL OPPORTUNITIES

1. Knowledge development and diffusion (provision of R&D, creating new knowledge)
2. Competence building (provision of education and training, creation of human capital, production and reproduction of skills)
3. Knowledge networks (institutes and value chain partners)

MARKET OPPORTUNITIES

1. Demand-side activities (growth and structure of demand for new products and services; formation of new product markets; articulation of quality requirements)
2. Financing of innovation projects and other activities that can facilitate commercialization of knowledge and its adoption (equity market; loans of different maturity and conditions; self-retained earnings; business angels)
3. Market of knowledge-based services and provision of consultancy services of relevance to innovation processes, e.g. technology transfer, commercial information, and legal advice

INSTITUTIONAL OPPORTUNITIES

1. Creating and changing institutions – e.g. intellectual property rights laws, tax laws, environment and safety regulations, R&D subsidies, etc. – that influence innovating organizations and innovation processes by providing incentives or obstacles to innovation
2. Incubating activities, e.g. providing access to facilities, administrative support, etc. for new innovative efforts
3. Public acceptance, other regulatory opportunities and constraints

National level: entrepreneurial propensity

Industry level: entrepreneurial propensity

Firms

Knowledge-intensive entrepreneurship: new firms, innovations, new knowledge

Source: Radosevic et al. (2010), p. 23 and Radosevic and Yoruk (2013), p. 1021.

Figure 6.1   Entrepreneurial propensity of the innovation systems

$$IKIEO = ITO + IMO + IIO$$

In both cases, the indicators included in each of the components that constitute the IKIE and IKIEO indices are multiplied by their corresponding indicator weight, so the values of the corresponding components can then be directly added. The weights for each of these sub-indices, components and their indicators are given in Table 6.1 (see also Radosevic & Yoruk, 2013, pp. 1019–20). The data for each of the indicators outlined in Table 6.1 is gathered from a variety of publicly available sources, including Eurostat, the OECD, World Bank, the World Economic Forum's Global Competitiveness Report (WEF GCR) and the Innobarometer of the European Commission.

Although the chapter focuses on the case of Sweden, we also aim to set a ground for the application of the methodology described in this section to other countries and regions. Hence, the methodology outlined here could also be used to explore the entrepreneurial propensity of any other innovation system and the opportunities that can be further developed in them.

6.4   ENTREPRENEURIAL PROPENSITY OF THE SWEDISH NATIONAL INNOVATION SERVICE

Table 6.2 provides the values observed for the indices, sub-indices and indicators that help us assess the entrepreneurial propensity of the Swedish NIS and the opportunities found in it. In all cases the year used for each indicator corresponds to the latest available year, which is indicated in brackets next to the value of each indicator.[4]

In general terms, Sweden shows a very high performance in all three components of the IKIE. In fact, based on the results reported by Radosevic and Yoruk (2013), Sweden ranks first in Europe in regards to its IKIE, followed by Finland, Germany and Denmark. The values achieved by Sweden in each of the three components that constitute the IKIE suggest that its NIS is comprehensive and balanced, supporting the development of the KIE in it. The major strength of the Swedish NIS concerning its entrepreneurial orientation lies in its KI (32,38). This is in line with the above-mentioned discussion of the Swedish Paradox. As discussed in the introductory section of this chapter, Sweden is characterized by its large investments in the S&T, particularly by multinational corporations and universities. While this could be regarded as one of the major strengths and key representative characteristics of the NIS, it also questions the overall efficiency of the system as a whole in translating investments into concrete outputs and outcomes (see Edquist et al., 2018).

The high value achieved by Sweden in the KI index is the main reason why the country ranks first in the IKIE. The KI is associated with three indicators. Swedish residents submitted 283 applications (per million inhabitants) to the

Table 6.1   Composite indices and indicators for measuring the entrepreneurial propensity of national innovation systems

Index	Sub-index	Component	Quantitative indicators	Source	Component weight	Indicator weight*
Index of knowledge-intensive entrepreneurship (IKIE) IKIE = NE + NTI + KI		New enterprises (NE)	1. Birth rate: number of enterprise births in the reference period (t) divided by the number of enterprises active in (t)	Eurostat	1/3	1/12
			2. Five-year-old enterprises' employment growth rate: number of persons employed in the reference period (t) among enterprises newly born in t-5 having survived to t divided by the number of persons employed in t-5 by the same enterprises, expressed as a percentage growth rate			1/12
			3. Survival rate 5: number of enterprises in the reference period (t) newly born in t-5 having survived to t divided by the number of enterprise births in t-5			1/12
			4. Five-year-old enterprises' share of the business population			1/12
		New technology and innovations (NTI)	5. Percentage of innovative enterprises	Eurostat	1/3	1/6
			6. Percentage of innovation expenditures (in GDP or turnover)			1/6
		Knowledge intensity (KI)	7. European Patent Office patent applications (per M inhabitant)	Eurostat	1/3	1/9
			8. Royalty and license fee receipts (% of GDP)	World Bank		1/9
			9. Knowledge-intensive services value added (% of GDP)	Eurostat		1/9

Index	Sub-index	Component	Quantitative indicators	Source	Component weight	Indicator weight*
Index of knowledge-intensive entrepreneurial opportunities (IKIEO) IKIEO = ITO + IMO + IIO	Technological opportunities (ITO) ITO = RD + SKILL + KNWK	Knowledge development and diffusion (RD)	10. Gross domestic expenditure on R&D GERD – (% GDP)	Eurostat	1/3	1/6
			11. Business expenditure on R&D (BERD) – (% of GDP)			1/6
		Competence building (SKILL)	12. Percentage of R&D personnel (% in total employment)	Eurostat	1/3	1/12
			13. Percentage of population with tertiary education: 25–64 years	WEF		1/12
			14. Quality of scientific research institutions	GCR		1/12
			15. Availability of scientists and engineers			1/12
		Knowledge networks (KNWK)	16. Firms involved in innovation cooperation (% in total)	Eurostat	1/3	1/9
			17. Job-to-job mobility of human resources in science and technology: 25–64 years (% in total employment)	WEF		1/9
			18. Value chain breadth	GCR		1/9

Index	Sub-index	Component	Quantitative indicators	Source	Component weight	Indicator weight*
Index of knowledge-intensive entrepreneurial opportunities (IKIEO) IKIEO = ITO + IMO + IIO	Market opportunities (IMO) IMO = DEMAND + FINANCE + MKIS	Demand-side activities (DEMAND)	19. GDP per capita (USD) (proxy for quality of demand)	World Bank	1/3	1/12
			20. GDP growth (annual %)	Eurostat		1/12
			21. Openness = share of trade (X + M) in GDP	WEF		1/12
			22. Buyer sophistication: buyer's purchasing decision	GCR		1/12
		Financing of innovation processes and other activities (FINANCE)	23. Domestic credit to private sector (% of GDP)	World Bank	1/3	1/12
			24. Stocks traded (% in GDP)	OECD		1/12
			25.1. Venture capital (early and expansion and replacement) (% of GDP)	WEF		1/12
			25.2. Venture capital availability	GCR		1/12

Index	Sub-index	Component	Quantitative indicators	Source	Component weight	Indicator weight*
Index of knowledge-intensive entrepreneurial opportunities (IKIEO) IKIEO = ITO + IMO + IIO	Market opportunities (IMO) IMO = DEMAND + FINANCE + MKIS	Market for knowledge-intensive services (MKIS)	26. High-tech sector enterprises (manufacturing and knowledge-intensive services) (% in total enterprises)	Eurostat	1/3	1/9
			27. High-tech exports (% in total exports)			1/9
			28. Employment in knowledge-intensive sectors (% in total employment)			1/9

Index	Sub-index	Component	Quantitative indicators	Source	Component weight	Indicator weight*
Index of knowledge-intensive entrepreneurial opportunities (IKIEO) IKIEO = ITO + IMO + IIO	Institutional opportunities (IIO) IIO = REGULATION + SUPPORT	Regulatory environment (REGULATION)	29. Number of procedures required to start a business	WEF GCR	1/2	1/12
			30. Time (days) required to start a business			1/12
			31. Intellectual property rights protection			1/12
			32. Burden of government regulation			1/12
			33. Efficiency of legal framework in challenging regulations			1/12
			34. Transparency of government policy-making			1/12

Index	Sub-index	Component	Quantitative indicators	Source	Component weight	Indicator weight*
Index of knowledge-intensive entrepreneurial opportunities (IKIEO) IKIEO = ITO + IMO + IIO	Institutional opportunities (IIO) IIO = REGULATION + SUPPORT	Public support to incubating and other supporting activities (SUPPORT)	35. State of cluster development	WEF GCR Innobarometer	1/2	1/8
			36. Declared clustered membership among enterprises in cluster-like environment (%)			1/8
			37. Interest in public procurement (% of firms in total)			1/8
			38. Opportunity to sell innovations on public tenders (% in enterprises with direct experience with public tenders)			1/8

Table 6.2   *Composite indices and indicators for measuring the entrepreneurial propensity of the Swedish national innovation system*

Index	Sub-index	Component	Quantitative indicators	Value	Sub-index value	Component value
Index of knowledge-intensive entrepreneurship (IKIE) $IKIE = NE + NTI + KI = 52.67$		New enterprises (NE)	1. Birth rate: number of enterprise births in the reference period (t) divided by the number of enterprises active in (t)	7.52 (2010)		
			2. Five-year-old enterprises employment growth rate: number of persons employed in the reference period (t) among enterprises newly born in t-5 having survived to t divided by the number of persons employed in t-5 by the same enterprises, expressed as a percentage growth rate	52.17 (2007)		10.43
			3. Survival rate 5: number of enterprises in the reference period (t) newly born in t-5 having survived to t divided by the number of enterprise births in t-5	61.70 (2010)		
			4. Five-year-old enterprises' share of the business population	3.81 (2010)		
		New technology and innovations (NTI)	5. Percentage of innovative enterprises	54.2 (2014)		
			6. Percentage of innovation expenditures (in GDP or turnover)	5 (2016)		9.86
		Knowledge intensity (KI)	7. European Patent Office patent applications (per M inhabitant)	283.46 (2017)		
			8. Royalty and license fees receipts (% of GDP)	1.40 (2017)		32.38
			9. Knowledge-intensive services value added (% of GDP)	6.53 (2014)		

Entrepreneurial ecosystems meet innovation systems

Index	Sub-index	Component	Quantitative indicators	Value	Sub-index value	Component value
Index of knowledge-intensive entrepreneurial opportunities (IKIEO) IKIEO = ITO + IMO + IIO = 76.87	Technological opportunities (ITO) ITO = RD + SKILL + KNWK	Knowledge development and diffusion (RD)	10. GERD % of GDP	3.4 (2017)	0.97	
			11. BERD % of GDP	2.42 (2017)		
		Competence building (SKILL)	12. Percentage of R&D personnel (% in total employment)	1.82 (2017)	4.52	10.51
			13. Percentage of population with tertiary education	41.94 (2017)		
			14. Quality of scientific research institutions	5.66 (2018)		
			15. Availability of scientists and engineers	4.80 (2018)		
		Knowledge networks (KNWK)	16. Firms involved in innovation cooperation (% in total)	33.3 (2016)	5.02	
			17. Job-to-job mobility of human resources in science and technology (% in total employment)	6.2 (2017)		
			18. Value chain breadth	5.70 (2018)		

Index	Sub-index	Component	Quantitative indicators	Value	Sub-index value	Component value
Index of knowledge-intensive entrepreneurial opportunities (IKIEO) IKIEO = ITO + IMO + IIO = 76.87	Market opportunities (IMO) IMO = DEMAND + FINANCE +	Demand-side activities (DEMAND)	19. GDP per capita (USD)	54.112 (2018)	12.68	
			20. GDP growth (annual %)	2.4 (2018		
			21. Openness = share of trade (X + M) in GDP	90.9 (2018)		
			22. Buyer sophistication: buyer's purchasing decision	4.7 (2018)		
			21. Openness = share of trade (X + M) in GDP	90.9 (2018)		
	MKIS	Financing of innovation processes and other activities (FINANCE)	23. Domestic credit to private sector (% of GDP)	133.1 (2018)	23.57	43.11
			24. Stocks traded (% in GDP)	145.2 (2017)		
			25.1. Venture capital (early and expansion and replacement) (% of GDP)	0.060 (2017)		
			25.2. Venture capital availability	4.5 (2018)		

Index	Sub-index	Component	Quantitative indicators	Value	Sub-index value	Component value
Index of knowledge-intensive entrepreneurial opportunities (IKIEO) IKIEO = ITO + IMO + IIO = 76.87	Market opportunities (IMO) IMO = DEMAND + FINANCE + MKIS	Market for knowledge-intensive services (MKIS)	26. High-tech sector enterprises (manufacturing and KIS) (% in total enterprises)	4.77 (2013)	6.86	43.11
			27. High-tech exports (% in total exports)	11.3 (2018)		
			28. Employment in knowledge-intensive sectors (% in total employment)	45.7 (2018)		

Index	Sub-index	Component	Quantitative indicators	Value	Sub-index value	Component value
Index of knowledge-intensive entrepreneurial opportunities (IKIEO) IKIEO = ITO + IMO + IIO = 76.87	Institutional opportunities (IIO) IIO = REGULATION + SUPPORT	Regulatory environment (REGULATION)	29. Number of procedures required to start a business	3 (2018)		
			30. Time required to start a business	7 (2018)		
			31. Intellectual property rights protection	5.8 (2018)		
			32. Burden of government regulation	4.1 (2018)	2.5	
			33. Efficiency of legal framework	4.6 (2018)		
			34. Transparency of government policy-making	5.5 (2018)		23.25

Index	Sub-index	Component	Quantitative indicators	Value	Sub-index value	Component value
Index of knowledge-intensive entrepreneurial opportunities (IKIEO) IKIEO = ITO + IMO + IIO = 76.87	Institutional opportunities (IIO) IIO = REGULATION + SUPPORT	Public support to incubating and other supporting activities (SUPPORT)	35. State of cluster development	5 (2018)		
			36. Declared clustered membership among enterprises in cluster-like environment (%)	81 (2006)		
			37. Interest in public procurement (% of firms in total)	38 (2009)	20.75	23.25
			38. Opportunity to sell innovations on public tenders (% in enterprises with direct experience with public tenders)	42 (2009)		

European Patent Office in 2017. The second measure denotes the percentage of GDP represented by royalty and license fee receipts (1.4 percent in year 2017). Finally, the last indicator measures the percentage of GDP derived from the value added by knowledge-intensive service firms (6.53 percent in year 2014). A possible explanation for these high levels observed in the KI may be that knowledge generation-related activities are mostly undertaken within large enterprises, which is one of the main structural characteristics of the Swedish NIS (Chaminade, Zabala & Treccani, 2010). While being a strength in the short run, this can handicap the potential of growth of new entrepreneurial ventures, as we will discuss next.

The NTI component (9.86) is characterized by two indicators. With reference to the first of these two measures, 54.2 percent of companies in Sweden (year 2014) are identified as innovative. This is an intermediate value in the European context (Zabala & Edquist, 2011). The second represents the share of the turnover devoted to innovation expenditures, which amounted to 5 percent in year 2016.

Finally, the NE component (10.43) is built from four indicators. The first indicator aims to capture the extent to which the creation of new companies thrives in the economy. This is measured through the number of enterprise births in the reference period divided by the number of enterprises active in this period (7.52 percent in year 2010). The second indicator is directly related to the previous one, as it captures the number of five-year-old enterprises as a share of the entire business population (3.81 percent in 2010). These two measures indicate that despite the fact that a large share of companies is created on a yearly basis, their representatives on the overall economy is low and decreasing as new start-ups get older.

This directly leads us to discuss the survival rate of the new ventures. The survival rate of start-ups to the five-year mark was 61.70 percent in 2010, which is regarded as a very large value in the European context (Zabala & Edquist, 2011). This constitutes one of the major strengths of the Swedish NIS and illustrates the sound network of organizations and infrastructures related to entrepreneurial support in the country. However, in spite of the high survival rate of entrepreneurial ventures in Sweden, their growth remains a challenge, as evidenced by relatively low employment growth prevalence. Only 52.17 percent of the five-year-old companies grew in year 2007, which was one of the lowest in Europe (Zabala & Edquist, 2011).

Table 6.3 summarizes the main characteristics of the Swedish NIS based on the conclusions that can be drawn from the analysis of the IKIE index and its different constituents. As discussed above, the knowledge intensity of the Swedish NIS is very large, which facilitates the development of a high innovation potential, particularly among large firms. One of the effects of having a comprehensive and mature innovation system is that it facilitates the high

Table 6.3　　Main characteristics of the Swedish national innovation system

Component of the IKIE index	Conclusion
New enterprises (NE): low	High survival rate → consolidated entrepreneurial support infrastructures Difficulties for small firms to grow
New technology and innovations (NTI): intermediate	Dominant role of large multinational corporations can hamper the growth potential of new firms
Knowledge intensity (KI): very high	High innovation capacity, particularly among large enterprises Difficulties to transform innovation inputs into outputs

Source: Own elaboration.

survival rate of entrepreneurial ventures. However, the NIS also shows difficulties to transform innovation inputs into outputs and facilitate the growth of small firms, which may be hampered due to the dominant role played by large multinational corporations in the NIS.

When it comes to the measures used to assess the entrepreneurial propensity of an innovation system, Sweden demonstrates a strong performance in all components of the IKIEO (76.87). As discussed in Radosevic and Yoruk (2013), Sweden ranks third in Europe on its entrepreneurial opportunities, with Finland and Denmark leading the IKIEO ranking. The general good health of the Swedish NIS is driven by high investments in R&D activities (3.4 percent GERD in 2017), a high share of the population with tertiary education (41.94 percent in 2017) and the high quality of scientific research institutions (5.66 in 2018), among others (see Table 6.2). All of these are areas of a relative comparative advantage of Sweden over other countries (Zabala-Iturriagagoitia, 2018).

On the other hand, the Swedish NIS shows a need for improvement in several areas, which include: firms involved in innovation cooperation (33.3 percent in 2016), job-to-job mobility (6.2 percent in 2017), venture capital (0.06 percent in 2017), interest in public procurement (38 percent in 2009) and the opportunity to sell innovations on public tenders (42 percent in 2009), which could be indicative of a lack of the demand-side activities in the innovation system.

The analysis of the results achieved by Sweden in its IKIEO and the corresponding components and sub-indices leads to the following conclusions. Table 6.4 summarizes the main opportunities of the Swedish NIS, based on the conclusions that can be drawn from the analysis of the IKIEO index and its different constituents. As interactions are at the core of innovation (Wincent, Anokhin & Boter, 2009), the low share of firms engaged in innovation coop-

Table 6.4   *Main opportunities of the Swedish national innovation system*

Component of the IKIEO index	Conclusion
Technological opportunities (ITO): high	Need to foster cooperation in innovation activities among stakeholders
Market opportunities (IMO): very high	Need to further increase venture capital availability
Institutional opportunities (IIO): high	Need to introduce schemes to boost the demand side of innovation

Source: Own elaboration.

eration and the extremely low job-to-job mobility of workers in the S&T industries calls for policies to improve Swedish performance in these areas. The policy-making should, thus, aim at generating an institutional setting that provides the right incentives and schemes to boost cooperative behavior, that would eventually lead to advancing the entrepreneurial orientation of the NIS and its overall performance. Another area for systemic improvement concerns the financing of innovation processes, and in particular, venture capital availability. This may be one of the explanations why Swedish entrepreneurial firms find it difficult to grow above a certain threshold (around 20) in the number of employees.

The last factor we would like to put emphasis on is the lack of interest shown by firms in public procurement and the low opportunities identified by firms to sell innovations on public tenders. Edquist and Zabala-Iturriagagoitia (2012) discuss at length the strong tradition Sweden has in the use of demand-side policies as a stimulus for the development of innovation. The low values achieved by Sweden in these two measures point to the opportunities that the system may be missing due to the lack of innovation-related demand.

6.5   CONCLUSIONS AND DISCUSSION

This chapter aims to link entrepreneurship with innovation systems. In much of the literature on entrepreneurship, this phenomenon is understood from an individual perspective (Shane & Venkataraman, 2000). However, in the literature on innovation systems, entrepreneurship is often regarded as a determinant or function of a system (Edquist, 2005). In order to link these two streams of the literature, and following Radosevic and Yoruk (2013), the chapter introduces the notion of entrepreneurial propensity of innovation systems, which is defined as the degree to which innovation systems are conducive to entrepreneurship, creating contexts for the emergence of new firms, which are able to generate sales and to grow, based on their innovation activities, and which also help improve the overall system to be more conducive to innovation. The entrepreneurial propensity of innovation systems is measured through two indices: the IKIE and the IKIEO. These two indices were used to identify the main entrepreneurial opportunities of the Swedish innovation system, in order to improve its overall performance. This final section discusses the type of policies that could be implemented to overcome the weaknesses identified in the Swedish innovation system.

Sweden is often referred to as a country with a consolidated innovation system (Edquist et al., 2018). This is due to, among other factors, its industrial structure dominated by large R&D-intensive multinational groups, a high specialization in high-tech industries and services and internationally oriented universities with a strong emphasis on basic research (Chaminade et al., 2010; Edquist & Hommen, 2008). As discussed in this chapter, and suggested by Zabala and Edquist (2011) and Radosevic and Yoruk (2013), Sweden is also one of the countries with the highest entrepreneurial propensity.

The Swedish NIS enjoys a comprehensive institutional and organizational setting supportive of entrepreneurship. In this regard, the role of business incubators, intermediary organizations such as technology transfer offices, funding support organizations (e.g. Tillväxtverket, ALMI, Innovationsbron, the knowledge foundation, Mistra), public agencies supporting innovation (i.e. VINNOVA) and favorable intellectual property rights regulations needs to be stressed.

However, due to the significance of large corporations, new entrepreneurial ventures face many challenges in their growth, which leads to a lack of structural change at the systemic level. This is not a Sweden-specific issue. Due to the speed of technological change and the reduction of barriers to its transfer through mass digitalization, economic environments are changing more and more rapidly (Gómez-Uranga, Zabala-Iturriagagoitia & Barrutia, 2016). In this context, companies (particularly the large ones) adopt defensive and risk-averse innovation strategies in order to keep their market power (Arbuthnott, Eriksson, Thorgren & Wincent, 2011), which calls for the need to reinforce competition laws. Consequently, the role entrepreneurship plays in an innovation system may be changing from being a determinant that fosters innovation and structural change to a function used by large companies to defend themselves from the competition of entrepreneurial firms through mergers and acquisitions of firms, or their intellectual property rights (Arbuthnott et al., 2011).

The offshoring strategy that many large Swedish companies are following (see Chaminade et al., 2010) can lead to a potential threat to the sustainability of the Swedish NIS, if there are no new start-ups able to take the lead. This requires promoting holistic policies that do not only focus on the development of new technologies or start-ups, but also on their growth and diffusion (and absorption) across the whole economy, so that the value added is produced across the whole economy rather than within very few leading firms (Borras & Edquist, 2019).

As underscored by Grillitsch, Hansen, Coenen, Miörner and Moodysson (2019), for the innovation systems to continuously adapt to the new (economic, social, technological, environmental) circumstances, policies should provide directionality to the system, while guaranteeing experimentation (i.e. entrepreneurship leading to industry renewal) and demand articulation. This final issue is crucial in many innovation systems. Traditionally, S&T policies have been viewed mostly from the supply side, aiming to create the (institutional, legal, organizational) conditions for the emergence of innovations. However, reaching and supplying the marketplace is a necessary but not sufficient condition for innovation to survive. Indeed, there is no innovation if there is no demand for it.

An example of a policy instrument that can be used to promote a holistic approach to policy-making is public procurement for innovation (Edquist & Zabala-Iturriagagoitia, 2012). One of the greatest challenges (entrepreneurial) firms face on their way to growth is the (initial) market delivery. A potentially successful way to enable new firms to position themselves in (new or existing) markets and to foster their growth (and, hence, their consolidation) may be by using procurement policies, due to the strong complementarity it offers with other (supply and demand) policy instruments (see Edquist & Zabala-Iturriagagoitia, 2015). This directly points to the need for a policy mix supporting not only the consolidation of Swedish companies, but also the industrial renewal and growth of new ventures, which cannot be achieved by providing R&D subsidies or by implementing supply-side policy measures only. If the Swedish economy is, thus, to rely more on new entrepreneurial companies, this needs to be done through the promotion of user–producer relations (i.e. fostering cooperation among universities, research centers, firms and venture capital organizations) and through the use of public policies for stimulating not only the generation of technologies, but also their diffusion and the demand for innovative products. This calls for a potential reallocation of funds in the Swedish NIS, moving away from traditional linear approaches to innovation policy-making based on supporting science-based activities through R&D investments, and moving toward a holistic approach to innovation policy-making in which funding is directed toward other innovation-support activities such as venture capital, supply chain policies, demand subsidies and tax incentives or public procurement.

NOTES

1. See the profile provided by the 2017–18 edition of the World Economic Forum's Global Competitiveness Report: http://reports.weforum.org/global -competitiveness-index-2017-2018/countryeconomy-profiles/.
2. See for example the discussion by Fragkandreas (2013) about the existence of a European Paradox.
3. For a more detailed discussion of the methodological approach followed to measure the entrepreneurial propensity of an innovation system, see Radosevic et al. (2010). For an alternative methodology on how to measure entrepreneurship in the context of NIS, the reading of Marcotte (2013) and Acs, Autio and Szerb (2014) is recommended.
4. For a more detailed discussion see Zabala and Edquist (2011), where the values observed for every indicator in year 2007 are reported. It is worth mentioning that due to their structural character, most indicators remain rather constant.

REFERENCES

Acs, Z. J., Autio, E., & Szerb, L. (2014). National systems of entrepreneurship: Measurement issues and policy implications. *Research Policy, 43*, 476–94.

Arbuthnott, A., Eriksson, J., Thorgren, S., & Wincent, J. (2011). Reduced opportunities for regional renewal: The role of rigid threat responses among a region's established firms. *Entrepreneurship and Regional Development, 23*(7–8), 603–35.

Bergek, A., Jacobsson, S., Carlsson, B., Lindmark, S., & Rickne, A. (2008). Analyzing the functional dynamics of technological innovation systems: A scheme of analysis. *Research Policy, 37*(3), 407–29.

Borras, S., & Edquist, C. (2019). *Holistic Innovation Policy: Theoretical Foundations, Policy Problems and Instrument Choices*. Oxford: Oxford University Press.

Braunerhjelm, P., Acs, Z. J., Audretsch, D. B., & Carlsson, B. (2010). The missing link: Knowledge diffusion and entrepreneurship in endogenous growth. *Small Business Economics, 34*, 105–25.

Chaminade, C., Zabala, J. M., & Treccani, A. (2010). The Swedish national innovation system and its relevance for the emergence of global innovation networks. *CIRCLE Electronic working papers 2010/09*. Lund: Lund University. www.circle.lu.se/ publications/.

Chen, P.-C., Chan, W.-C., Hung, S.-W., & Lin, D.-Z. (2019). How entrepreneurs recognise entrepreneurial opportunity and its gaps: A cognitive theory perspective. *Technology Analysis and Strategic Management, 32*(2), 223–38.

Dopfer, K., Foster, J., & Potts, J. (2004). Micro-meso-macro. *Journal of Evolutionary Economics, 14*(3), 263–79.

Dutta, S., Lanvin, B., & Wunsch-Vincent, S. (2017). *The Global Innovation Index 2017: Innovation feeding the world*, 10th ed. www.wipo.int/edocs/pubdocs/en/wipo _pub_gii_2017.pdf.

Edquist, C. (2005). Systems of innovation: Perspectives and challenges. In: J. Fagerberg, D. C. Mowery & R. R. Nelson (Eds), *The Oxford Handbook of Innovation* (pp. 181–208). Oxford: Oxford University Press.

Edquist, C. (2010). The Swedish Paradox: Unexploited opportunities! *CIRCLE electronic working papers 2010/05*. Lund: Lund University. www.circle.lu.se/ publications/.

Edquist, C. (2011). Design of innovation policy through diagnostic analysis: Identification of systemic problems (or failures). *Industrial and Corporate Change*, *20*(6), 1725–53.

Edquist, C., & Hommen, L. (Eds) (2008). *Small Country Innovation Systems: Globalization, change and policy in Asia and Europe*. Cheltenham, UK and Northampton, MA, USA: Edward Elgar Publishing.

Edquist, C., & McKelvey, M. (1998). High R&D intensity without high tech products: A Swedish Paradox? In: K. Nielsen & B. Johnson (Eds), *Institutions and Economic Change: New perspectives on markets, firms and technology* (pp. 131–49). Cheltenham, UK and Northampton, MA, USA: Edward Elgar Publishing.

Edquist, C., & Zabala-Iturriagagoitia, J. M. (2012). Public procurement for innovation (PPI) as mission-oriented innovation policy. *Research Policy*, *41*(10), 1757–69.

Edquist, C., & Zabala-Iturriagagoitia, J. M. (2015). Pre-commercial procurement: A demand or supply policy instrument in relation to innovation? *R&D Management*, *45*(2), 147–60.

Edquist, C., Zabala-Iturriagagoitia, J. M., Barbero, J., & Zofio, J. L. (2018). On the meaning of innovation performance: Is the synthetic indicator of the Innovation Union Scoreboard flawed? *Research Evaluation*, *27*(3), 196–211.

Ejermo, O., & Kander, A. (2011). Swedish business research productivity. *Industrial and Corporate Change*, 20(4), 1081–118.

Ejermo, O., Kander, A., & Svensson Henning, M. (2011). The R&D-growth paradox arises in fast-growing sectors. *Research Policy*, *40*(5), 664–72.

European Union (2018). *European Innovation Scoreboard 2018*. Brussels: European Commission.

Fragkandreas, T. (2013). When innovation does not pay off: Introducing the "European Regional Paradox". *European Planning Studies*, *21*(12), 2078–86.

Gómez-Uranga, M., Zabala-Iturriagagoitia, J. M., & Barrutia, J. (Eds) (2016). *Dynamics of Big Internet Industry Groups and Future Trends: A view from epigenetic economics*. Heidelberg: Springer.

Granberg, A., & Jacobsson, S. (2006). Myths or reality: A scrutiny of dominant beliefs in the Swedish science policy debate. *Science and Public Policy*, *33*(5), 321–40.

Grillitsch, M., Hansen, T., Coenen, L., Miörner, J., & Moodysson, J. (2019). Innovation policy for system-wide transformation: The case of strategic innovation programmes (SIPs) in Sweden. *Research Policy*, *48*(4), 1048–61.

Growth Analysis (2011). *The Performance and Challenges of the Swedish Innovation System: A background report to the OECD*. Stockholm: Swedish Agency for Growth Policy Analysis.

Hekkert, M. P., Suurs, R. A. A., Negro, S. O., Kuhlmann, S., & Smits, R. E. H. M. (2007). Functions of innovation systems: A new approach for analyzing technological change. *Technological Forecasting and Social Change*, *74*, 413–32.

Jones, M. V., Coviello, N., & Tang, Y. K. (2011). International entrepreneurship research (1989–2009): A domain ontology and thematic analysis. *Journal of Business Venturing*, *26*, 632–59.

Landström, H. (2005). *Pioneers in Entrepreneurship and Small Business Research*. Heidelberg: Springer.

Marcotte, C. (2013). Measuring entrepreneurship at the country level: A review and research agenda. *Entrepreneurship and Regional Development*, *25*(3–4), 174–94.

Metcalfe, J. S. (1995). Technology systems and technology policy in an evolutionary framework. *Cambridge Journal of Economics*, *19*, 25–46.

132 *Entrepreneurial ecosystems meet innovation systems*

Palmberg, C. (2006). The sources and success of innovations: Determinants of commercialisation and break-even times. *Technovation, 26*, 1253–67.

Radosevic, S. (2010). What makes entrepreneurship systemic? In: F. Malerba (Ed.), *Knowledge-Intensive Entrepreneurship and Innovation Systems: Evidence from Europe* (pp. 52–76). Abingdon: Routledge.

Radosevic, S., & Yoruk, E. (2013). Entrepreneurial propensity of innovation systems: Theory, methodology and evidence. *Research Policy, 42*(5), 1015–38.

Radosevic, S., Yoruk, E., Edquist, C., & Zabala, J. M. (2010). *Innovation Systems and Knowledge-Intensive Entrepreneurship: Analytical framework and guidelines for case study research*. Deliverable 2.2.1 of the AEGIS Project. Advancing Knowledge-Intensive Entrepreneurship and Innovation for Economic Growth and Social Well-Being in Europe.

Shane, S., & Venkataraman, S. (2000). The promise of entrepreneurship as a field of research. *Academy of Management Review, 25*(1), 217–26.

Uygur, U. (2019). An analogy explanation for the evaluation of entrepreneurial opportunities. *Journal of Small Business Management, 57*(3), 757–79.

Wincent, J., Anokhin, S., & Boter, H. (2009). Network board continuity and effectiveness of open innovation in Swedish strategic small-firm networks. *R&D Management, 39*(1), 55–67.

Zabala, J. M., & Edquist, C. (2011). *Innovation System and Knowledge-Intensive Entrepreneurship: Sweden*. Deliverable 2.2.5 of the AEGIS Project. Advancing Knowledge-Intensive Entrepreneurship and Innovation for Economic Growth and Social Well-Being in Europe.

Zabala-Iturriagagoitia, J. M. (2018). Emprendimiento intensivo en conocimiento y sistemas nacionales de innovación en la UE. In: A. López López, J. Guimón de Ros & J. C. Salazar-Elena (Eds), *Innovación, capital intelectual y desarrollo económico. Ensayos en honor a Paloma Sánchez* (pp. 93–106). Madrid: UAM Ediciones.

7. Territory, development and systemic innovation: A Southern perspective

José Eduardo Cassiolato, Maria Gabriela v. B. Podcameni, Helena Maria Martins Lastres and Maria Cecília Junqueira Lustosa

7.1 INTRODUCTION

At the beginning of the twenty-first century, the lack of a better understanding of the transformative nature of the world economy and society has given room to several interpretations that sometimes seem contradictory. One is the perception that localization forces have accompanied globalization trends. This global-local dialectic has led to a renewed interest in the territorial aspects of production and innovation.

Since the 1990s, a variety of conceptual approaches aimed at analyzing new forms of organizing economic activities and relationships among firms and other organizations at the local level have been introduced both in academic and policy debates. Most of these analyses have focused on groups of agents and their interactions, recognizing them as important sources of economic dynamism. Different analytical frameworks have been developed.

Notions of industrial districts, clusters, *milieu innovateurs* and systems of innovation (SI) have all stressed the importance of the spatial dimension, proximity and interactions among firms to explain the specificities of their performance under globalization. Such concepts have been extensively used, during the last 20 years, in policy actions in different parts of the world. Arguably, the concept of SI, introduced by Christopher Freeman (1982), has been the most influential. It is used as an analytical tool and as a framework for policy analysis in both developed and underdeveloped countries. However, it may be argued that most of the time, the design and implementation of policies labeled as systemic have been rather rhetoric. That is, "only as a new label of traditional postures [...] (with) policies continuing to be horizontal and focusing either on the business entity in isolation (through the granting of tax and credit benefits) or on the university-enterprise relationship" (Cassiolato & Lastres, 2005, pp. 1225–46).

The failure of policies[1] has triggered the search for new ideas. One of these that gained significant attention in policy circles is the notion of entrepreneurial ecosystems of innovation (EEI).

In Brazil, a conceptual and analytical framework capable of dealing with local production and innovation structures was developed by RedeSist, the Research Network on Local Production and Innovation Systems, which was set up in the late 1990s. This framework, local production and innovation systems (LIPS), derived from the SI and Latin American structuralist approaches has been widely used both by network researchers and other scholars in Brazil, Latin America and other parts of the world.

The main objectives of this chapter are to present the LIPS approach and to discuss its differences with the EEI framework. Section 7.2 discusses, in a critical way, the entrepreneurial ecosystem framework. Section 7.3 details the LIPS approach and Section 7.4 provides the concluding remarks.

7.2   THE ENTREPRENEURIAL ECOSYSTEM OF INNOVATION APPROACH: A CRITIQUE

During the last few years, the EEI approach has gained ground on policy discourses, with an impact on entrepreneurial leaders and policy makers and on the academic community. The concept forms part of public policies that aim at creating an atmosphere where, according to Holtz-Eakin (2000), "the entrepreneurial virtues of new businesses are often assumed rather than examined" (p. 284). The concept contains two main components.

The first refers to the role of entrepreneurs as economic agents and entrepreneurship as a process in which opportunities for creating new goods and services are explored, evaluated and exploited (Shane & Venkatamaran, 2000). It is acknowledged that the emphasis of entrepreneurs as relevant economic agents started with Richard Cantillon, an eighteenth-century Irish-French economist, who introduced the concept of the entrepreneur as a risk bearer (Wennekers & Thurik, 1999).

The recent renewal of interest in the theme is linked to the works of Joseph Schumpeter. As pointed out by Jones and Murtola (2012), "if ever there was a consensus in the analysis of entrepreneurship, it must be that Schumpeter's contribution to it has been widely recognized as the most influential" (p. 117). And here is an important convergence among the different approaches focusing on innovation as a transformative force towards development. Indeed, the Schumpeterian view about the role of entrepreneurship refers to the notion – explicit in his *Theory of Economic Development* – that innovation (putting together already existing elements into new combinations) is linked to entrepreneurs (Schumpeter, 1911). The entrepreneur was always seen as a part, albeit a very important one, of the innovation process.

However, it cannot be ignored that the emphasis of the young Schumpeter on the role of entrepreneurs for innovation was certainly misplaced, as it is also well known that he modified his view on the subject. In later works he practically abandoned his former view about entrepreneurship and never really decided which institutions would be more relevant for triggering innovation in capitalist societies (Schumpeter, 1943).

In his first works, he pointed out that innovation upsurges in competitive industries were characterized by low entry barriers and creative destruction, by which new innovative firms substituted incumbent firms using outdated technologies. Later, Schumpeter (1943) described a radically different pattern: a small, relatively stable group of firms with considerable market power, and operating in markets with high entry barriers and creative accumulation (instead of destruction), play the most significant role for innovation. In a capitalist system, in which oligopolies predominate, the vision of the single entrepreneur (and entrepreneurship) as a dominant figure for innovation simply disappears.

Also, a more detailed reading of Schumpeter could lead to an opposite conclusion about the role of the entrepreneur. The central point in Schumpeter's work was to understand the functioning of capitalism. The fetishization of the modern entrepreneur that claims to be based on his ideas totally abstracts from such comprehension. As pointed out by Jones and Murtola (2012), "although entrepreneurship research is often taken to have developed out of the work of Schumpeter, perhaps the most egregious mistake of this literature has been to omit the reality of the relationship between entrepreneurship and capitalism" (p. 128). It is also important to note that most entrepreneurship research and policy prescriptions separate entrepreneurial activity from its territorial contexts, therefore ignoring its social, economic, environmental and political dimensions.

Another problem that shows how Schumpeter has been misquoted in the discussion of entrepreneurship refers to his foundational concept of "creative destruction" and how this notion and that of entrepreneurship "are fundamentally connected with the crisis tendencies of capitalism" (Jones & Murtola, 2012, p. 117). These authors also argue that one of the greatest critical contributions to this debate is the revelation that entrepreneurship does not necessarily offer a solution to a crisis but it is structurally linked with the emergence of crises (Jones & Murtola, 2012, pp. 121–2), even though the discourse as stated, for example in World Bank reports, "portrays entrepreneurs on the one hand as hapless victims of macroeconomic forces, and on the other as agents expected to resolve the current crisis" (Jones & Murtola, 2012, p. 121).

Max Weber, with his emphasis on the role of the entrepreneur for economic transformation and growth, has also significantly influenced the entrepreneurship literature (Howard, 1972). Weber's idea about the Puritan rational and frugal businessman geared towards achievements has been instrumental on what should be expected of entrepreneurs "particularly in peripheral countries". In this sense, the emphasis on the role of entrepreneurship reflects the bias of explaining underdevelopment by "cultural reasons as opposed to, for example, historical theories of development", as proposed by Furtado (1964) and other Latin American structuralist authors.

This Weberian explanation has been used to negatively compare local entrepreneurs in the developing world to their Western or United States counterparts. As pointed out by Howard (1972), the "differences in their values and behaviour can be used to explain the differences in the levels of economic development [...] (with the) [...] assumption made that certain cultural conditions existed in the West at the time of its great expansion in the eighteenth and nineteenth centuries, and that similar conditions [...] in countries presently underdeveloped, would cause similar expansion" (p. 2). Along this line, Van de Ven (1993) argues that the conventional discourse on entrepreneurship is rooted in the heroic myth that defines the dominant, rational, European/ North American male model. Ogbor (2000) has gone even further indicating that such narrative favors the dominance of the Western male mentality and has been used to increase "the divisions among humans, race, ethnicity and gender, through processes of classification, codification, categorization and taxonomies" (p. 607).

Some have argued that despite an almost universally accepted belief outside academia that entrepreneurial firms are beneficial to the economy, the accumulated evidence suggests otherwise (Nightingale & Coad, 2011). There is scarce evidence about its impact and "even taking into account the positive impact of these atypical [gazelle] firms, small firm jobs are more volatile, less productive and less well-paid, have fewer benefits, and have higher rates of accidents" (p. 3).

The second component of the term is ecosystems of innovation. Similarly to the SI perspective, the EEI literature emphasizes the relevance of the territory, which connects also with other frames of reference including the LIPS approach developed in Brazil. Although similarities with these conceptual frameworks exist (such as the focus on the external, localized environment), the EEI approach differs in some important aspects. For one, in the EEI, the entrepreneur is the focus point rather than the firm. Additionally, the EEI literature points out that entrepreneurship takes place in a community of interdependent agents and focuses on the role of the context in providing either favoring or constricting entrepreneurship (Jones & Murtola, 2012). In this sense, even if there are initiatives aiming at connecting the SI framework with entrepreneurship studies, the literature perceives the context as externalities to the entrepreneur and not as everything being part of the same system.

Oh, Phillips, Park and Lee (2016), in a review of the concept, suggest that nothing is gained from adding "eco" to our treatment of national and regional innovation systems and, on the contrary, the risks of using a flawed analogy to natural ecosystems outweigh any possible benefits. Therefore, it can be argued that EEI is neither a clearly defined concept nor a theory and that "its causal depth and evidence base is rather limited [...] (providing) [...] only long laundry lists of relevant factors without a clear reasoning of cause and effect" (Stam, 2015, p. 1761). This author also notes that the idea carries significant pitfalls, notably for its overemphasis on market forces, and it is mostly tautological as successful EEI are those that produce successful entrepreneurship, and where there is a lot of successful entrepreneurship, there is apparently a good entrepreneurial ecosystem of innovation.

7.3 THE LOCAL INNOVATION AND PRODUCTION SYSTEM APPROACH

The LIPS framework is a focusing device resulting from the combination of the SI approach with the contributions of the Latin American Structuralist School. As part of the Latin American literature on innovation systems (Arocena & Sutz, 2003; Cassiolato & Lastres, 2005), the LIPS approach is based on a broad perspective of SI.[2] Thus, besides firms, science and technology (S&T) institutions and explicit policies, it considers other types of agents, the implicit policies, history and culture, the demand and insertion pattern in the global economic and political system, as important features that influence innovation, learning and capability building. Furthermore, what differentiates this approach is its focus on the territory, where systemic structural specificities are defined, interactions are established and knowledge is created, absorbed, used and disseminated.

This section will discuss the relevance of the central elements in the LIPS framework for development: knowledge, systemic innovation and territory. It will also present RedeSist's methodology for the analysis of LIPS, stressing its main building blocks at two levels: the LIPS external context and the structures and processes intrinsic to the local environment.

7.3.1 Conceptual Basis of Local Production and Innovation Systems

Among the few consensuses established in the intense debate on globalization and the diffusion – partial and skewed – of information and communications technologies, two were fundamental in defining the intellectual framework and research agenda of RedeSist: the understanding that knowledge and innovation are the main factors, which define the development possibilities of nations, regions, sectors, companies and even individuals, as well as the notion that changes in the geography of world production reasserted the relevance of different territorial scales, in particular the local dimension. The following subsections provide a quick overview of the contributions that helped to shape these consensuses.

7.3.1.1 Innovation, knowledge and development
We argue that the neo-Schumpeterian approach of Innovation Systems (Freeman, 1987; Lundvall, 1992) and the Latin American structuralist tradition have strong connection points since both conceptual frameworks understand that development processes are characterized by structural changes, resulting from technological discontinuities that affect and are also affected by the social, cultural, political and institutional structures (Cassiolato & Lastres, 1999, 2008). Thus, development is a unique, specific systemic process, with theory and policy recommendations being highly dependent on each particular context (Furtado, 1964; Freeman, 1987).

These propositions diverge from the prevailing argument at the end of the 1990s – amid a political and economic debate still strongly influenced by the neoliberal agenda and the Washington consensus – which suggested that technological globalization would render national S&T policies irrelevant. In clear contrast, the national systems of innovation approach (Freeman, 1987) showed that the action of policy makers and other agents and institutions shape the elements and relationships that make up the systems. Therefore, the importance of public and private institutional arrangements for the creation and support of skills in national and regional economies was reaffirmed.

In the Latin American tradition, we find a similar emphasis, which also (1) stressed the importance of accumulating resources and knowledge for sustainable development; and (2) highlighted the negative results of the policies, adopted in the 1980s in the region, based on the so-called traditional comparative advantages. The latter were labeled by Fajnzylber (1988) as promoters of "spurious competitiveness" (a specialization in the low cost of labor and the intensive use of natural resources without a long-term vision).

The notions of knowledge, innovation and development derive from the combination of both contributions.[3] Innovation is understood as a systemic and contextualized process of a marked social and cultural nature. It is the result of collective and interactive actions between individuals and organizations generated and sustained by a complex network of interpersonal, interagency and interinstitutional relations.

Another main point of connection between the two literatures resides in the relevance assigned to complex relationships between the micro, meso and macro levels. As pointed out by Latin American scholars, the process of innovation is deeply influenced by the macro-economic environment and policies (Herrera, 1973; Katz, 1996; Coutinho, 2003). They significantly interfere with production and innovation strategies and capacities, eventually neutralizing explicit public and private innovation policies and restricting investment decisions, especially high-risk inversions, such as those aimed at innovation and technological development. Even if most of the SI literature ignores such relationships, Freeman (1987) emphasized the connections of micro, meso and macro levels in his explanation of the Japanese national system of innovation.

The relationship between innovation systems and finance is another important component of our agenda since the early 2000s that has been rooted in both literatures (Cassiolato, Lastres & Maciel, 2003). Metcalfe and Ramlogan (2008) already noticed its importance as they pointed out that "from whatever angle one approaches the problem, innovation systems and financial systems are inevitably interwoven" (p. 434).

Hence, one of the basic tenets of the LIPS analytical framework is that production and innovation capacities are negatively influenced by a finance-dominated accumulation regime that generates crisis and instability. Such a regime also challenges industrial and science, technology and innovation policies (Cassiolato, Lastres & Matos, 2014).

7.3.1.2 The relevance of focusing on different territorial scales
In a clear contrast to arguments in vogue about the alleged and supposedly inexorable deterritorialization of productive and innovative activities in the contemporary economy, induced by the phenomenon of globalization and technoglobalism, RedeSist's perception was from the outset diametrically opposed, namely that the global and the local are dialectically complementary and nourish each other. Hence, the emphasis placed on the relationship between geographical proximity and on the diversity and specificities that characterize the different local productive systems and their economic, social, political and institutional contexts as central elements in the analysis of technological dynamism and competitiveness of entrepreneurs, companies, regions and countries.

The recognition of the importance of the territorial dimension of globalization ignited a renewal of academic interest about local processes of economic and social transformation. But arguably it is the cluster literature that has attracted more attention, particularly in policy circles. Elsewhere (Lastres & Cassiolato, 2005), we argued that some points of partial convergence among distinct approaches could be found. They are mostly related to the recognition that (1) the specificities of the environment are critical to the survival and development of the different LIPS; (2) the focus on local activities can never ignore the global dimension; and that (3) a variety of economic and non-economic agents are important elements of any local system. But we also highlighted the notable differences that exist between these approaches and the LIPS perspective. Among these differences it is possible to single out the specific connotations of key central tenets of each theoretical approach, such as development and innovation.

Most important is the use of the LIPS framework as a focusing device capable of encompassing all types of production and innovation structures, and not only structured and specialized agglomerations that can be identified by traditional indicators and that are normally associated with the notions of clusters.[4] Of course, this is one of the reasons that grant the concept of LIPS a wider applicability to broader ranges of production activities and to different territories and countries. As the notion of cluster automatically emphasizes structured and specialized agglomerations, its use leaves aside others that may also require better understanding and also policy support. As a matter of fact, emerging and less structured systems are frequently very important everywhere and industrial and technological policies cannot ignore them.

7.3.1.3 Local production and innovation systems and sustainability

As pointed out above, for RedeSist, innovation is a systemic and contextualized process of social and cultural nature resulting from collective and interactive actions. Emphasis is placed on the importance of accumulating resources and knowledge for sustainable development. The LIPS framework adopts a definition of sustainable development which focuses on its manifold dimensions such as social, cultural, environmental, economic and political. In previous work, Lustosa et al. (2017) explored the affinity between LIPS and sustainability, identifying four main points of convergence between them: the focus of the territory/space; the focus on dynamic and evolutionary processes; the systemic perspective (which focuses on interactions and context specificities); and the understanding of the object analysed as an open system. According to the authors, these four convergence points are directly related to crucial theoretical foundations of both frameworks.

Especially fruitful are the contributions that explore the environmental and social features within a multidimensional perspective of sustainability in the LIPS analyses. However, it is still an open challenge to advance in two complementary fronts. First, in articulating the many dimensions of sustainability – namely social, cultural, environmental and economic – in a comprehensive theoretical framework, which establishes them as the main metric for determining success in terms of development. Second, in consolidating this perspective within an analytical and methodological framework, applying this multidimensional perspective of sustainable development to the analysis of any innovation system or LIPS. This could also provide very relevant policy implications.

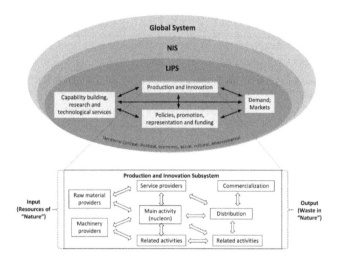

Source: Own elaboration, based on Matos et al. (2017).

Figure 7.1   Schematic representation of the LIPS framework

Figure 7.1 presents a schematic representation of the LIPS framework, including an element to shed light on sustainability issues. The aim is to include nature as the main resource provider and waste receiver resulting from production and innovation in the model. As such, innovation and production are understood as social and systemic processes, which depend upon environmental resources for their proper functioning. In other words, the productive processes of LIPS must be understood from the point of view of the exchange between society and nature.

The model in Figure 7.1 shows that a LIPS encompasses a local production chain, a diverse set of social, political and economic organizations and interactions among the agents that constitutes them. The importance of the territorial context is evident, represented as the axis where agents and interactions are inserted. The local productive system is highlighted, as well as the local productive chain and its links. The emphasis lies in the interactions between the agents involving knowledge and learning, and thus reinforcing the focus on collective aspects instead of the individual entrepreneur. The role of policy institutions is stressed in the scheme as well, making the influence of explicit and implicit policies over a LIPS dynamic clear. Finally, the representation of

LIPS inserted in the national system of innovations and in the global system reflects the importance of the national and international roles on local and national economies.

7.3.2   Main Characteristics of the Local Production and Innovation Systems Framework

The development and consolidation of the conceptual and methodological approach of RedeSist's LIPS results from the application of the concepts described above during more than two decades for both research and policy purposes. The approach encompasses economic, political and social agents and their interactions, including companies producing final goods and services and suppliers of raw materials, equipment and other inputs; distributors and marketers; workers and consumers; organizations focused on the training of human resources, information provision, research, development and engineering; support, regulation and financing; cooperatives, associations, unions and other representative bodies. It includes agents and production and innovation activities with different dynamics and trajectories, from the most knowledge intensive to those using endogenous or traditional knowledge; and of different sizes, originating in the primary, secondary and tertiary sectors, operating locally, nationally or internationally.

As a result, in sharp contrast with the frameworks that focus on the most structured and economically visible cases, the concept of LIPS assumes that some kind of system always exists around every production activity, however fragmented and unstructured it may be. In this sense, LIPS can be understood as a synonym of a local production and innovation structure with particular attention on the capacity to generate and use innovations fostered by the articulations of producers and users of goods, services and technologies. Along this line of argumentation, the broad unit of analysis offered by the LIPS framework – besides encompassing all production activities – focuses on the space in which learning takes place, productive and innovative capacities are created and tacit knowledge flows (Lastres & Cassiolato, 2005). It is a distinctive feature to focus on a set of agents and their interactions.

From a conceptual and analytical point of view, RedeSist's research efforts have succeeded in advancing the understanding of the different local and regional Brazilian production systems. More than 300 cases of LIPS have been studied, providing a rich set of empirical evidence. Initially the focus was on manufacturing activities in the southern (and richer) regions of Brazil. This perspective was gradually enriched with the incorporation of new activities performed in all regions of the country: LIPS of agriculture and services, namely family agriculture; essential public services, such as health; and tourism and cultural activities, including small-scale and informal entrepreneurs. The parallel advancement of the research agenda required a continuous improvement of the framework in order to incorporate nuances related to different types of activities and structures.

From the normative point of view, it is important to highlight that the term LIPS was used as a policy framework by various governmental and non-governmental agencies at the federal, national and local levels. This has reinforced the extremely rich process of experimentation, learning and fine-tuning of conceptual and methodological frameworks.

7.3.3 RedeSist's Methodology for the Analysis of Local Production and Innovation Systems

There are diverse sources and ways through which knowledge is developed, acquired, used and disseminated. They are often complementary and simultaneous. It is not surprising, therefore, that attempts to map and measure them are still very incipient worldwide (Cassiolato & Stallivieri, 2010). For RedeSist, the use of the LIPS approach requires an investigation of (1) articulations among companies and between them and other agents; (2) knowledge flows (including their tacit dimension); (3) a basis for generating production, organizational and innovation capacities; and (4) relevance of geographical proximity and historical, institutional, social and cultural identity. We also underline the importance of understanding the role of LIPS within the local, national and international levels.

Therefore, the analytical tool used by RedeSist starts with the observation that the transformation of a local system is influenced by elements on two interrelated levels. The first refers to the environment and context external to LIPS. This adheres to an understanding of LIPS as an open system with diversified and complex interconnections of agents and dimensions that often extrapolate the local sphere. The second level concerns the structures and processes largely intrinsic to the local environment and its specificities. The subsequent subsections explore the main aspects related to these analytical levels that are fundamental to the LIPS methodology.

7.3.3.1 The international and national influence on the trajectory of local production and innovation systems

As seen above, most LIPS have national and international linkages and RedeSist's analytical framework emphasizes their relevance; we need to understand how these articulations occur and affect the LIPS development. Thus, the first analytical stage focuses on how transformations of territorial production and innovation structures can be limited by global geopolitical and power constraints. We start by analyzing the influence of the organizational pattern of production and competition on a global and national scale and the associated technological regime in conditioning strategies of local agents and the development of LIPS. As described in more detail in Cassiolato et al. (2017, 2018), the methodological framework of LIPS takes the multiscale learning dimensions as a central element of analysis. We aim at covering all these international and national dimensions predominantly through bibliographic research and the analysis of secondary data on production, innovation processes and intellectual property, flows of products and services, investments flows, etc.

7.3.3.2   Local production and innovation systems and its endogenous conditions

In straight articulation with the analysis of the external elements, we focus on the structures and processes that are inherently endogenous to each LIPS. This requires procedures for gathering primary information in field research. Here, we explore the main research elements and present the instruments for gathering this information. As innovation is a central determinant of the LIPS development, the application of this framework requires a broader understanding of what constitutes innovation, and especially in areas such as highly innovative service and cultural activities. Similarly, broadening the scope of analysis to small-scale and informal activities also challenges our understanding of innovation. Advancement of the research agenda of RedeSist sought to incorporate these nuances, undertaking successive rounds of improvement and adaptation of the conceptual and methodological framework.

This framework, therefore, utilizes different strategies for information gathering seeking to identify and evaluate the following dimensions related to the innovative process: (1) efforts to search for innovation – activities of organizations from distinct entangled production segments aimed at promoting changes in production and organizational processes, as well as at developing, producing and introducing new products; (2) resource sources and the role of financing strategies – use of their own and third-party resources, exploring the support instruments used, the capital structure of firms and the influence of different arrangements of financial institutions on production and innovation strategies; (3) strategies for the introduction of innovations; (4) pecuniary impacts – reduction in costs and in the utilization of inputs, as well as the impact on revenues; (5) broad impacts – perennial impacts, such as succeeding in entering new markets, expansion of firms' capabilities, strategic diversification, greater visibility and recognition, etc.; and (6) obstacles – factors that hindered or hampered innovation efforts.

The second main topic of analysis refers to learning, i.e. the processes of production and innovation capacity building. These are conditioned by the LIPS historical trajectory and individual and collective learning capacity in connection with their external possibilities and constraints. Particular emphasis is given to tacit knowledge, which consists of skills, competencies, rules, beliefs, values and behavior of agents and organizations. Several forms of learning are investigated: those that are internal (learning with their own experiences in production, commercialization and use, as well as in search of new internal solutions, etc.) and those that are essentially external, including process of purchase, cooperation and other interactions.

As the processes of generation, diffusion and use of knowledge do not occur in a vacuum, their analysis necessarily requires a consideration of the environment that influences them. Thus, information gathering and analytical procedures in the methodology seek to cover internal learning processes, incorporation of knowledge and skills through human resources, external learning processes and relevance of interaction with agents from the local environment, the region, the rest of the country and from abroad, profile, performance and contribution of the organizations of the subsystem of S&T and capacity building in the generation and diffusion of information, education and professional qualification and, finally, social and economic impacts.

Another main focus of analysis lies in the cooperation processes among local agents. RedeSist's methodology considers the analysis of the systematic exchange of production, technological and market information (with customers, suppliers, competitors and others); interactions of various types of actors, involving companies and other institutions, through common training programs, events, fairs, courses and seminars, among others; integration of competencies, through the execution of joint projects, ranging from product and process improvement to research and development itself, between companies and between them and other institutions; and impacts on the firm's capabilities and on the strengthening of trust and collective strategies.

A fourth set of topics includes aspects of territorialization, embeddedness and governance. Understanding levels of territorialization requires an analysis of the articulation between the agents and the local environment and, specifically, with the organizations that conform to the local innovation system. We investigate to what extent the characteristics of the workers, organizations, physical, financing and knowledge infrastructure, as well as other facets of the territory influence and contribute to the development of LIPS.

The degree of embeddedness refers to the intensity and quality of articulation of organizations with the local environment and its social, natural, cultural, S&T and economic contexts. A multidimensional perspective of sustainability comes in and objective factors analyzed include the level of value aggregation, quality of jobs and working conditions, origin and control (local, national and foreign) of the organizations and the destination of production, technology and other inputs, use and impacts on natural endowments, urban space, etc. Governance refers to the different mechanisms that characterize and guide the decision-making processes within LIPS. It encompasses modes of coordination between different agents, such as local companies, representation and promotion organizations operating at its different levels, citizens and workers, civil society organizations, etc. In this sense, governance is related both to the coordination of production and market relations and the manifestation of the exercise of power by organizations and individuals.

Apart from firms and their strategies, understanding territorialization, embeddedness and governance requires analyzing the role played by public and private representation and promotion organizations. These exert important influences in creating and strengthening spaces for dialogue and the construction of collective strategies, influencing the directions and priorities in the scope of these collective actions, mobilizing and directing promotion instruments, acting on infrastructure dimensions, etc.

Thus, the methodology of RedeSist focuses on the importance of different factors inherent to the local environment for the competitiveness of companies; degree of articulation with the local economy in terms of the intensity of transactions with different agents of the system; degree of articulation with the local economy through subcontracting relations; morphology of the productive and organizational structure and the power exercised by different agents; use and impact on the natural, rural and urban environments; and the role of representation and promotion organizations.

A final set of issues focuses on LIPS' performance, by examining the qualification of labor, output and revenue levels, access to regional, national and foreign markets (including destination of exports and origin of imports), as well as the main competitive strategies. We also analyze, from the perspective both of support organizations and potential beneficiaries, government and private promotion policies. Finally, the perspectives for LIPS are addressed and the policy implications are discussed.

7.4   CONCLUSIONS

In this chapter we aimed to retrieve and synthesize the experience accumulated in more than 20 years by RedeSist in creating, improving and using the concept of LIPS both for analytical and policy-orientation purposes. As emphasized above, this research effort has succeeded in advancing the understanding of the dynamics of competence building and innovation of local production systems in the five macro regions of Brazil, with its considerable socio-economic heterogeneity and diverse political and institutional environments. The different LIPS studies carried out and the pragmatic use of this approach to support production and innovation development have generated an intensive learning process, which has contributed to enrich both research and policy initiatives. This effort has significantly benefited from joint research activities performed with partners in Latin America and the BRICS countries (Brazil, Russia, India, China and South Africa), and involved the research network Globelics.

We argue that the approach developed and used in such collaboration allows for a broader and proper understanding of the dynamics of any production and innovation structure. In particular, it is argued that a better comprehension of the dynamics of a particular system – and the proposition of suggestions for how to promote it – requires not only to know in depth its particular characteristics but also its weight and role within the economic, social and political contexts in which they are inserted, at local, regional, national and international levels.

Summing up, the main advantages of the framework developed by RedeSist refer chiefly to the fact that the concept of LIPS:

- represents a practical unit of research that establishes a bridge between territory and economic activities, going beyond classic spatial and sectorial cuts;
- focuses on groups of agents and related activities (organizations in charge of producing goods and services, research and development, education, training, promotion, financing, representation, coordination, etc.) and their interactions;
- encompasses the locus where the main production and innovation capacities are created and used and where tacit knowledge flows;
- focuses on the territorial context, including society and nature, as crucial elements to innovation and local development;
- implies the establishing of a bridge between the micro, meso and macro spheres, and integrates social, economic and political dimensions;
- represents the level in which public and private policies can be more effective;
- takes into account the influence of power conflicts in defining and implementing innovation and development policies, highlighting the relevance of understanding the mode of international insertion of each specific LIPS in the world economy; and
- provides companies, promotion agencies and other agents with a more comprehensive vision of the reality these structures face, helping to define more appropriate strategies.

By highlighting these advantages of the LIPS conceptual and methodological framework, we reinforce three streams of arguments. In the first place, despite a few points of convergence, notable differences exist between the LIPS perspective and other related approaches: (1) the systemic vision (by definition multidimensional, trans-sectorial and multiscale) provides a better understanding of the production and innovation structures than the traditional single-organization, sector and scale perspective; (2) a variety of economic and non-economic agents are important elements of any system; and (3) apprehending the specificities of the LIPS context is critical to the survival and development of the different production and innovation structures and cannot be ignored, in the same way that the focus on local activities can never disregard the global dimension as well as hierarchies and power elements.

Second, the LIPS framework is a focusing device capable of encompassing all types of production and innovation structures, and not only specialized agglomerations that can be identified by traditional indicators. As a matter of fact, emerging and less structured systems – often invisible and "below the radar" – are frequently very important everywhere and industrial and technological policies cannot ignore them. Of course this is one of the reasons that grant the concept of LIPS a wider applicability to a broader range of production activities and to different territories and countries.[5]

Third, it is worth emphasizing that the pressures for new sustainable modes of development require the effective incorporation of a multidimensional sustainability perspective in all production and innovation analyses. Those theories, concepts, indicators and policy models that adopt a broad, systemic and contextualized perspective of development are fertile and suited for this task; especially those that focus on – and are capable of – exploring the environmental and the social dimensions of the production and innovation structures.[6]

It also seems worth noting that the Brazilian policy experience based on the LIPS framework has been considered "the main novelty and most relevant industrial policy initiative in Latin America in recent decades" (Peres, 2011, p. 3). In the same way, the approach is perceived by international specialized literature as one that has had "notable success in the academic literature and in decision-making centres and promotion policies and in their means of impact communication" (Torre & Zimmermann, 2015, p. 25). Mazzucato and Penna (2016) also singled out its importance as "those productive structures that have been left out of major programs are targeted through the LIPS policy" (p. 71).

The results of the RedeSist investigations also confirm these conclusions, revealing substantial evidence on how the focus on LIPS has (1) allowed groups of informal and small producers and their activities to be supported by industrial and science, technology and innovation policies, in many cases for the first time in the history of the country; and (2) has become a "passport for inclusion" and a reference for policies committed with production inclusiveness, reduction of inequalities and with the promotion of cohesive development.

These are some of the main reasons that justify our arguments that the LIPS conceptual and methodological framework is more robust, suitable and instrumental than others that restrict approaches and that ignore some (or all) of the elements, which, in the twenty-first century, are considered essential to understand and orient the dynamics of production, innovation and entrepreneurship within a sustainable perspective.

NOTES

1. We have argued that although policies apparently focus on variables such as knowledge and innovation, they in fact continue to conceive of the state's intervention based only on the need to compensate for or mend market imperfections (Lastres, Cassiolato, Laplane & Sarti, 2016). See also Mazzucato and Penna (2016).
2. It has been argued (Lundvall, 1992; Cassiolato & Lastres, 2008) that the SI framework has two approaches, the narrow and the wide or broad. A follow up of earlier analyses of national science systems and technology policies, the narrow version concentrates on the analysis of research and development and S&T organizations. The policy issues raised are typically related almost exclusively to explicit S&T policy focusing on research and development and interactions between the scientific and technological infrastructure and the productive sector. Although it brings important information regarding the SI, the narrow version provides only an incomplete account of its structure and evolution. The wide (or broad) approach is inclusive, incorporating the narrow dimension and going beyond it (Freeman,1987; Lundvall, 1992). Emphasis is put on the role of cultural, geographical and historical processes, which account for differences in socio-economic capabilities and for different development trajectories and institutional evolution, creating SI with very specific local features and dynamics.
3. See Cassiolato and Lastres (2008) and Lastres and Cassiolato (2017).
4. For a detailed critique of use of traditional secondary indicators to "identify" local patterns of specialization and define what is (or is not) a cluster including the use and abuse of locational quotients, see Cassiolato and Stallivieri (2010) and Lastres and Cassiolato (2005). For a critique of the cluster approach, see Martin and Sunley (2003).
5. See Lastres et al. (2003); Lastres and Cassiolato (2005).
6. See Lustosa et al. (2017); Cassiolato, Podcameni and Soares (2015).

REFERENCES

Arocena, R., & Sutz, J. (2003). Inequality and innovation as seen from the South. *Technology in Society*, *25*(2), 171–82.

Cassiolato, J. E., & Lastres, H. M. M. (Eds) (1999). *Globalização e Inovação Localizada: experiências de sistemas locais de inovação no Mercosul*. Brasília: IBICT/MCT.

Cassiolato, J. E., & Lastres, H. M. M. (2005). Tecnoglobalismo e o papel dos esforços de P&D&I das multinacionais no Brasil. *Parcerias Estratégicas*, *22*, 1225–46.

Cassiolato, J. E., & Lastres, H. M. M. (2008). Discussing innovation and development: Converging points between the Latin American school and the innovation systems perspective? *GLOBELICS Working Paper Series*, *1*. www.globelics.org

Cassiolato, J. E., Lastres, H. M. M., & Maciel, M. L. (Eds) (2003). *Systems of Innovation and Development*. Cheltenham, UK and Northampton, MA, USA: Edward Elgar Publishing.

Cassiolato, J. E., Lastres, H. M. M., & Matos, M. (Eds) (2014). *Desenvolvimento e Mundialização: O Brasil e o pensamento de François Chesnais*. Rio de Janeiro: E-Papers.

Cassiolato, J., Lastres, H., Matos, M. & Szapiro, M. (2018). *Desemaranhando a tecnologia do êxito em políticas de desenvolvimento produtivo: estudos de caso narrados a partir da perspectiva de seus protagonistas*. Brasilia: International Labor Organization.

Cassiolato, J. E., Podcameni, M. G., & Soares, M. C. C. (2015). *Sustentabilidade Socioambiental em um Contexto de Crise Políticas Estratégicas de Inovação e Mudança Estrutural*. Rio de Janeiro: E-papers.

Cassiolato, J. E., & Stallivieri, F. (2010). Indicadores de inovação: dimensões relacionadas à aprendizagem. In: CGEE (Eds), *Bases conceituais em pesquisa, desenvolvimento e inovação: implicações políticas no Brasil*, Vol. 1. Brasília: Centro de Gestão e Estudos Estratégicos, 119–63.

Cassiolato, J., Zucoloto, G. F., Gonzalo, M., & Hausmann Tavares, J. (2017). APLs, a crise atual do capitalismo e a globalização dominada pelas finanças. In: M. Matos, J. Cassiolato, H. Lastres, C. Lemos & M. Szapiro (Eds), *Arranjos Produtivos Locais: Referencial, experiências e políticas em 20 anos da RedeSist* (pp. 265–88). Rio de Janeiro: E-Papers.

Coutinho, L. (2003). Macroeconomic regimes and business strategies: An alternative industrial policy for Brazil in the wake of the 21st century. In: J. Cassiolato, H. Lastres & M. L. Maciel (Eds), *Systems of Innovation and Development: Evidence from Brazil* (pp. 429–48). Cheltenham, UK and Northampton, MA, USA: Edward Elgar Publishing.

Fajnzylber, F. (1988). Latin-American industrialization: From the black box to the empty box. *International Social Science Journal*, *40*(4), 469–75.

Freeman, C. (1982). Innovation and long cycles of economic development. International Seminar on Innovation and Development at the Industrial Sector. Campinas: Departamento de Economia da Universidade de Campinas.

Freeman, C. (1987). *Technology Policy and Economic Performance: Lessons from Japan*. London: Pinter.

Furtado, C. (1964). *Development and Underdevelopment*. Los Angeles: University of California Press.

Herrera, A. (1973). Los determinantes sociales de la política científica en América Latina: Política científica explícita y política científica implícita. *Desarrollo Económico*, *13*(49), 113–34.

Holtz-Eakin, D. (2000). Public policy toward entrepreneurship. *Small Business Economics*, *15*(4), 283–91.

Howard, R. E. (1972). *Entrepreneurship and Economic Development: A critique of the theory*. Master's thesis, McGill University, Montreal, Canada. http://digitool.Library .McGill.CA:80/R/-?func=dbin-jump-full&object_id=50239&silo_library=GEN01

Jones, C., & Murtola, A.-M. (2012). Entrepreneurship, crisis, critique. In: D. Hjorth (Ed.), *Handbook of Organisational Entrepreneurship* (pp. 116–33). Cheltenham, UK and Northampton, MA, USA: Edward Elgar Publishing.

Katz, J. (1996). *National Innovation Systems in Latin America*. Santiago: ECLAC.

Lastres, H. M. M., & Cassiolato, J. E. (2005). Innovation systems and local productive arrangements: New strategies to promote the generation, acquisition and diffusion of knowledge. *Innovation: Management Policy and Practice*, *7*(2–3), 172–87.

Lastres, H. M. M., & Cassiolato, J. E. (2017). Development and innovation: Learning from the legacies of Freeman and Furtado. *Innovation and Development*, *7*(2), 271–86.

Lastres, H. M. M., Cassiolato, J. E., Laplane, G., & Sarti, F. (Eds) (2016). *O Futuro do Desenvolvimento*. Campinas: Editora da Unicamp. www.redesist.ie.ufrj.br

Lundvall, B.-Å. (Ed.) (1992). *National Systems of Innovation: Towards a theory of innovation and interactive learning*. London: Pinter.

Lustosa, C., Podcameni, M. G., Marcellino, I., Tomassini, C., Andreatta, A., & Queiroz, J. (2017). Desenvolvimento local inclusivo e sustentável: Revisitando a sustentabilidade a partir da perspectiva sistêmica de arranjos produtivos locais. In: M. Matos, J. Cassiolato, H. Lastres, C. Lemos & M. Szapiro (Eds), *Arranjos Produtivos Locais: Referencial, experiências e políticas em 20 anos da RedeSist*. Rio de Janeiro: E-Papers.

Martin, R., & Sunley, P. (2003). Deconstructing clusters: Chaotic concept or policy panacea? *Journal of Economic Geography*, *3*(1), 5–35.

Mazzucato, M., & Penna, C. (2016). The Brazilian innovation system: A mission-oriented policy proposal. *Temas Estratégicos para o Desenvolvimento do Brasil*, *1*, 120.

Metcalfe, S. & Ramlogan, R. (2008). Innovation systems and the competitive process in developing economies. *Quarterly Review of Economics and Finance*, *48*(2), 433–46.

Nightingale, P., & Coad, A. (2011). *Muppets and Gazelles: Rooting out ideological and methodological biases in entrepreneurship research*. Brighton: University of Sussex. www.finnov-fp7. eu/sites/default/files/FINNOV_DP8

Ogbor, J. O. (2000). Mythicizing and reification in entrepreneurial discourse: Ideology-critique of entrepreneurial studies. *Journal of Management Studies*, *37*(5), 605–35.

Oh, D. S., Phillips, F., Park, S., & Lee, E. (2016). Innovation ecosystems: A critical examination. *Technovation*, *54*, 1–6.

Peres, W. (2011). Industrial policies in Latin America. Working Paper, World Institute for Development Economics Research, 48.

Schumpeter, J. (1911). *Theorie der wirtschaftlichen Entwicklung*. Berlin: Duncker und Humblot.

Schumpeter, J. (1943). *Capitalism, Socialism and Democracy*. New York: Routledge.

Shane, S., & Venkataraman, S. (2000). The promise of entrepreneurship as a field of research. *Academy of Management Review*, *25*(1), 217–26.

Stam, E. (2015). Entrepreneurial ecosystems and regional policy: A sympathetic critique. *European Planning Studies*, *23*(9), 1759–69.

Torre, A., & Zimmermann, J. B. (2015). Des clusters aux ecosystems industriels locaux. *Revue d'Économie Industrielle*, *152*, 13–38.

Van de Ven, A. (1993). The development of an infrastructure for entrepreneurship. *Journal of Business Venturing*, *8*, 211–30.

Wennekers, S., & Thurik, R. (1999). Linking entrepreneurship and economic growth. *Small Business Economics*, *13*, 27–55.

8. The complementarity approach to understanding entrepreneurship and innovation ecosystems taxonomy

Maksim Belitski and Andrew Godley

8.1 INTRODUCTION

In recent years, entrepreneurial ecosystems (EE) has become a popular way to further explain why some places grow and agglomerate while others deteriorate and slowly stagnate (Isenberg, 2010). This idea was already implicit in the literature on innovation systems. There are a number of differences between them, particularly in the units of analysis used, context mechanisms, roles of individual agents in regional economic development and the ways by which entrepreneurial opportunities emerge (Autio, Kenney, Mustar, Siegel & Wright, 2014; Autio, Nambisan, Thomas & Wright, 2018; Adner & Kapoor, 2010).

The entrepreneurship ecosystem framework builds on Marshall's (1890) legacy and reawakens the "new economic geography" (Feldman & Braunerhjelm, 2006; Buenstorf & Fornahl, 2009). EE benefit from local industrial specialization so knowledge spillovers across ecosystem actors are stimulated, which results in broader economic benefits (Stam, 2015).

While the EE framework is intuitively appealing, its rapid adoption has tended to overlook the heterogeneous nature of specific EE (Isenberg & Onyemah, 2016). There are several ground-breaking studies highlighting the importance of accounting for the systemic nature of EE (Autio et al., 2014; Spigel, 2017; Stam, 2015) and the need to develop an EE taxonomy (Mason & Brown, 2017). We define "EE taxonomy" as the set of common characteristics that could be applied to territories with different types of EE.

EE taxonomy offers a practice-based (bottom-up) approach by Mason and Brown (2017) which includes four distinct components: entrepreneurial actors, resource providers, entrepreneurial connectors and entrepreneurial culture. Entrepreneurial actors are not always connected to each other. In fact, the major difference between an entrepreneurial and innovation ecosystem is that actors may or may not be connected at all.

Entrepreneurial resource providers fill up an ecosystem with debt and financial capital. They also coordinate supply and demand of resources, and enable the transfer of resources between entrepreneurs, firms and other stakeholders. Financial connectors comprise banks, venture capital firms, accelerators, business angels and other financial institutions (Clarysse, Wright & Van Hove, 2015).

Entrepreneurial connectors are represented by networks of nascent ventures and stakeholders in other EE (Granovetter, 1973; Sullivan & Ford, 2014). Entrepreneurial culture and orientation represent societal norms and attitudes towards entrepreneurship activity, entrepreneurial aspirations and attitudes of individuals to entrepreneurship. Despite the long-standing theoretical and empirical relationship between entrepreneurship and innovation, the question of the components which facilitate EE and innovation ecosystems has received little attention.

Acs, Autio and Szerb (2014) argue that the innovation ecosystems literature hardly mentions entrepreneurship ecosystems, and even the most influential concept – national systems of innovation – has been unable to explain the process of new venture creation. This is because of the institutional tradition of the innovation ecosystems literature, which reinforces countries' institutions effect in creation and dissemination of new ideas and knowledge. The EE draws our attention to individual-level entrepreneurs and firms as well as to the micro-processes of entrepreneurial innovation.

While the structure and institutions are present as in innovation ecosystems, the EE literature has increasingly focused on entrepreneurship quality, high-quality jobs, opportunity self-employment and growth ambitions. This contrast calls our attention to how institutional characteristics contrast EE components, in particular the role of capital availability, connectivity and entrepreneurial actors in EE (Bowen & De Clercq, 2008; Levie & Autio, 2011). Still, the gap remains: although increased availability of data on entrepreneurship opened new opportunities for comparative EE research, identification of the combinations of components related to entrepreneurship and innovation ecosystems remains much in its infancy (Autio & Acs, 2010; Autio et al., 2014; Stam & Spigel, 2016).

There has been criticism of the concept of innovation and entrepreneurship systems and its focus on the national level, which is heterogeneous in terms of geography and sectors (Malerba & Breschi, 1997; Autio et al., 2014). As a result, the concept has been extended to cities and regions (Szerb, Acs, Autio, Ortega-Argilés & Komlósi, 2013; Charron, Dijkstra & Lapuente, 2014).

There are a number of other gaps in the literature. Firstly, existing EE taxonomy lacks an explanation in regards to absent components and the ability of the

EE to complement those components to different EE (Mason & Brown, 2017). Secondly, it is unclear which components and combinations of components are more efficient in channeling knowledge to market and supporting entrepreneurial strategies across heterogeneous EE (Isenberg & Onyemah, 2016). Thirdly, while the network perspective is often used to analyze ecosystems, it is not enough to explain how EE function (Stangler & Bell-Masterson, 2015).

Bridging this theoretical gap (Williamson & De Meyer, 2012; Autio et al., 2018; Adner & Kapoor, 2010) we distinguish EE components and explain how regions which lack several of the components of EE taxonomy may still be successful in supporting entrepreneurship.

We introduce the complementarity perspective to EE taxonomy and use the example of Greater Reading as a case which describes how a combination of complementors within the EE taxonomy facilitates EE growth while discussing the factors that may impede it.

This study is particularly important for EE which aim to innovate with limited resources and exploit existing capabilities rather than engage in exploration activities.

This study makes the following contributions to the literature on entrepreneurship, small business economics and the resource-based approach.

Our first contribution is in critically analyzing and demonstrating that EE are a distinctive unit of analysis in the management, entrepreneurship and economic geography literatures with a complex system of complementors. Although the complementarity approach has been extensively used in industrial economics and management, its application in small business economies and management has been limited (Stangler & Bell-Masterson, 2015). More theoretical and empirical work is needed to better explain how various combinations of EE taxonomy may work as complementors.

Our second contribution is expanding the entrepreneurship, management and economic geography literatures by explaining how different types of complementarities and combinations of four components of EE taxonomy can be used to predict the performance of heterogeneous EE. We apply a complex system of complementors to the case of the Greater Reading EE in the United Kingdom (UK).

The remainder of this chapter is organized as follows. Section 8.2 describes the existing literature and theories, and introduces the complementarity approach to EE taxonomy. Section 8.3 illustrates the case of the Greater Reading area. Section 8.4 discusses EE taxonomy as applied to Greater Reading, while Section 8.5 concludes.

8.2 THEORETICAL FRAMEWORK

8.2.1 Entrepreneurship Ecosystem

The concept of the EE has evolved rapidly over the last few years, and has helped researchers and policy-makers to think in systemic terms when considering the entrepreneurial activity of regions and countries. As a new unit of analysis, the EE provides a more realistic portrayal of the entrepreneurial phenomenon. It also allows researchers to adopt a much broader perspective when considering the role of each economic actor (Audretsch, Keilbach & Lehmann, 2006).

Mason and Brown (2014, p. 5) defined EE as a "set of interconnected entrepreneurial actors, entrepreneurial organizations, institutions and entrepreneurial processes which formally and informally coalesce to connect, mediate and govern the performance within the local entrepreneurial environment". Clearly, the dynamic and systemic nature of the concept encompasses multiple actors, institutions and processes.

However, the majority of innovation and entrepreneurship scholars view ecosystems primarily as a spatial concept (Feldman & Braunerhjelm, 2006; Mason & Brown, 2014, 2017) to explain why certain places have high levels of entrepreneurial activity (Stam, 2015). So rather than having innovation at its core, entrepreneurship is the fundamental driver behind the concept. Radosevic and Yoruk (2013) discussed the entrepreneurial propensity of innovation systems by integrating knowledge-intensive entrepreneurship and innovation system concepts. The authors were the first to assess the influence of a system's complementary activities on the emergence of knowledge-intensive entrepreneurship, and confirmed that technological innovation is an important determinant of entrepreneurial opportunity and performance (Audretsch, Bönte & Keilbach, 2008; Eckhardt & Shane, 2010). At the same time, the concept of innovation systems has been criticized because the literature is based on a relatively narrow conception of innovation, with a focus on patentable technological innovation.

Another criticism is that the concept provides only limited insight into the factors driving change in the innovation system, with a limited explanation as to its evolution over time (Hung & Whittington, 2011). The literature calls for the systemic perspective to account for multi-level factors which influence the capacity to generate entrepreneurial activity. These include personal factors (individual level), interpersonal (team level), organizational (firm level), networks (industry level) and spatial factors (regional level) which can influence both innovation and entrepreneurship.

From the innovation systems perspective, entrepreneurship is the property of systems of innovation and depends on both structural features of the economic system and on social mechanisms. From an entrepreneurship perspective, the key structural feature of an economic system is its capacity to generate entrepreneurial opportunities independent of individuals' capacity to recognize them (Radosevic & Yoruk, 2013). However, a well-known gap in the entrepreneurship literature is its narrow focus on the entrepreneur and firm while paying little attention to how components of the ecosystem and the local context regulate the behavior of entrepreneurs and the choices they make (Phan, 2004). This is a significant omission, since we know that entrepreneurial action occurs in institutional contexts which affect the outcomes of entrepreneurial choices. The EE perspective thus views entrepreneurial activities as deriving directly from entrepreneurial behavior and the traits that characterize entrepreneurial actors, such as entrepreneurial cognition (McMullen & Shepherd, 2006; Autio, Frederiksen & Dahlander, 2013), and from the external environment as represented by systemic conditions.

In contrast to the innovation systems literature, the dimensions portrayed in the EE literature demonstrate differences in the unit of analysis, context mechanisms and the role of individual agents in regional economic development. Whereas the innovation systems literature portrays entrepreneurship cognition as something of a "black box" (Stam, 2015), it recognizes the importance of the contextual mechanisms facilitating entrepreneurial choices. The EE literature uses the individual pursuing a new venture creation as a core unit of analysis, while in the innovation systems literature the role of individual agents was not considered to appear automatically, being instead influenced by institutions (Baumol, 1993).

Finally, the context mechanisms in innovation systems are top down (i.e. government policy) and complex sets of interactions. Meanwhile, in EE the context mechanisms are bottom up (i.e. individual entrepreneurs, firms, communities) and decentralized. Resource endowments and government support is substituted with resource orchestration instead.

Various innovation and entrepreneurship scholars have attempted to explore and interpret EE with a focus on individuals and firms and with respect to their multi-actor networks. However, it is the fusion of diverse perspectives which has proved to be the strongest asset of EE. At the same time, the fusion of diverse perspectives to EE as a unit of analysis and their hybrid nature makes the measurement of EE complex (Acs et al., 2014; Stangler & Bell-Masterson, 2015; Isenberg & Onyemah, 2016; Audretsch & Belitski, 2017). Case studies have remained one of the most logical and comprehensive ways to address the genesis of EE in local contexts (Best, 2015). Although there is some evidence of EE in European cities and regions (Stam, 2015), there is a lack of case studies in emerging metropolitan areas and in countries adjunct to Europe.

8.2.2 Complementarity Approach to Entrepreneurship Ecosystem Taxonomy

To date, there has been little explicit theorization around EE components and the outcome of EE (Stam, 2015). Given the ability of entrepreneurs to achieve complex tasks with limited resources, applying the resource-based view to EE could be helpful in understanding how resources are distributed within an EE. The ability to accumulate and effectively use financial resources across different EE depends on both entrepreneurial actors' endowment and the contextual factors where entrepreneurs (firms) operate. The interdependency between entrepreneurial actors and financial resource providers could be expressed as functional congruence, with the main function to provide resources for entrepreneurial opportunity recognition and commercialization of ideas. The interdependency between entrepreneurial actors and resource providers (EE stakeholders) on the one hand and the external environment, as represented by entrepreneurial regulations, culture, networks and institutions, on the other hand, can be called strategic congruence. This implies that the design and implementation of a successful EE strategy in a region requires a strategic congruence of an entrepreneurial actor's strengths and weaknesses to the wider contextual factors that may complement each other. Both institutional and individual (firm) levels aim to achieve productive entrepreneurship (Desai, Acs & Weitzel, 2013; Stam & Spiegel, 2016) as the outcome of EE.

The conceptual model which comprises entrepreneurial culture and networks as well as actors and resource providers embedded within an institutional environment (Autio et al., 2014; Mason & Brown, 2017) can influence complementarities between each component of EE (Szerb et al., 2014; Charron et al., 2014). While individual entrepreneurs respond to external opportunities created by the EE, they are also considered important in the exploitation of opportunities. The opportunities to which entrepreneurs "respond" may not be exogenous but can also be shaped and created by entrepreneurs (Radosevic & Yoruk, 2013).

The individual dimension of the EE comprises entrepreneurial actors and resource providers such as governments, corporations, entrepreneurs, angel investors and universities (Audretsch & Belitski, 2017; REAP MIT, 2016) who are responsible for creating and commercializing market opportunities. The institutional dimension is represented by regulation for entrepreneurship, networks, entrepreneurial orientation and culture which shapes the mindset of entrepreneurs and affects their responses to the exogenous factors (Autio & Acs, 2010). The conceptual model of EE taxonomy and the complementarities between them is illustrated in Figure 8.1.

The traditional innovation system approach focuses on the components within the innovation systems, such as entrepreneurial actors and institu-

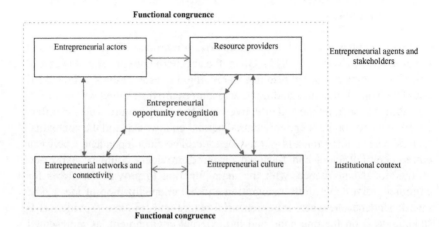

*Figure 8.1   Synergy approach of the entrepreneurial ecosystems
             framework*

tions (Nelson, 1993; Malerba & Breschi, 1997). We take an EE perspective (Isenberg, 2010) and demonstrate that EE influence entrepreneurship processes through the networks of stakeholders, interdependences and by changing the institutions. Entrepreneurial actors are not independent of each other, but instead support and interact with one another. In order to understand EE functionality we should thus allow for the interactions between stakeholders of EE and their embeddedness into institutional context.

It is unlikely that a region has all components at the stakeholder level and institutional context needed to facilitate the congruence between all components of the EE taxonomy. Complementarity between taxonomy components can leverage the missing components and result in new entrepreneurial opportunities being recognized and commercialized (Acs et al., 2014).

Highly complementary components create a highly interdependent EE, while mismatched components weaken the EE. Higher levels of congruency among the different components in the EE lead to higher levels of entrepreneurial opportunity (Figure 8.1) and more efficient EE. This resonates with the long-term perspective on economic growth based on complementarities as described by Freeman and Louca (2001) and with Kremer's (1993) O-ring theory of economic development as well as the entrepreneurial propensity of an innovation ecosystem (Radosevic & Yoruk, 2013).

Building on Radosevic (2010), we argue that EE and entrepreneurial opportunities should be explored from a complementary perspective. This perspective is based on complementarity between the EE components, and can explain how heterogeneous EE with different combinations of entrepreneurial agents and stakeholders can generate entrepreneurial opportunities and contribute to regional economic development.

Interdependencies between entrepreneurial agents and their embeddedness in institutions (Adner & Kapoor, 2010; Autio et al., 2014) constitute entrepreneurial opportunities. Shane's (2000) three sources of opportunities are technological change, political/regulatory change and social/demographic change. Within these, the complementarity perspective (Radosevic, 2010) can demonstrate that interactions between entrepreneurial agents within an EE constitute technological and market opportunities, while entrepreneurial culture and networks lead to institutional opportunities.

As the degree of complementarity between each of the four components of EE is different, it changes the entrepreneurial opportunities and thus the performance of the entire EE.

As one would expect in the ecosystem, entrepreneurial actors are not always connected to each other. In fact, the major difference between an EE and an innovation ecosystem is that entrepreneurial actors may or may not be connected at all (Baum, Cowan & Jonard, 2014). Both entrepreneurial actors and institutional environments will create entrepreneurial opportunities (Shane, 2000) that affect entrepreneurial choices.

Our main hypothesis is that EE are driven by complementarities arising from the interaction of all four components of taxonomy and result in the creation of entrepreneurial opportunities. This perspective is indeed an integration of three views on entrepreneurial and innovation ecosystems: Mason and Brown (2017), Adner and Kapoor (2010) and Radosevic (2010). In each of these views, the EE is the result of different driving factors:

- Mason and Brown (2017): actors, connectors, finance resource providers and entrepreneurial orientation as four elements of taxonomy;
- Adner and Kapoor (2010) and Autio et al. (2014): institutional context, complementarities or synergies; and
- Radosevic (2010): the systemic approach to the entrepreneurial propensity of innovation ecosystems.

In EE no single entrepreneurship actor can work independently of another actor in addressing customer needs (Williamson & De Meyer, 2012). This means that the EE should include analysis of the complementarity of EE components (Adner & Kapoor, 2010). This is because these four EE components cannot generate entrepreneurial opportunities on their own, but only through their mutual interaction. Accordingly, an EE is able to nurture and exploit the interactions of these four components.

The channels that link the four components with entrepreneurial outcomes in terms of entrepreneurial activities are interactions between components, i.e. complementarities. In general, complementarities are defined as processes (Radosevic & Yoruk, 2013) where two or more components of the taxonomy reinforce each other. More formally, Milgrom and Roberts (1995) define complementarities as situations where doing more of any activity increases the returns of other activities.

The mechanism within an EE is triggered when there is a mutually compatible set of opportunities (Shane, 2000) to be pursued by actors. If there is no mutually compatible set of opportunities, actors will not be able to create opportunities as the EE will not have sufficient critical mass to emerge. Entrepreneurship activity is a function of stakeholder characteristics along with other systemic features, including the institutional environment.

Figure 8.1 depicts the conceptual differences between mainstream and complementarity perspectives on EE. In the mainstream perspective, entrepreneurship opportunities (technological, market and institutional) and new firm formation is explained as an outcome of the framework and systemic conditions (Stam, 2015; Audretsch & Belitski, 2017). In the complementarity perspective, entrepreneurial opportunities are the outcome molded through complementarities and interactions between the different components of the EE taxonomy. This includes entrepreneurial experimentation by actors, availability of financial capital, networking and the institutional environment that includes entrepreneurial culture.

The conceptual model in Figure 8.1 illustrates the logic of our approach by depicting the relationships between the different components of the EE taxonomy. These components shape different combinations of entrepreneurial outcomes which are not exogenous (as in the mainstream approach) but are also constitutive of the EE.

Additional support for the complementarity perspective of EE comes from the economic geography literature, where a region is seen as a space which contains numerous entrepreneurial actors (Kenney & Von Burg, 1999). Changes among entrepreneurial actors may affect how resource providers change the functionality of EE (Figure 8.1) as well as how entrepreneurial culture affects the overall strategic congruence between entrepreneurial agent and contextual levels of taxonomy. Intra-ecosystem changes, contextual factors (Autio et al., 2014) and regional entrepreneurial culture (Stuetzer et al., 2018) affect entrepreneurial behavior.

8.3 THE CASE OF GREATER READING AND RESEARCH METHOD

Greater Reading is a sub-region of south-east England which is centered on the River Thames. It is to the west of London and covers the urban areas of Slough/Windsor, Reading in Berkshire and (to the north) Oxford and south Oxfordshire, as well as largely rural Buckinghamshire. This westwards arc of about 50 miles around the western section of the M25 motorway from St Albans to Guildford represents the sweet spot of post-crisis economic growth in the UK. Within the broad Thames Valley region, Reading (historically the county town of Berkshire) has emerged as a thriving urban area with over 320,000 inhabitants and is the area's dominant commercial center. Of all the major satellite towns surrounding London, only Reading has emerged as a net commuter destination in recent years. Unlike the economies of Cambridge and Oxford, Reading has higher inward than outward commuter trips as it is greatly embedded in London's economy. At the same time Reading has emerged as an important center to compete with London as a commuter destination in the south east of England (TVB, 2014).

To date the Thames Valley region with the Greater Reading area at its heart has secured and allocated £182 million of UK and European public funds to deliver a wide range of initiatives in the Thames Valley Berkshire area. Alongside London, the area is the UK's economic powerhouse contributing over £37 billion in gross value added to the national economy (TVB, 2014).

In order to gain a deeper understanding of the Greater Reading region and thus the complementarity of its EE elements, we approached this study with an interpretivist lens. We decided to follow the REAP MIT (2016) approach and interviewed seven potential stakeholders of the Reading EE (see Table 8A.2). Interview questions are provided in Table 8A.1.

Their subjective evaluation of the EE in Reading with respect to their businesses and roles in the region was important as it allowed us to apply the taxonomy. Furthermore, the interpretivist lens of the interviews allowed us to exploit our own expertise within the Greater Reading region, as well as our access to and understanding of Thames Valley/Berkshire-specific documents obtained for this study.

For this research, we identified and interviewed seven representative stakeholders in the Greater Reading area. Our selection of interviewees used purposive sampling logic, which is the purposeful selection of participants based on their unique characteristics which can "inform an understanding of the research problem and central phenomenon in the study" (Creswell, 2007, p. 125). To maintain originality of thought, we provide verbatim quotes from interviewees which directly speak about the Reading EE and can be used to justify the analytic evaluations we made in this study (Corden & Sainsbury, 2005).

8.4   COMPLEMENTARITY PERSPECTIVE OF GREATER READING'S ENTREPRENEURIAL ECOSYSTEM

8.4.1   Entrepreneurial Actors

In recognition of the role large organizations and multinationals play in Greater Reading's EE, the ecosystems literature highlights the importance of knowledge spillovers (Napier and Hansen, 2011; Coutu, 2014; Audretsch & Belitski, 2017). These spillovers come from scale-ups, which Mason and Brown (2014) refer to as "blockbuster entrepreneurs", entrepreneurial community, local government and capital-generating positive externalities for entrepreneur firms (Buenstorf & Fornahl, 2009).

Scale-up firms are the most important entrepreneurial actors in the Greater Reading EE. Scale-ups are businesses which have achieved a 20 percent growth rate year on year for the past three years and have an annual turnover of over £1 million (Scaleup Berkshire, 2019).

Start-ups in Reading serve as a role model for other new entrepreneurial firms as well as large incumbent firms in the Greater Reading area, such as Microsoft, Verizon and Cisco.

The Thames Valley Local Enterprise Partnership (LEP) agency was established to promote regional economic development and support scale-ups, and has started focusing more on supporting policies for scale-ups in Reading. Frances Campbell, head of business environment at LEP, states that "Reading EE is maturing and evolving. It is very fragmented." In order to decrease the fragmentation, the Business Environment Programme Group was created and given responsibility for the business environment. The Berkshire Local Industrial Strategy has also been developed, where scale-ups are explicitly described as the "drivers" of Reading's regional economy. Louize Clarke, head of ConnecTVT business incubator in Reading, adds: "Entrepreneurial actors in Reading are lacking, instead their role is performed by business coaches running programmes, rather than scale-ups themselves".

The Scaleup Advisory Group was established to support and advise businesses (Scaleup Berkshire, 2019). The main issue for Reading is that entrepreneurial actors who should be helping EE development are reluctant to change. Sharon Cunnington, director of Santander Bank's Reading branch, notes "There are many shared office spaces, but actors such as the Chamber of Commerce are still very traditional". Tom Fox, a c-level manager at KPMG

Tech Growth in Reading, said "Connections between actors are not in a great place now".

8.4.2   Entrepreneurial Resource Providers

Reading is closely connected with London and has a number of financial channels for entrepreneurs to build on. Along with debt financing, accelerators are important sources of EE finance in Reading and provide additional support to businesses becoming so-called "start-up factories" (Miller & Bound, 2011). These have grown very rapidly in recent years in large cities such as London, Chicago and Berlin (e.g. Y Combinator, Rocket Internet, Barclays Techstars, Innovation Warehouse, Funlab and Wayra). The start-up grid incubator also known as ConnecTVT for business is located in one of Reading's three international business parks. It has brought accelerator culture and the ConnecTVT project from large cities to smaller innovation hubs such as Greater Reading.

However, the following issues remain. Louize Clarke, head of ConnecTVT, states that "We need entrepreneur-led activity and investment in the risky companies who will innovate. We don't have any real incubation in Reading and most of the co-working is more expensive than London. The only affordable co-working spaces are outside of town which are not the best for start-ups who often need to be connected directly into London." Knowledge spillover and resources are available from software development companies located within Reading, and through debt financing with a general lack of equity capital. The Reading Santander Bank branch director highlights the help available for start-ups as "Working capital, asset funding, machinery".

Tim Martin, chief executive officer of WorkInConfidence, adds that "More angel networks outside of London are needed, but still not particularly. Non recourse banking capital is the same as everywhere in the UK, it's non-existent. Crowdfunding platforms – you don't really need to be in an area to tap these VCs and Angels." This thesis highlights the importance of the digitalization of finance (Cumming, Meoli & Vismara, 2019) which significantly expands access to capital for distant EE. Thomas Henderson, head of HSBC branch in Reading, confirms this: "There is a struggle for funding. I would say it's less than 10 years ago cyclical thing – funding goes up and down. Lack of marketing!!! What funding is available is not advertised properly to entrepreneurs and there is a lot of austerity. We also have less state funding (opportunities) than before." Unlike banks and venture capital, scale-ups in Reading between themselves have accumulated entrepreneurship financing.

8.4.3 Entrepreneurial Connectors

The Greater Reading EE is characterized by a "nested geography" with a higher embeddedness in the south east of England area between Oxford and London. It involves multi-scaler interactions with entrepreneurial actors in both cities.

Incubators and accelerators are known as the main "connectors" for EE in cities. However, their location relative to transport links is important. Frances Campbell, head of business environment at LEP, states that "There are less incubators than in other places. For example, in Bristol, they invested in a LEP and it has been constructed right next to the train station – Engine Shed (university was also involved). We need more hubs of innovation!"

Incubators and co-working spaces may create the information and communication environment needed for all EE actors, in particular incumbents and scale-ups, to enable face-to-face interactions and the co-location of people and firms within the same area (Bathelt, Malmberg & Maskell, 2004). Tim Martin, chief executive officer of the WorkInConfidence scale-up, adds "Better than most parts of UK we have incubators but still limited. We approached local government about our service to connect us to other actors and they don't respond, while incubators somewhat limited – all offer the same old advice you may not need plus limited access to funding for companies which grow."

"Greater Reading is perhaps the region with the largest numbers of dealmakers," says Jurek Sikorski, head of the Henley Centre for Entrepreneurship. The relational dealmakers are individuals with "valuable social capital, who have deep fiduciary ties within regional economies and act in the role of mediating relationships, making connections and facilitating new firm formation" (Feldman & Zoller, 2012, p. 24). Dealmakers were also described by Napier and Hansen (2011) as a specific type of entrepreneurial connector that facilitate networks. At the same time, entrepreneurial connectors complain about limited collaboration with the local university. Louize Clarke, head of the ConnecTVT business incubator in Reading, laments that: "To date Reading University has largely not wanted to collaborate with our business incubator, but I do see a change with the appointment of a new Commercial Director at the University." The main reason for this is that EE stakeholders aim to connect to incubation facilities, such as the Thames Valley science park as an extension of the University of Reading.

8.4.4 Entrepreneurial Culture

Entrepreneurial orientation and culture is still developing and is distinct from the incumbent firm's culture. Over time incumbents work as attractors of skilled labor and customers for many scale-ups which have yet to become incubation springboards for entrepreneurs. The development of the software sector triggered the development of diversity and corporate orientation, and not quite entrepreneurial culture as discussed in Mason and Brown (2017). Large multinationals recruited highly skilled workers, some of whom went on to found successful businesses. Frances Campbell argues that "The universities are key to ecosystem culture," while Thomas Henderson, head of Reading's HSBC branch, stated: "People seem willing to take risks despite Brexit. The hub of activity is growing and this is how we see the culture." The casual inference is that the local area has benefited from the accumulation in local skills and inward investments, as the individuals who left incumbents have then created their own businesses in Reading and London.

Overall this component of the EE taxonomy has remained weak in Reading. Tom Fox, head of the KPMG branch in Reading, believes this is because "The fear of failure is present and people take less risks. They don't go as big as they wish they did. Academic strength – University of Reading, developing the business culture locally, but definitely there is a prestige for self-employment." Positive attitudes and understanding the character of a place is missing in the EE, in addition to risk aversion there is also a perceived lack of regional identity as an entrepreneurial hub of the Thames Valley region.

8.5   CONCLUSIONS

A growing number of policy-makers around the world are actively promoting the systemic approach to entrepreneurship policy. However, adopting the exploratory-based approach when advising policy may be dangerous as it runs ahead of its theoretical underpinnings.

In this study we built on complementarity theory to develop a taxonomy which could analyze and compare heterogeneous EE (Adner & Kapoor, 2010), the entrepreneurial propensity approach to innovation systems (Radosevic & Yoruk, 2013) and the resource-based approach. Our model can help policy-makers to compare and contrast ecosystems as well as explain that the complementarity perspective to EE can be used by policy-makers as a location-based tool to bestow entrepreneurial opportunities in places with a mix of available resources.

Our work is particularly valuable for territories that lack one of the four components considered. The role played by these elements within the system could potentially be provided by the complementarity between the components that are in place.

We used a case study of the Greater Reading area in the UK and conducted semi-structured interviews with seven relevant stakeholders in Reading to corroborate our theoretical model.

One of our most interesting findings for the Greater Reading EE is that knowledge exploitation by small businesses and scale-ups may take place through a system of complementarities and information technology-enabled services (Li, Liu, Belitski, Ghobadian & O'Regan, 2016).

This study's limitations lie in the lack of a mixed-methods approach in developing the concept, in particular the mix of qualitative and quantitative methods. Further primary data should be collected from a broader range of stakeholders that describe each level of the entrepreneurial action and allow for a greater diversity of resource providers, connectors and corporations. Future research could address this issue by seeking to gain access to primary and secondary data across a variety of EE. This taxonomy could then be used to compare them and to use the causality approach to link these four components of EE to entrepreneurial opportunity identification, entrepreneurial outcomes and economic growth. Subsequent research will also benefit from natural experimental analysis, whether with one EE within the same country or two or three EE within several countries with different entrepreneurial policies, institutional histories and cultures of entrepreneurship.

ACKNOWLEDGEMENTS

We would like to thank Dr Sara Amoroso, Joint Research Centre European Commission, Sevilla, Spain and Dr Lebene Soga at the University of Reading for helpful comments and support at the earlier stage of this project.

REFERENCES

Acs, Z. J., Autio, E., & Szerb, L. (2014). National systems of entrepreneurship: Measurement issues and policy implications. *Research Policy, 43*(3), 476–94.

Adner, R., & Kapoor, R. (2010). Value creation in innovation ecosystems: How the structure of technological interdependence affects firm performance in new technology generations. *Strategic Management Journal, 31*(3), 306–33.

Audretsch, D. B., & Belitski, M. (2017). Entrepreneurial ecosystems in cities: Establishing the framework conditions. *Journal of Technology Transfer, 42*(5), 1030–51.

Audretsch, D. B., Bönte, W., & Keilbach, M. (2008). Entrepreneurship capital and its impact on knowledge diffusion and economic performance. *Journal of Business Venturing, 23*, 687–98.

Audretsch, D. B., Keilbach, M. C., & Lehmann, E. E. (2006). *Entrepreneurship and Economic Growth*. Oxford: Oxford University Press.

Autio, E., & Acs, Z. (2010). Intellectual property protection and the formation of entrepreneurial growth aspirations. *Strategic Entrepreneurship Journal, 4*(3), 234–51.

Autio, E., Frederiksen, L., & Dahlander, L. (2013). Information exposure, opportunity evaluation and entrepreneurial action: an empirical investigation of an online user community. *Academy of Management Journal, 56*(5), 1348–71.

Autio, E., Kenney, M., Mustar, P., Siegel, D., & Wright, M. (2014). Entrepreneurial innovation: The importance of context. *Research Policy, 43*(7), 1097–108.

Autio, E., Nambisan, S., Thomas, L. D., & Wright, M. (2018). Digital affordances, spatial affordances, and the genesis of entrepreneurial ecosystems. *Strategic Entrepreneurship Journal, 12*(1), 72–95.

Bathelt, H., Malmberg, A., & Maskell, P. (2004). Clusters and knowledge: Local buzz, global pipelines and the process of knowledge creation. *Progress in Human Geography, 28*(1), 31–56.

Baum, J., Cowan, R., & Jonard, N. (2014). Does evidence of network effects on firm performance in pooled cross-section support prescriptions for network strategy? *Strategic Management Journal, 35,* 652–67.

Baumol, W. J. (1993). Formal entrepreneurship theory in economics: Existence and bounds. *Journal of Business Venturing, 8*(3), 197–210.

Best, M. H. (2015). Greater Boston's industrial ecosystem: A manufactory of sectors. *Technovation, 39,* 4–13.

Bowen, H., & De Clercq, D. (2008). Institutional context and the allocation of entrepreneurial effort. *Journal of International Business Studies, 39*(1), 1–21.

Buenstorf, G., & Fornahl, D. (2009). B2C-bubble to cluster: The dot-com boom, spin-off entrepreneurship, and regional agglomeration. *Journal of Evolutionary Economics, 19*(3), 349–78.

Charron, N., Dijkstra, L., & Lapuente, V. (2014). Regional governance matters: Quality of government within European Union member states. *Regional Studies, 48*(1), 68–90.

Clarysse, B., Wright, M., & Van Hove, J. (2015). *A Look inside Accelerators*. London: Nesta.

Corden, A., & Sainsbury, R. (2005). Verbatim quotations: Whose views count? *Qualitative Research, 1*(1), 4–6.

Coutu, S. (2014). The scale-up report on UK economic growth. August 1. www .scaleupreport.org/scaleup-report.pdf

Creswell, J. W. (2007). *Qualitative Inquiry and Research Design: Choosing among Five Approaches*. Thousand Oaks, CA: SAGE.

Cumming, D., Meoli, M., & Vismara, S. (2019). Investors' choices between cash and voting rights: Evidence from dual-class equity crowdfunding. *Research Policy, 48*(8), 1037–40.

Desai, S., Acs, Z. J., & Weitzel, U. (2013). A model of destructive entrepreneurship: Insight for conflict and postconflict recovery. *Journal of Conflict Resolution, 57*(1), 20–40.

Eckhardt, J. T., & Shane, S. A. (2010). Industry changes in technology and complementary assets and the creation of high-growth firms. *Journal of Business Venturing, 26*(4), 412–30.

Feldman, M., & Braunerhjelm, P. (2006). The genesis of industrial clusters. *Cluster Genesis: Technology-Based Industrial Development, 1,* 1–13.

Feldman, M., & Zoller, T. D. (2012). Dealmakers in place: Social capital connections in regional entrepreneurial economies. *Regional Studies, 46*(1), 23–37.

Freeman, C., & Louca, F. (2001). *As Times Goes By: From the Industrial Revolutions to the Information Revolution*. Oxford: Oxford University Press.

Granovetter, M. S. (1973). The strength of weak ties. *American Journal of Sociology, 78*(6), 1360–80.

Hung, S. C., & Whittington, R. (2011). Agency in national innovation systems: Institutional entrepreneurship and the professionalization of Taiwanese IT. *Research Policy*, *40*(4), 526–38.

Isenberg, D. J. (2010). How to start an entrepreneurial revolution. *Harvard Business Review*, *88*(6), 40–50.

Isenberg, D. J., & Onyemah, V. (2016). Fostering scaleup ecosystems for regional economic growth (innovations case narrative: Manizales-Mas and Scale Up Milwaukee). *Innovations: Technology, Governance, Globalization*, *11*(1–2), 60–79.

Kenney, M., & Von Burg, U. (1999). Technology, entrepreneurship and path dependence: Industrial clustering in Silicon Valley and Route 128. *Industrial and Corporate Change*, *8*(1), 67–103.

Kremer, M. (1993). The O-ring theory of economic development. *Quarterly Journal of Economics*, *108*, 551–75.

Levie, J., & Autio, E. (2011). Regulatory burden, rule of law, and entry of strategic entrepreneurs: An international panel study. *Journal of Management Studies*, *48*(6), 1392–419.

Li, W., Liu, K., Belitski, M., Ghobadian, A., & O'Regan, N. (2016). e-Leadership through strategic alignment: An empirical study of small-and medium-sized enterprises in the digital age. *Journal of Information Technology*, *31*(2), 185–206.

Malerba, F., & Breschi, S. (1997). Sectoral innovation systems. In: C. Edquist (Ed.), *Innovation System* (pp. 130–56). Cheltenham, UK and Northampton, MA, USA: Edward Elgar Publishing.

Marshall, A. (1890). *Principles of Economics*. London: Macmillan.

Mason, C., & Brown, R. (2014). Entrepreneurial ecosystems and growth oriented entrepreneurship. *Final Report to OECD* (pp. 1–38). Paris: OECD Publishing.

Mason, C., & Brown, R. (2017). Looking inside the spiky bits: A critical review and conceptualisation of entrepreneurial ecosystems. *Small Business Economics*, *49*, 11–30.

McMullen, J. S., & Shepherd, D. A. (2006). Entrepreneurial action and the role of uncertainty in the theory of the entrepreneur. *Academy of Management Review*, *31*(1), 132–52.

Milgrom, P., & Roberts, J. (1995). Complementarities and fit strategy, structure, and organizational change in manufacturing. *Journal of Accounting and Economics*, *19*(2), 179–208.

Miller, P., & Bound, K. (2011). *The Startup Factories*. London: NESTA.Napier, G., & Hansen, C. (2011). *Ecosystems for Young Scaleable Firms*. Copenhagen: FORA Group.

Nelson, R. (1993). *National Innovation Systems: A comparative analysis*. New York: Oxford University Press.

Phan, P. (2004). Entrepreneurship theory: Possibilities and future directions. *Journal of Business Venturing*, *19*(5), 617–20.

Radosevic, S. (2010). What makes entrepreneurship systemic? In: F. Malerba (Ed.), *Knowledge-Intensive Entrepreneurship and Innovation Systems* (pp. 52–76). London: Routledge.

Radosevic, S., & Yoruk, E. (2013). Entrepreneurial propensity of innovation systems: Theory, methodology and evidence. *Research Policy*, *42*(5), 1015–38.

REAP MIT (2016). Regional Entrepreneurship Acceleration Programme MIT. June 3. https://reap.mit.edu/

Scaleup Berkshire (2019). Business Growth Hub. January 20. www.berkshirebusinesshub.co.uk/scaleup-berkshire-programme

Shane, S. (2000). Prior knowledge and the discovery of entrepreneurial opportunities. *Organization Science*, *1*(4), 448–69.

Spigel, B. (2017). The relational organization of entrepreneurial ecosystems. *Entrepreneurship Theory and Practice*, *41*(1), 49–72.

Stam, E. (2015). Entrepreneurial ecosystems and regional policy: A sympathetic critique. *European Planning Studies*, *23*(9), 1759–69.

Stam, F. C., & Spigel, B. (2016). Entrepreneurial ecosystems. *USE Discussion Paper Series*, *16*(13).

Stangler, D., & Bell-Masterson, J. (2015). *Measuring an Entrepreneurial Ecosystem*. Kansas City, MI: Kauffman Foundation.

Stuetzer, M., Audretsch, D. B., Obschonka, M., Gosling, S. D., Rentfrow, P. J., & Potter, J. (2018). Entrepreneurship culture, knowledge spillovers and the growth of regions. *Regional Studies*, *52*(5), 608–18.

Sullivan, D. M., & Ford, C. M. (2014). How entrepreneurs use networks to address changing resource requirements during early venture development. *Entrepreneurship Theory and Practice*, *38*(3), 551–74.

Szerb, L., Acs, Z. J., Autio, E., Ortega-Argilés, R., & Komlósi, É. (2014). REDI: The Regional Entrepreneurship and Development Index: Measuring regional entrepreneurship Report for the European Commission Directorate-General Regional and Urban Policy under contract number 2012. www.projectfires.eu/wp-content/uploads/2017/07/

TVB (2014). Thames Valley Berkshire. Delivering national growth, locally, strategic economic plan 2015/16–2020/21. *Evidence Base*, October 10, 2.

Williamson, P. J., & De Meyer, A. (2012). Ecosystem advantage: How to successfully harness the power of partners. *California Management Review*, *55*(1), 24–46.

APPENDIX

Table 8A.1   *Interview protocol establishing the entrepreneurship ecosystem framework*

Questions	EE taxonomy element	Indicative reason	Justification from the literature/study objective
How has your location in the Thames Valley been of influence for your business?	Entrepreneurial orientation	Broad answer expected for analysis. Might include EE elements	Economy of place literature
How has the presence of other businesses in the Thames Valley influenced you and your business? Any role models?	Entrepreneurial actors		A show of EE element interaction *Role model question targeted as per argument in the paper*
How would you describe the development of entrepreneurial actors in Reading (such as incubators, local and national government, chamber of commerce, IKEA, serial entrepreneurs)	Entrepreneurial actors and connectors	Answers to show who does mentoring services, what is government program support, incubation activity	Paper's objective: we argue that not all EE components must necessarily be present
How would you describe the development of entrepreneurial resource providers?	Financial resource providers	Answers to demonstrate the role of large firms, crowdfunding platforms, research and development centers, equity (angel and venture capital), banking capital in funding ideas	Understanding resources to entrepreneurship

Questions	EE taxonomy element	Indicative reason	Justification from the literature/study objective
How would you describe the development of entrepreneurial connectors?	All	Answers here expected reveal investment – investee matching, entrepreneurship and business clubs, university–business school networks	Paper's objective
How would you describe the entrepreneurship culture in the Thames Valley?	Orientation and culture	Answers to confirm prestige of self-employment, role models, entrepreneurship education	Addresses one element of the EE: culture

Table 8A.2   List of expert interviewees

Full name	Role in the company	Company	Company description
Frances Campbell	Head of Business Environment	Thames Valley Berkshire LEP	Thames Valley Berkshire Local Enterprise Partnership is a business-led, multi-sector partnership mandated by government to lead activities that drive local economic growth
Louize Clarke	Director	ConnecTVT	The vision for ConnecTVT was to give an amplified voice to the innovative companies in the Thames Valley through a rich events program
Sharon Cunnington	Branch Director	Santander Bank	Santander Bank (financial services to business and entrepreneurs)
Tom Fox	Senior Manager	KPMG Tech Growth	KPMG is a network of professional service firms and one of the Big Four auditors
Thomas Henderson	Branch Director	HSBC	Bank (financial services to business and entrepreneurs)
Tim Martin	Chief Executive Officer	WorkInConfidence	WorkInConfidence is a scale-up that delivers solutions which help organizations and stakeholders to connect (information technology communications)
Jurek Sikorski	Head	Henley Centre for Entrepreneurship	University of Reading – business and educational services

PART III

The overlooked dimensions of the systems perspectives

9. Beyond entrepreneurial culture in the entrepreneurial ecosystems framework: Contributions from economic anthropology

Maria Giulia Pezzi and Félix Modrego

9.1 INTRODUCTION

In spite of decades of implementation worldwide, the traditional support policies have fallen short in realizing the promise of entrepreneurship as a tool for economic prosperity (Mason & Brown, 2014; Shane, 2009). Influenced by the literature on systems of innovation (Nelson, 1993; Cooke, 1992), the search for new approaches to the understanding and promotion of high-potential entrepreneurship has shifted to the more holistic approaches where entrepreneurship is deemed as deeply embedded in its socio-economic and institutional context (Acs, Autio & Szerb, 2014; Audretsch & Belitski, 2017). One of the most promising new approaches is the entrepreneurial ecosystems (EE) framework (Isenberg, 2010, 2011; Mason & Brown, 2014; Roundy, Bradshaw & Brockman, 2018). The EE model focuses on the identification and strengthening of key local framework conditions enabling high-growth potential endeavors, based on a view of entrepreneurship as the outcome of a complex network of interrelated actors, policies, political and economic institutions and supplemental conditions (Isenberg, 2011; Mason & Brown, 2014; Mack & Mayer, 2016).

The systemic approach to entrepreneurship has had a large intellectual influence, which is reflected in major international research projects, such as the Babson Ecosystem Entrepreneurship Project (Isenberg, 2011),[1] the Global Entrepreneurship and Development Index (GEDI) (Acs et al., 2014)[2] and the Regional Entrepreneurship and Development Index (Szerb, Acs, Ortega-Argilés & Komlosi, 2015).[3] The approach has also been embraced by influential international organizations such as the Organisation for Economic Co-operation and Development (Mason & Brown, 2014) and the World Economic Forum (WEF, 2013). However, the systemic model of entrepreneurship is still not fully developed (Acs et al., 2014; Audretsch & Beliski, 2017) and has been subject to criticism due to a yet unripe conceptual elaboration limiting its capacity to provide clear policy prescriptions tailored to specific regional and local contexts (e.g. Stam, 2014, 2015; Mack & Mayer, 2016; Brown & Mason, 2017; Roundy et al., 2018).

This chapter aims at contributing to the development of the EE framework by highlighting some key insights from economic anthropology (e.g. Rencher, 2014; Bjerregaard & Lauring, 2012; Anderson, 2000; Stewart, 1992, 2003; Barth, 1963, 1967; Rosa & Caulkins, 2013), which partially tackle these sources of criticism and add to the well-established results in management sciences and economics. We focus on conceptualizations of entrepreneurship and culture – two central concepts in the EE where we believe economic anthropology can make substantial contributions through theory development and evidence from ethnographic research – and on the paramount role of these two concepts for ecosystems' structure, functioning and evolution.

We argue that the EE framework can benefit from a broader conceptualization of entrepreneurship, culture and of their relationships with other ecosystem elements. While the EE largely bounds entrepreneurship to the creation of high-growth businesses, the anthropological view casts it as a dynamic process of social change led by entrepreneurial human agency. Likewise, whereas the EE limits culture to a set of socially established structures that influence the behavior of entrepreneurs with regard to business creation, anthropology understands culture as an enduring set of shared values and beliefs, which direct both entrepreneurial cognition and the whole construction of the social structures in which entrepreneurship is embedded. Thus, our stance is that culture and entrepreneurial agency are more structural elements than currently acknowledged by the EE model, both exerting a strong influence over the other system components and driving the systems' outcomes and evolution.

From the discussion, we highlight some entry points to integrate the EE and agency-based models in economic anthropology, two still disparate approaches to entrepreneurship, advancing towards a more comprehensive, anthropology-sensitive systemic framework of entrepreneurship. We argue that further consideration of insights from economic anthropology carry some important implications, both intellectual and with regard to prescriptions for informing both entrepreneurship support policies and entrepreneurs' strategies.

9.2 THE ENTREPRENEURIAL ECOSYSTEMS FRAMEWORK

The EE framework is both a conceptual model to understand the key contextual conditions stimulating entrepreneurial activity and an approach to inform policies to the support of entrepreneurship, particularly the growth-oriented one (Isenberg, 2010; Mason & Brown, 2014). Its main premises are the following. First, entrepreneurial activity cannot be understood independently of the context in which it is embedded (Isenberg, 2010; Moore, 1993). Second, the multiplicity of elements making up the entrepreneurial environment, and the complex relationships among them, require approaching entrepreneurship in a holistic and systemic way (Isenberg, 2011; Acs et al., 2014; Mason & Brown, 2014). Third, due to the specificity of contextual conditions influencing entrepreneurial activity, the EE is inherently local/regional in scale (Isenberg, 2011; Stam, 2015). Fourth, the ecosystems are intrinsically dynamic; they emerge as a result of multiple concurrent events and co-evolve organically due to complex interactions among entrepreneurs, framework conditions, systemic conditions and outcomes (Stam, 2014; Mason & Brown, 2014; Roundy et al., 2018).

In its original formulation, the EE framework is comprised of six elements (including 12 sub-elements) identified as the framework conditions for entrepreneurship, namely (Figure 9.1): (1) *human capital*; (2) *markets*; (3) *funding*; (4) *entrepreneurship support*; (5) *policies*; and (6) *culture*. The details of the EE framework can be found in the literature (Isenberg, 2010, 2011; Mason & Brown, 2014; Stam, 2014, 2015; Mack & Mayer, 2016; Roundy et al., 2018) and other chapters of this volume.

Although generally accepted among scholars and policymakers, the EE framework is not free of criticism, which often focuses on its inability to determine causality and the limited evidence base (e.g. Stam, 2015; Roundy et al., 2018). The set of key mechanisms governing the functioning and outcomes of an EE are, to a large extent, still to be conceptually developed and empirically verified. In addition, there is still a largely static application of the EE model (Mason & Brown, 2014; Stam, 2014; Mack & Mayer, 2016); the framework does not provide precise testable implications on the way in which the interactions among the elements (the structural conditions and the outcomes) and the feedback mechanisms shape alternative ecosystem dynamics (Mack & Mayer, 2016; Roundy et al., 2018). As remarked by Stam (2014, 2015), these conceptual gaps limit the potential of the EE model to become a clear roadmap for the design of effective policies in support of entrepreneurship, particularly those that are tailored to specific socio-economic and institutional local contexts.

In our view, the inherent complexity of a holistic approach like the EE framework should encourage intellectual efforts to abstract the key mechanisms governing the functioning and outcomes of the ecosystem. In the rest of this chapter, we endeavor to argue that a cross-disciplinary approach that borrows insights from economic anthropology could greatly contribute to unravel this complexity.

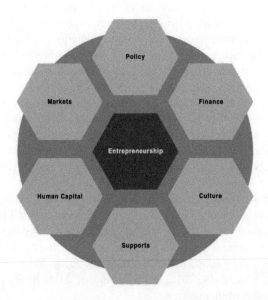

Source: Adapted from Isenberg (2011).

Figure 9.1   Entrepreneurial ecosystem

9.3   BEYOND ENTREPRENEURIAL CULTURE: CONTRIBUTIONS FROM ECONOMIC ANTHROPOLOGY

Anthropology is arguably the social science most concerned with culture, and has a long tradition of studies dealing with culture and social organization (see, for instance, Ruttan, 1988). Moreover, entrepreneurship has been an active area of anthropological research since the second part of the twentieth century, particularly within the broader framework of economic anthropology (e.g. Barth, 1963; Firth, 1967). Since most anthropological accounts on entrepreneurship focus on the cultural embeddedness of economic relations, the discipline is best suited to contribute to research and practice, by conceptualizing and operationalizing the concept of entrepreneurship within the cultural domain (Bjerregaard & Lauring, 2012; Rencher, 2014). In addition, the dominant epistemological paradigm in anthropology is fundamentally holistic (Dana & Dana, 2005) and, therefore, useful to generate theory about entrepreneurship (Stewart, 1990, 1992), a still fragmented epistemic field (e.g. Roundy et al., 2018). Furthermore, anthropology could bring a theoretical perspective focused on the social action into the systemic view of entrepreneurship, which is criticized as a model of social organization due to its deterministic, "stimulus-response" orientation (see Reed, 1988; Lundvall, 2007). Finally, the descriptive realism anthropology pursuit is valuable for economists and management scientists in order to reinterpret their conceptual frameworks and empirical evidence (Ruttan, 1988), and their ethnographic methods are useful to approach EE from a complexity theory resting in mixed-empirical methods (Roundy et al., 2018).

9.3.1   Entrepreneurship as an Agency-Led Process of Social Change

Due to its explicit economic policy orientation, the EE framework has largely considered the entrepreneur as an initiator of high-growth businesses (i.e. the *aspirational entrepreneur*). As put by Isenberg (2011, p. 2):

> I am referring very narrowly and classically to the entrepreneur as a person who is continually pursuing economic value through growth and as a result is always dissatisfied with the status quo. Entrepreneurship is aspirational and risk-taking, and, as I shall argue, intrinsically contrarian. Self-employment per se, is not entre- preneurship: self-employment-plus-aspiration, usually is; aspiration, not business ownership per se, is the continental divide between the entrepreneur and the non-entrepreneur.

The economic anthropology, in turn, understands entrepreneurship as a process of social change driven by the purposeful action of the entrepreneur (Anderson, 2000). This notion fundamentally departs from the rather essentialist views found in other social sciences; before the individual standing out for their innate or acquired managerial skills in economics (e.g. Silva, 2007) or having certain distinctive personality traits in psychology (e.g. McClelland, 1961), entrepreneurs in economic anthropology are individuals performing a specific *role* (Barth, 1963) or *function* (Belshaw, 1965; Greenfield & Strickon, 1986) in the wider socio-economic system. This function is the creative manipulation of a wide array of resources (both tangible and intangible) in the pursuit of profits and following an expansive private economic policy (Stewart, 1992, 2010).

Such conceptualization warrants a deeper inspection of the – often subtle – conditioning factors enabling and hindering the expression of the entre- preneurial role. The anthropological research focuses on two dimensions of distinct hierarchical nature. First, the individuals' cognition, including subjective and formally acquired knowledge, motivations, interests and back- ground shaping entrepreneurs' perceptions of their own ability and of value and opportunity (Bjerregaard & Lauring, 2012; Anderson, 2000; Oxfeld,

1992). Second, the structure of social relationships in which entrepreneurship is embedded, including social networks, institutional and governance arrangements, politics, rituals, social conventions and so on (see Bjerregaard & Lauring, 2012; Rencher, 2014). The two dimensions influence each other. The environmental conditions frame the cognitive processes that shape the entrepreneurial decisions (Roundy et al., 2018), but also the possibilities of accessing entrepreneurial support and resources, accepted patterns of behavior and specific tactics available to the entrepreneur (Stewart, 2003, 2010; Bjerregaard & Lauring, 2012). The entrepreneur's cognition, in turn, directs the way in which the entrepreneur perceives value, opportunity and sets out the strategies to carry out her entrepreneurial role by modifying social structures (Anderson, 2000; Barth, 1963). Barth (1963, p. 6) illustrates this view: "To the extent that persons take the initiative, and in the pursuit of profit in some discernible form manipulate other persons and resources, they are acting as entrepreneurs."

Thus, for economic anthropologists, before entrepreneurs, what we observe is people *acting entrepreneurially*, which makes it hard to type-case the character of an entrepreneur in rigid definitions and typologies (Stewart, 1992). In this dynamic, human action-based approach, the individuals' *agency* is the key capability making possible the translation of the entrepreneurial intention into entrepreneurial action (see Bjerregaard & Lauring, 2012; Anderson, 2000). By agency, we refer to "the actor's capacity to reinterpret and mobilize an array of resources in terms of rules other than those that initially constituted the array" (Sewell, 1989, p. 22), which, due to the embeddedness of entrepreneurship in the broad structure of social relationships, is a socially embedded agency (Garud & Karnøe, 2003).

The anthropological view of entrepreneurship allows articulating in a coherent, multi-level framework the role of social relations – particularly conditioning social practices and institutions (Reed, 1988) – and the cognitive elements driving the entrepreneurial decision. In this articulation, the concept of culture plays a key mediating role. Anthropology poses culture as a pervasive aspect of social organization, influencing both the patterns of social relationing (Geertz, 1973; Roundy et al., 2018) as well as entrepreneurs' cognitive processes shaping individual choices (Anderson, 2000; Bjerregaard & Lauring, 2012). Further, culture brings coherence to individuals' actions and gathers agency (Roundy et al., 2018). Thus, at the interplay between the two, culture shapes entrepreneurial agency.

9.3.2 Culture and Entrepreneurship: Beyond "Entrepreneurial Culture"

The EE framework provides no precise definition of culture or entrepreneurial culture. Instead, it limits itself to the description of a set of societal values, which are frequently found in ecosystems, easing the creation of growth-oriented ventures, such as social openness, creativity, tolerance to failure, the encouragement of experimentation and collaborative innovation, the promotion of risk taking, a positive attitude towards wealth creation, individual entrepreneurial hunger and drive and the public recognition and social status of entrepreneurs (Isenberg, 2010, 2011; Feld, 2012). To illustrate, the Babson Ecosystem Entrepreneurship Project proposes the following questions as a way to diagnose the strength of culture in a particular ecosystem (Isenberg, 2010, p. 5):

> Does the culture at large:
> Tolerate[s] honest mistakes, honorable failure, risk taking, and contrarian thinking?
> Respect[s] entrepreneurship as a worthy occupation?

Put this way, the culture is bounded to a set of socially established values and patterns of behavior that influence the strategies of individuals with regard to business creation. According to George and Zahra (2002), the way in which culture has been addressed in most of the entrepreneurship literature bypasses substantial aspects conditioning entrepreneurial outcomes, such as the construction of governance structures, gender relationships or the role of the family in business creation and development.

In anthropology, there are almost as many definitions of culture as studies utilizing the concept (i.e. Wagner, 2016). Anthropologists concerned with entrepreneurship tend to conceptualize it as an enduring set of values and beliefs, which are shared by members of a given social group and distinguish them from others, which provide collective meaning, mold their worldviews and, thus, shape the whole social, historical, institutional and economic context in which human agency takes place. Culture "denotes a historically transmitted pattern of meanings embodied in symbols, a system of inherited conceptions expressed in symbolic forms by means of which men communicate, perpetuate, and develop their knowledge about and attitudes toward life" (Geertz, 1973, p. 89).

Thus, whereas the EE model proposes a view of culture (or entrepreneurial culture) which is largely centered on favorable norms and attitudes towards business creation, the broader view of culture in economic anthropology brings to the forefront the complex ways in which entrepreneurial agency is contingent on the social values, norms, conventions and practices prevailing in the broad ecosystem's cultural system.

9.3.3   Culture as a Social Conditioning Mechanism

A central aspect of the relationship between culture and entrepreneurship is its social-conditioning role. One way is through the culturally imposed constraints to entrepreneurship, which go well beyond the EE's view of acknowledging the detrimental effects of social discredit of an entrepreneurial failure (Isenberg, 2011; Feld, 2012; Mason & Brown, 2014).

The culture's conditioning role may impose sizeable costs to entrepreneurship (Stewart, 2003), and limit the extent and scope of tactics available to the entrepreneur (Stewart, 2010). Moreover, cultural constraints may operate selectively, excluding specific agents and/or social groups from entrepreneurship, while preserving the privileged position of the others (Hale, 1978; Oxfeld, 1992).

An example is the culturally imposed *gender* roles. Gender stereotypes typically operate against the entrepreneurial agency of women, for instance, due to male dominance in the business heirship rules and the exclusion of women from decision-making positions in businesses (Bennedsen, Nielsen, Pérez-González & Wolfenzon, 2007; Joos, 2017). This gender bias translates into a restricted use of talent and an underutilization of networks (Stewart, 2010). Similarly, there is social stratification[4] and *ethnicity*. For example, whereas venture capital allocation in the United States (US) is highly biased towards white entrepreneurs (see Rencher, 2014), minority ethnic groups typically face big barriers for accessing entrepreneurial resources (Thornton, Ribeiro-Soriano & Urbano, 2011). Further, the culturally imposed ethnic roles may also limit the scope of activities entrepreneurs belonging to minorities can undertake, a point thoroughly documented, for instance, in the literature of Chinese minorities in North America (Oxfeld, 1992; Wong, 1998).

Other aspects of culture inhibiting entrepreneurial agency are *kinship* and *familism*. Stewart (2003), for instance, argues that kinship may carry sizeable costs (but also benefits) to businesses. Examples are relatedness against meritocracy as a recruitment criterion, the imperative of supporting extended family members through the firm, social legitimacy losses arising from non-compliance to kinship norms and the need to compensate members of the community to regain lost social legitimacy. Family firms and entrepreneurial familism (Jones, 2005) are also particularly relevant cultural constructions that condition entrepreneurial action. Ghezzi (2015), for instance, in his study of the Brianza (Lombardy, Italy) argues that by establishing a fuzzy separation between business and family life, familism strongly conditions entrepreneurs' choices. Entrepreneurs in Brianza often make sub-optimal decisions, such as delaying investments, favoring family members instead of more qualified external workers or choosing sub-optimal locations to keep physical proximity with the family house.

The social-conditioning role of culture may, however, also bring opportunities, which are perceived by the alert entrepreneurs capable of mobilizing their entrepreneurial resources and individuating the best strategies and tactics at hand (Stewart, 2003, 2010). One example is the use of kinship ties to access a wide range of resources, such as capital, networks, moral support for risk taking, information and even entrepreneurial drive – either to consolidate kinship leadership or to escape from it (Stewart, 2003). In the case of Brianza, Ghezzi (2015) argues that in a strongly familial cultural context, the immediate family becomes the major source of resources for the business, including funding and labor, but also emotional support and consolation over failure. Further, family conflicts ending up in broken partnerships are an important catalyzer for the creation of new ventures, which would be a main reason behind a thriving local economy characterized by an abundance of small enterprises.

9.3.4   Culture and Entrepreneurs' Cognition

Culture also shapes entrepreneurial cognition. The entrepreneurial process of opportunity perception and recognition is largely shaped by individuals' experiential and acquired knowledge (Bjerregaard & Lauring, 2012), which is, in turn, shaped by the cultural meaning systems in which the individual is immersed. Manifestations of culture such as artifacts, practices, rules and knowledge provide shared meanings and, thus, shape the behavior of entrepreneurs in a "correlated" way, rendering ecosystems truly interconnected systems (Roundy et al., 2018; Garud & Karnøe, 2003). The linguistic, symbolic and ideological aspects of culture shape the way in which the entrepreneur perceives the environment and opportunities (Anderson, 2000), having the potential of "impelling men to action" (Pettigrew, 1979, p. 575). Following Barth et al. (2002), knowledge is not only a corpus of assertions, but also a communicative medium and social organization, which co-determine each other in a particular cultural context and are turned into entrepreneurial activity by the purposeful action of the entrepreneur. Furthermore, entrepreneurial processes are contingent on cultural interpretations of profit opportunities (Montoya, 2000; Ana & Lubiński, 2018). This depends on two mutually dependent aspects: the entrepreneurs' embeddedness in the local culture, and their ability to "read" situations and spot opportunities. In this sense, entrepreneurship is linked with discovery and creation more than sudden inspiration.

One further example is provided by Anderson (2000): localness and cosmopolitanism is a highly discriminating dichotomy with regard to the way rural entrepreneurs in Scotland perceive and use value and exploit such value through the ventures they set up. The "cosmopolitan" entrepreneurs – crudely put as those having an urban background – show a wider perception of value that allows them to visualize business opportunities in the exploitation of rural assets and amenities, setting up niche-oriented undertakings such as thematic museums, boutique hotels or rural art galleries. The "locals", not perceiving such opportunities, pursue the satisfaction of the local demand, setting up more "mundane", imitative businesses, such as hair dressing or car-repair shops.

Together, the subjective perception of entrepreneurs' ability, value and opportunity and the mediating role of culture in shaping entrepreneurs' cognition call for paying greater attention to contingency and ambiguity as inherent aspects of entrepreneurial action (Reed, 1988), both being the features of entrepreneurial agency not yet incorporated in the EE framework.

9.3.5   Culture and the Other Ecosystems Components

In a paper laying out the conceptual bases of the GEDI, Acs et al. (2014, p. 491) state on an ecosystem-based model of entrepreneurship:

> Case studies are therefore important, not only to shed more light on the systemic interactions implied in the GEDI model, but also, identify causal mechanisms underlying (or not!) those interactions. We still know too little about the contributions of and constraints upon entrepreneurial action in different systemic contexts [...] although we have argued for systemic characteristics of entrepreneurial processes, we have not provided a detailed discussion of interactions between individual pillars of systems of entrepreneurship.

Several other studies identify a lack of understanding of the relationships among EE's components as a priority area of the EE framework development (Stam, 2015; Audretsch & Belitski, 2016; Mack & Mayer, 2016; Roundy et al., 2018). We argue that anthropology and ethnographic research can be particularly useful in describing the mechanisms in the relationships involving culture. With EE being rooted in specific socio-historical contexts, and with culture being a main conditioning factor of social organization, culture naturally exerts a strong influence over all other ecosystem components.

Anthropology has described the preeminent role of culture in directing the social construction of institutions by framing their normative content within the structure of social values, beliefs and practices (Geertz, 1973; Verver & Dahles, 2013). Such institutional framing has a direct expression in the design and implementation of entrepreneurship support policies. This may lead to failures by design, when cultural frameworks of beneficiaries are not aligned to those in which the policy was crafted. Kelman (2018), for instance, describes the case of an emergent start-up ecosystem in Malaysia targeted at the socio-economic wellbeing of disadvantaged Malay-Muslims. In such a policy framework, Malay entrepreneurs found themselves in a dilemma of using these benefits, while being viewed by their communities as lacking the entrepreneurial spirit for doing so.

Social conventions ruled by particular cultural systems also bound the extent and direct the particular styles of entrepreneurial leadership (Pettigrew, 1979). In a pre-industrial setting, Stewart (1990) describes the Bigmanship system – a powerful metaphor for contemporary entrepreneurship – as a meritocratic, enacted career of political and economic leadership, exerted in the social functions of communities' political representation and trading. In the contemporaneous start-up communities of the US, entrepreneurial leadership manifests itself in the realm of creativity and ideas, and the entrepreneur is no longer a social and political leader, but a 20-year-old nerd drop-out from a university who looks like having no social life (Rencher, 2014).

But the entrepreneurs' strategies and tactics are also conditioned by and have to be accommodated to the cultural system in which the entrepreneurial action unfolds. Economic anthropology and ethnographic research have illustrated the ways in which culture guides the entrepreneurial task of building and managing business networks and thus the building and functioning of markets and entrepreneurship support. Ahlstrom and Bruton (2002), for example, illustrate how Chinese entrepreneurs resort to their capacity of building and managing *guanxi* – personal relationships based on mutual knowledge and trust – to succeed in the Chinese business environment. The *guanxi* is such a powerful cultural construct that it may even condition strategic decisions such as the geographic location of businesses. Similarly, Stewart (2010) describes the use of marriage relationships as a tactic for mobilizing resources in situations of strong kinship ties and Rencher (2014), in her study of start-up communities' culture in the US, discusses the use of material representations such as business plans and prototypes, as well as specialized entrepreneurial skills unfolded in highly stereotyped situations, such as the "ritual" of pitching.

Finally, the ecosystem's formation and accretion of human capital is also mediated by culture. Knowledge generation is itself a cultural construction strongly shaped by shared practices within a given epistemic community (Rabinow, 1992). Further, the entrepreneurial spirit is always nurtured in socially constructed communities with their own prevailing values and rhetoric. The introduction of entrepreneurship into educational programs of many universities of the Western world is largely a reflection of a widely shared pro-entrepreneurship social discourse, which permeates both the practices of entrepreneurship educators and the learning process of students (Robinson & Shumar, 2014). Nevertheless, the social and community learning settings such as family, rituals or apprenticeships are also important. The ethnographic work on the Melanesian Bigman (e.g. Stewart, 1990) illustrated how Bigmanship is instilled in children at a very early age, with fathers stimulating the interest of their sons for economic transactions, encouraging their practice and teaching respect for the Bigmen.

In summary, an anthropological approach to the study of EE can shed light on key mechanisms through which culture exerts its pervasive influence over all the other ecosystems elements and, thus, contribute to what has been identified as one of the key conceptual gaps of the EE framework.

9.3.6 Entrepreneurial Agency and Ecosystems Dynamics

The EE model still lacks a sufficient consideration of the mechanisms governing the emergence and evolution of EE (Roundy et al., 2018; Mason & Brown, 2014). According to Stam (2014, p.6): "The entrepreneurial ecosystem approach lacks a dynamic view on entrepreneurial ecosystems: how do they emerge, what keeps them 'vital' and what causes their decline." In the same vein, Mack and Mayer (2016) point out the co-evolution of the ecosystems component as among the most neglected aspects of EE theory.

The EE are described as complex, path-dependent systems, which evolve throughout their life-cycle (Mack and Mayer, 2016) in trajectories which are sensitive to initial conditions and largely shaped by the historical context, as specific events (often serendipitous) tend to lock in and define specific ecosystem cultures (Roundy et al., 2018). The information and communications technology cluster in the Capitol region of the US, for instance, would probably not have developed without the downsizing of the federal government and the outsourcing of critical informatics services (Feldman, 2001). Mack and Mayer (2016) describe how an entrepreneurial culture in Phoenix consolidated along its ecosystem's life-cycle.

Following Martin and Sunley (2006), one of the main sources of path dependence is institutional hysteresis, understood as the tendency of social, cultural and institutional arrangements to self-sustain in order to support the social organization they coordinate. Anthropology points at the entrepreneurs' agency as a main driver of social change both in modern (Barth, 1963; Steyaert & Hjorth, 2006) and pre-industrial (Brown, 1987; Belshaw, 1965) societies alike. This view of entrepreneurial action goes well beyond the contagion effects stressed by the EE framework (e.g. Isenberg, 2011), and entails looking also at the ways entrepreneurial agency shapes the whole set of structural elements and outcomes of the ecosystem. From a systemic point of view, acknowledging the transformative nature of entrepreneurial agency allows making explicit a still absent feedback mechanism running not only from the outcomes to the outcomes (i.e. an endogenous entrepreneurial agency), but from the outcomes to the system's constitutive elements (e.g. Roundy et al., 2018).

An example is the creation of an economic opportunity, which for economic anthropologists is itself a form of cultural change. Entrepreneurs find opportunities by identifying interpretive discrepancies of valuation between spheres of exchange (i.e. a set of socially acceptable exchanges) and exploit them by carrying out the most valuable transactions (Stewart, 1990; Barth, 1967b). In doing so, entrepreneurs modify the structure of social values, in particular, the value society assigns to exchanged goods and services, thus becoming "cultural brokers" (Moench, 1971). Markowska and López-Vega (2018) illustrate this point with the case of "Winepreneurs" in the Priorat region, Spain. By building collective identity stories around the distinctiveness of the *terroir*, Priorat Winepreneurs managed to position a local wine industry, which was virtually dismantled at the beginning of the 1990s, in international markets.

But entrepreneurs also play a key role in the creation and functioning of markets. By setting up and engaging in transactions, entrepreneurs bridge previously disconnected groups (Barth, 1967b; Montoya, 2000), including entrepreneurs and customers, but also suppliers, developers of entrepreneurial support and institutional actors, often having different interpretive frames of a given product or technology (Garud & Karnøe, 2003). Thus, entrepreneurs act as a conduit for the exchange of information, systems of valuation, practices and conventions, be it through the transaction itself or through the goods and services that are exchanged (Firth, 1967; Rencher, 2014; Barth, 1967). Further, this connecting role would also help gather agency, which is distributed across actors embedded in the entrepreneurial networks (e.g. Tsoukas, 1996).

The potentially bridging role of entrepreneurial agency is well illustrated in the case of the wind turbines industry in Denmark, which was largely developed in response to the energy crises in the 1970s. The crises motivated multiple actors to recontextualize prototypes developed 20 years prior (Garud & Karnøe, 2003). The development of this technology required no radical technological breakthrough at the time, but on the contrary, the synthesis of knowledge from many professions and the gathering of efforts and inputs from many kinds of actors. Here, particular entrepreneurs played a key bridging role in updating previous developments, in organizing industry meetings and in pushing for institutional changes (laws and certifications). These actions created the necessary conditions, which helped to develop what is now a leading industry worldwide.

The economic anthropologists also stress how entrepreneurial agency disrupts the structure of entrepreneurship support, to the extent that new supplemental structures may be needed in order to link the different spheres of exchange (Stewart, 1992; Barth, 1963). One notable example is provided by the case of sustainable urban development initiatives in the Netherlands (Woolthuis, Hooimeijer, Bossink, Mulder & Brouwer, 2013). Here, entrepreneurs exerted their agency, for instance, by teaming up with specialists in universities and certifying institutions to create a need for cradle-to-cradle building materials and get them rapidly certified in a country where such certification was still non-existent.

Equally important is the role of entrepreneurs as major policy actors (or *institutional entrepreneurs*, as described, for example, in Woolthuis et al., 2013). In the pursuit of economic opportunities, entrepreneurs utilize a broad set of resources to reshape current governance frameworks, including politics, policies, formal institutions and even informal institutions such as social norms and conventions (Keesing, 1976; Hale, 1978; Barth, 1967b). Berry and Flowers (1999) analyze the case of performance-based budgeting in Florida in the 1990s. Here, individuals and organizations from the private business sector (including groups of local business leaders, chambers of commerce and business lobbying groups) pushed for the adoption of a monitored and evaluated public budgeting scheme. Among the tactics they used were the formation of policy groups, agenda setting, the positioning of a public efficiency discourse, political lobbying and the gathering of broad public support. The policy process resulted in the passing of the 1994 Government Performance and Accountability Act, requiring the governor to submit performance-based program budgets for the executive agencies.

Agency is a capability that entrepreneurs may also use to shift the local supply of human capital, as a part of a broad set of tactics they utilize to develop supplemental resources and promote and protect their interests (Feldman, Francis & Bercovitz, 2005). This entails the entrepreneurs' active role in both the formation of the domestic and the attraction of foreign human capital. Regarding the former, the business sector is identified as one of three drivers (along with governments and students) of the rising demand for formal entrepreneurship education (Jack & Anderson, 1999). With respect to the latter, entrepreneurs attract external human capital tailored to their needs. This is well illustrated by the case of the biotech and information and communications technology clusters in the Capitol region of the US (Feldman, 2001). One of the factors explaining the rise of such industries in an area with no clear initial advantages is the local entrepreneurs' philanthropy. The transfer of sizeable private resources to local universities allowed them to bring high-profile scholars in and develop postgraduate educational programs focused on the technologies needed by emerging industries.

Overall, further consideration of the entrepreneur as a driver of ecosystems change could provide an analytic lens to tackle the complexity of EE dynamics from a social action perspective, in order to understand their self-organized, adaptive and geographically bounded nature (see Roundy et al., 2018). Embedding better systemic policies into the local socio-cultural context, which entrepreneurs to a large extent build, sustain and modify, may also help.

9.4   CONCLUSIONS AND POLICY IMPLICATIONS

The EE framework is a response to the ineffectiveness of the traditional policy approaches in promoting entrepreneurship of high economic and social impact. It proposes a holistic approach which focuses on getting the contextual conditions enabling the growth-oriented entrepreneurship in place, based on the premises that the local context matters and that efforts to tackle each of the local framework conditions in isolation are doomed to fail. While such systemic perspective represents a conceptual leap with respect to the previous generation of entrepreneurship theories and policies, the approach has been criticized due to a still feeble theoretical and empirical grounding and due to its still largely static application.

To contribute to the conceptual development of the EE framework, this chapter reviews some relevant insights from economic anthropology. We argue that theoretical advances in the discipline and findings from the ethnographic research can enlighten our understanding about entrepreneurship as a complex, multi-dimensional and dynamic phenomenon deeply rooted in the socio-economic, institutional and historical context.

Based on the previous review, we propose some entry points for an extended, anthropology-sensitive systemic approach to entrepreneurship, which could guide a more systematic, social action-based inquiry into contextual conditions and mechanisms enabling it. A first anthropological insight we highlight is a broader understanding of entrepreneurship *as a process of social change framed into two interrelated, hierarchically distinctive domains.* On the one hand, the individual's cognitive elements may or may not impel entrepreneurial action. On the other hand, the social structures define the functioning of all ecosystems elements, their relationships and the EE as a whole, such as gender and ethnic roles, social stratification, kinship or familism. Second, *the entrepreneurial agency should be understood as the key articulating concept that mediates these two domains.* Here, the entrepreneur is the actor of the social system performing the role or function of mobilizing resources in pursuing an expansive private economic policy; in doing so, she create new entrepreneurial opportunities, gathering distributed agency and modifying the ecosystem's framework conditions themselves. Third, *the role of culture as a moderator of entrepreneurial agency should be stressed.* An extended systemic approach should emphasize the ways in which culture influences agency, through the conditioning of entrepreneurs' cognition, but also the settings in which the entrepreneur enacts formal, informal and experiential knowledge. This entails paying greater attention to the many critical channels of influence linking culture and the other elements making up the EE.

These considerations call for a revised epistemology of EE, which puts the entrepreneurial agency at the center stage. Such an approach opens up avenues for a novel research agenda, where new mechanisms driving/constraining the selection into entrepreneurship and ventures' performance can be conceptualized and analyzed, both qualitatively and quantitatively, in a micro (entrepreneur) – macro (ecosystem) multi-level way (see Roundy et al., 2018). They can also illuminate a still incipient agenda on the evolutionary aspects of EE, which deals with their path-dependent, adaptive, self-organized and self-reinforcing nature. Here, entrepreneurs and their agency should be seen as a main catalyzer of ecosystems' emergence and a driver of their dynamics, either in maintaining their inertia or otherwise as a source of disruptive change.

We consider that anthropological insights about entrepreneurship and culture have relevant implications for systemic approaches aimed at informing policies and entrepreneurs' strategies. In the first place, the adoption of a broader view of entrepreneurship beyond the creation of growth-oriented businesses may expand the scope of support policies to other relevant targets, such as social (Alvord, Brown & Letts, 2004) and institutional (Woolthuis et al., 2013) entrepreneurship. Similarly, it may contribute to the rendering of entrepreneurship as a policy tool to achieve other important societal goals, which entrepreneurship, in a broader sense, can help fulfill, such as poverty and inequality reduction (particularly in developing countries, see Naudé, 2010) or regional economic resilience (Williams & Vorley, 2014).

Second, since it is hard for local policymakers to identify growth-oriented entrepreneurs *ex-ante*, a broader view of entrepreneurship in policy design could expand the targeting of policies beyond the usual suspects (e.g. spinoffs of large firms or the ready-made external start-ups) to many promising would-be entrepreneurs (particularly local) that are *a priori* unobservable. This is particularly relevant since often the growth-oriented firms develop from the simpler, more imitative endeavors (Stewart, 1992; Feldman et al., 2005).

Third, the EE framework prescribes a series of interventions aimed at strengthening the cultural dimension, which eases the emergence of (high-growth) entrepreneurship, but a narrow definition of culture leads to overlooking the important dimensions that should be tackled by the systemic entrepreneurship policies. Acknowledging culture as a strong precondition of entrepreneurial agency and identifying its key hampering mechanisms could signal new relevant areas of policy intervention, as well as novel policy levers aimed at removing cultural barriers to entrepreneurship. As cultural constraints are a source of costs and inefficiencies, a straightforward implication is that systemic entrepreneurship policy approaches should also target the release of gender, class and ethnic constraints to entrepreneurial agency and, more generally, to the entrepreneurial agency, which is within any individual but that is at the same time distributed across many actors of different types. In addition, such policies should point at the sensitization of entrepreneurs about the available tactics given the cultural systems in which entrepreneurs are embedded, in order to increase the degree of discretion, particularly in situations where normative orders are difficult, if not impossible, to modify as is the case with kinship and familism (see Stewart, 2010).

Fourth, wider conceptualizations of culture and entrepreneurship can help expand the geographic scope of application of the EE framework. Although the EE model promotes an essentially regional/local rationale (Isenberg, 2011; Mason & Brown, 2014; Stam, 2015), its current excessive focus on the growth-oriented firms (and often an implicit targeting at technology-intensive sectors) confines practical application to a narrow set of already advantaged regions, thus disregarding the latent potential of ecosystems in other kinds of places (as documented by many case studies reviewed here)[5] and at various stages of the life-cycle.

Fifth, internalizing the paramount importance of entrepreneurial agency motivates a review of the entrepreneurship education and training programs and the development of a broader range of capabilities beyond business strategy and management, such as political abilities to understand and adapt governance frameworks, the management of social networks and institutional relationships or the capacity to cope with uncertainty and complex adaptive contexts. Likewise, internalizing the ubiquitous influence of culture could help make such educational and training programs more tailored to the specific local systems.

In any case, such considerations warrant a more multi-sectoral approach to the design and management of entrepreneurship support policies, with a greater engagement of traditionally absent actors – such as ministries and agencies related to social development, education and gender equality – working articulately with private social actors and across sectors and levels of government.

NOTES

1. http://entrepreneurial-revolution.com/.
2. https://thegedi.org/global-entrepreneurship-and-development-index/.
3. https://ec.europa.eu/regional_policy/en/information/publications/studies/2014/redi-the-regional-entrepreneurship-and-development-index-measuring-regional-entrepreneurship.
4. For an illustration of entrepreneurial exclusion based on castes, see for instance Hale (1978).
5. See also Mack and Mayer (2016) and Roundy et al. (2018).

REFERENCES

Acs, Z. J., Autio, E., & Szerb, L. (2014). National systems of entrepreneurship: Measurement issues and policy implications. *Research Policy*, *43*(3), 449–76.

Ahlstrom, D., & Bruton, G. D. (2002). An institutional perspective on the role of culture in shaping strategic actions by technology-focused entrepreneurial firms in China. *Entrepreneurship Theory and Practice*, *26*(4), 53–68.

Alvord, S. H., Brown, L. D., & Letts, C. W. (2004). Social entrepreneurship and societal transformation: An exploratory study. *Journal of Applied Behavioral Science*, *40*(3), 260–82.

Ana, R., & Lubiński, O. (2018). Cuban private entrepreneurship: From periphery to key sector of the economy in tourism-oriented market socialism. *Regional Science Policy and Practice*, *11*(3), 467–77. https://doi.org/10.1111/rsp3.12154

Anderson, A. R. (2000). The protean entrepreneur: The entrepreneurial process as fitting self and circumstance. *Journal of Enterprising Culture*, *8*(3), 201–34.

Audretsch, D. B., & Belitski, M. (2017). Entrepreneurial ecosystems in cities: Establishing the framework conditions. *Journal of Technology Transfer*, *42*(5), 1030–51.

Barth, F. (1963). *The role of the entrepreneur in social change in northern Norway*. Bergen-Oslo: Norwegian Universities Press.

Barth, F. (1967). On the study of social change. *American Anthropologist*, *69*(6), 661–9.

Barth, F. (1967b). Economic spheres in Darfur. In: R. Firth (Ed.), *Themes in Economic Anthropology* (pp. 149–73). London: Tavistock.

Barth, F., Chiu, C., Rodseth, L., Robb, J., Rumsey, A., Simpson, B. (2002). An anthropology of knowledge. *Current Anthropology*, *43*(1), 1–18.

Belshaw, C. S. (1965). *Traditional Exchange and Modern Markets*. Englewood Cliffs, NJ: Prentice Hall.

Bennedsen, M., Nielsen, K. M., Pérez-González, F., & Wolfenzon, D. (2007). Inside the family firm: The role of families in succession decisions and performance. *Quarterly Journal of Economics*, *122*: 647–91.

Berry, F. S., & Flowers, G. (1999). Public entrepreneurs in the policy process: Performance-based budgeting reform in Florida. *Journal of Public Budgeting, Accounting and Financial Management*, *11*(4), 578–617.

Bjerregaard, T., & Lauring, J. (2012). The socially-dynamic entrepreneurial process: An anthropological approach. *International Journal of Entrepreneurial Venturing*, *4*(2), 132–47.

Brown, P. (1987). New men and big men: Emerging social stratification in the Third World: A case study from the New Guinea Highlands. *Ethnology*, *26*, 87–106.

Brown, R., & Mason, C. (2017). Looking inside the spiky bits: A critical review and conceptualisation of entrepreneurial ecosystems. *Small Business Economics*, *49*(1), 11–30.

Cooke, P. (1992). Regional innovation systems: Competitive regulation in the new Europe. *Geoforum*, *23*(3), 365–82.

Dana, L. P., & Dana, T. E. (2005). Expanding the scope of methodologies used in entrepreneurship research. *International Journal of Entrepreneurship and Small Business*, *2*(1), 79–88.

Feld, B. (2012). *Startup Communities: Building an entrepreneurial ecosystem in your city*. Hoboken, NJ: Wiley.

Feldman, M. P. (2001). The entrepreneurial event revisited: Firm formation in a regional context. *Industrial and Corporate Change, 10*(4), 861–91.

Feldman, M. P., Francis, J., & Bercovitz, J. (2005). Creating a cluster while building a firm: Entrepreneurs and the formation of industrial clusters. *Regional Studies, 39*(1), 129–41.

Firth, R. (Ed.) (1967). *Themes in Economic Anthropology*. London: Tavistock.

Garud, R., & Karnøe, P. (2003). Bricolage versus breakthrough: Distributed and embedded agency in technology entrepreneurship. *Research Policy, 32*(2), 277–300.

Geertz, C. (1973). *The Interpretation of Cultures*. New York: Basic Books.

George, G., & Zahra, S. A. (2002). Culture and its consequences for entrepreneurship. *Entrepreneurship Theory and Practice, 26*(4), 5–8.

Ghezzi, S. (2015). Familism as a context for entrepreneurship in northern Italy. *Human Affairs, 25*(1), 58–70.

Greenfield, M. S., Strickon, A. (Eds) (1986). *Entrepreneurship and Social Change*. Lanham, MD: University Press of America.

Hale, S. (1978). The politics of entrepreneurship in Indian villages. *Development and Change, 9*(2), 245–75.

Isenberg, D. J. (2010). How to start an entrepreneurial revolution. *Harvard Business Review, 88*(6), 40–50.

Isenberg, D. J. (2011). The entrepreneurship ecosystem strategy as a new paradigm for economic policy: Principles for cultivating entrepreneurship. *Presentation at the Institute of International and European Affairs*, 1–13.

Jack, S. L., & Anderson, A. R. (1999). Entrepreneurship education within the enterprise culture: Producing reflective practitioners. *International Journal of Entrepreneurial Behavior and Research, 5*(3), 110–25.

Jones, A. M. (2005). The elementary structures of the family firm: An anthropological perspective. *Human Organization, 64*(3), 276–85.

Joos, V. (2017). Space, female economies, and autonomy in the shotgun neighborhoods of Port-Au-Prince, Haiti. *Economic Anthropology, 4*, 37–49. doi:10.1002/sea2.12071

Keesing, R. M. (1976). *Cultural Anthropology*. New York: Holt, Rinehart, and Winston.

Kelman, S. (2018). The Bumipreneur dilemma and Malaysia's technology start-up ecosystem. *Economic Anthropology, 5*, 59–70. doi:10.1002/sea2.12102

Lundvall, B.-Å. (2007). National innovation systems: Analytical concept and development tool. *Industry and Innovation, 14*, 95–119.

Mack, E., & Mayer, H. (2016). The evolutionary dynamics of entrepreneurial ecosystems. *Urban Studies, 53*(10), 2118–33.

Markowska, M., & López-Vega, H. (2018). Entrepreneurial storying: Winepreneurs as crafters of regional identity stories. *International Journal of Entrepreneurship and Innovation, 19*(4), 282–97.

Martin, R., & Sunley, P. (2006). Path dependence and regional economic evolution. *Journal of Economic Geography, 6*(4), 395–437.

Mason, C., & Brown, R. (2014). *Entrepreneurial Ecosystems and Growth Oriented Entrepreneurship*. Paper prepared for the workshop organized by the OECD LEED Programme and the Dutch Ministry of Economic Affairs, November 2013. www.oecd.org/cfe/leed/ Entrepreneurial-ecosystems.pdf

McClelland, D. C. (1961). *The Achieving Society*. Princeton, NJ: Van Nostrand.

Moench, R. U. (1971). Wealth, expertise, and political entrepreneurship. *Journal of Asian and African Studies, 6*(1), 37.

Montoya, L. (2000). Entrepreneurship and culture: The case of Freddy the straw-
berry man. In: R. Swedberg (Ed.), *Entrepreneurship: The social science view*
(pp. 332–55). Oxford: Oxford University Press.
Moore, J. F. (1993). Predators and prey: A new ecology of competition. *Harvard
Business Review, 71*(3), 75–86.
Naudé, W. (2010). Entrepreneurship, developing countries, and development econom-
ics: New approaches and insights. *Small Business Economics, 34*(1), 1.
Nelson, R. R. (1993). *National Innovation Systems: A comparative analysis*. Oxford:
Oxford University Press.
Oxfeld, E. (1992). Individualism, holism, and the market mentality: Notes on the recol-
lections of a Chinese entrepreneur. *Cultural Anthropology, 7*(3), 267–300.
Pettigrew, A. M. (1979). On studying organizational cultures. *Administrative Science
Quarterly, 24*(4), 570–81.
Rabinow, P. (1992). Studies in the anthropology of reason. *Anthropology Today, 8*(5),
7–10.
Reed, M. I. (1988). The problem of human agency in organizational analysis.
Organization Studies, 9, 33–46.
Rencher, M. (2014). Value and the valley of death: Opportunities for anthropologists to
create and demonstrate value in entrepreneurial contexts. *Practicing Anthropology,
36*(2), 52–6.
Robinson, S., & Shumar, W. (2014). Ethnographic evaluation of entrepreneurship
education in higher education: A methodological conceptualization. *International
Journal of Management Education, 12*(3), 422–32.
Rosa, P., & Caulkins, D. D. (2013). Entrepreneurship studies. In: D. D. Caulkins &
A. T. Jordan (Eds), *A Companion to Organizational Anthropology* (pp. 98–121).
Oxford: Blackwell Publishing.
Roundy, P. T., Bradshaw, M., & Brockman, B. K. (2018). The emergence of entre-
preneurial ecosystems: A complex adaptive systems approach. *Journal of Business
Research, 86*, 1–10.
Ruttan, V. W. (1988). Cultural endowments and economic development: What can we
learn from anthropology? *Economic Development and Cultural Change, 36*(S3),
247–71.
Sewell, Jr., W. H. (1989). Toward a theory of structure: Duality, agency, and trans-
formation. Center for Research on Social Organization Working Paper #392, Ann
Arbor, MI.
Shane, S. (2009). Why encouraging more people to become entrepreneurs is bad public
policy. *Small Business Economics, 33*, 141–9.
Silva, O. (2007). The jack-of-all-trades entrepreneur: Innate talent or acquired skill?
Economics Letters, 97(2), 118–23.
Stam, E. (2014). The Dutch entrepreneurial ecosystem. SSRN. https://ssrn.com/abstract
=2473475 or http://dx.doi.org/10.2139/ssrn.2473475
Stam, E. (2015). Entrepreneurial ecosystems and regional policy: A sympathetic cri-
tique. *European Planning Studies, 23*(9), 1759–69.
Steyaert, C., & Hjorth, D. (2006). *Entrepreneurship as Social Change*. Cheltenham,
UK and Northampton, MA, USA: Edward Elgar Publishing.
Stewart, A. (1990). The Bigman metaphor for entrepreneurship: A "library tale" with
morals on alternatives for further research. *Organization Science, 1*(2), 143–59.
Stewart, A. (1992). A prospectus on the anthropology of entrepreneurship.
Entrepreneurship Theory and Practice, 16(2), 71–92.

Stewart, A. (2003). Help one another, use one another: Toward an anthropology of family business. *Entrepreneurship Theory and Practice, 27*(4), 383–96.

Stewart, A. (2010). Sources of entrepreneurial discretion in kinship systems. In: A. Stewart, G. Lumpkin & J. Katz (Eds), *Entrepreneurship and Family Business* (pp. 291–313). Bingley: Emerald Group Publishing. https://doi.org/10.1108/S1074 -7540(2010)0000012014

Szerb, L., Acs, Z. J., Ortega-Argilés, R., & Komlosi, E. (2015). *The Entrepreneurial Ecosystem: The regional entrepreneurship and development index.* SSRN: https:// ssrn.com/abstract=2642514 and http://dx.doi.org/10.2139/ssrn.2642514

Thornton, P. H., Ribeiro-Soriano, D., & Urbano, D. (2011). Socio-cultural factors and entrepreneurial activity: An overview. *International Small Business Journal, 29*(2), 105–18.

Tsoukas, H. (1996). The firm as a distributed knowledge system: A constructionist approach. *Strategic Management Journal, 17*(S2), 11–25.

Verver, M., & Dahles, H. (2013). The anthropology of Chinese capitalism in Southeast Asia: From culture to institution? *Journal of Business Anthropology, 2*(1), 93–114.

Wagner, R. (2016). *The Invention of Culture.* Chicago, IL: University of Chicago Press.

WEF (2013). *Entrepreneurial Ecosystems around the Globe and Company Growth Dynamics.* Davos: World Economic Forum.

Williams, N., & Vorley, T. (2014). Economic resilience and entrepreneurship: Lessons from the Sheffield City region. *Entrepreneurship and Regional Development, 26*(3–4), 257–81.

Wong, B. (1998). *Ethnicity and Entrepreneurship: The new Chinese immigrants in the San Francisco Bay area.* Boston, MA: Allyn and Bacon.

Woolthuis, R. K., Hooimeijer, F., Bossink, B., Mulder, G., & Brouwer, J. (2013). Institutional entrepreneurship in sustainable urban development: Dutch successes as inspiration for transformation. *Journal of Cleaner Production, 50*, 91–100.

10. Typifying latecomer social enterprises by ownership structure: Learning and building knowledge from innovation systems

Jahan Ara Peerally and Claudia De Fuentes

10.1 INTRODUCTION

Enterprises' ownership structure is a key basis for predicting their access to knowledge and thereby the nature of their innovation systems (Dunning, 1958, 1970; Lall & Streeten, 1977). This basis emanates from studies which examine the propensity of multinational (MNEs) versus domestic enterprises to contribute to economic development. Several studies[1] have shown that the subsidiaries of MNEs – hence *foreign-owned* entities – from more advanced locations contributed more to the economic development of poorer regions because they had access to better knowledge from more advanced innovation systems. Thus, unlike *domestic-owned* enterprises in developing countries, they were better placed to promote learning, knowledge and innovative capability building. The East Asian experience (Kim, 1980, 1997) and more recent evidence have shown that several developing country enterprises have closed the gap with developed ones and have nurtured improved innovation systems (Lorenzen, 2019), allowing them to positively impact their home country's economic development (Peerally & Cantwell, 2012).

Following from the above, we propose that a judicious understanding of social enterprises' (SEs') nature, and impact on economic development, also requires the integration of ownership structure in their analysis. Indeed, when we overlap the international business, innovation studies and social entrepreneurship literatures, key blind spots emerge related to ownership structure, innovative capability building and SEs. The innovation studies literature presents within the "innovation systems" framework (Freeman, 1987, 1995; Lundvall, 1988, 1992; Nelson, 1993; Nelson, Freeman, Lundvall & Pelikan, 1988; Dosi, Freeman, Nelson, Silverberg & Soete, 1988) the domestic and foreign links for learning and knowledge accumulation for innovative capability building. But this literature has so far overlooked the combination of SEs and equity structure in its analysis. The international business literature integrates the innovation systems framework with ownership structure to explain flows of knowledge and innovative capability development to and from MNEs and latecomer country enterprises, but it neglects SEs in its analysis. The social entrepreneurship literature advances the "innovation ecosystem" approach (Bloom & Dees, 2008) to explain SEs' strategies and competitiveness based on their external environment. However, it overlooks learning and knowledge creation for innovative capability building through links with actors within that system. Furthermore, the innovation ecosystem as developed within the social entrepreneurship literature was initially designed for advanced country contexts and tends to focus on SEs that already achieved a certain level of innovative capability. More specifically, the current learning and capability-centered studies (e.g. El Ebrashi, 2017; Smith, Gonin & Besharov, 2013; Bloom & Smith, 2010) in this field do not shed light on the activities that SEs engage in, or resources they use, to accumulate knowledge and learn *prior* to building innovative capabilities. However, the social entrepreneurship literature has conceptually and empirically documented the historical evolution of the diverse SE models, culminating to date in the most comprehensive set of attributes which reconciles these diverse models.

The first set of attributes is that SEs span the boundaries of the private, public and non-profit sectors, they bridge institutional fields (Tracey, Phillips & Jarvis, 2011) and face conflicting institutional logics (Pache & Santos, 2012). Second, SEs are concerned with fulfilling their dual mission of achieving sustainability, i.e. financial self-sufficiency, and socially desired outcomes[2] (Miller, Grimes, McMullen & Vogus, 2012). Third, achieving this dual mission is often incompatible in the short term and raises complexities which in the long term may undermine SEs' sustainability (Voltan & De Fuentes, 2016; Hockerts, 2015; Batillana, Lee, Walker & Dorsey, 2012). In line with this literature, we adopt the approach that SEs are those that fall within the attributes mentioned above. They represent a heterogeneous group of organizations, encompassing for-profit or non-profit organizations, non-governmental organizations (NGOs) or governmental agencies, charitable or philanthropic organizations, inclusive and/or social businesses (Yunus, Moingeon & Lehmann-Ortega, 2010). More specifically, we focus on latecomer SEs (LCSEs) which are, *inter alia*, SEs that operate in emerging, developing and less developing economies (Peerally et al., 2019).

While it is accepted that commercial enterprises create, through learning, a stock of knowledge-based assets that give them competitive edge, and that they seek to gain and maintain this stock of assets (Narula, 2004), it is unclear from existing evidence whether SEs make purposive efforts to develop such knowledge-based assets. Learning, knowledge and skills are required to build and accumulate the operational and then – potentially – innovative capabilities, which LCSEs need to operate and to conceptualize, produce and scale products (goods and/or services) for achieving socially desired outcomes, while simultaneously achieving financial sustainability (Peerally et al., De Fuentes, & Figueiredo, 2019). Thus, to better understand LCSEs, it is necessary to examine how, or even if, they learn and create knowledge for building innovative capabilities. By examining their sources of knowledge in a first instance, and their ability to learn and build innovative capabilities, researchers can further comprehend SEs' nature, sustainability issues and their social/developmental impact.

Cross-disciplinary studies have *not* shown how SEs – as based on different ownership structures – learn to build operational and then innovative capabilities. Indeed, adding ownership structure within the analysis allows for a holistic framing of LCSEs for future studies. In other words, what can be viewed as successful cases of purely endemic LCSEs can often be LCSEs launched by foreign social entrepreneurs, foreign investors or foreign parent companies belonging to more advanced innovation systems. Thus, we suggest that understanding the nature and success of LCSEs, and their impact on development, requires jointly examining their ownership structures with their innovation systems, their linkages and sources for learning and their technological capability creation paths.

Moreover, since LCSEs emerge or are launched, and thrive or fail in developing, less developing and emerging country contexts, it is informative to study them using different lenses than that used in developed countries. In this conceptual chapter, we demonstrate through a process of normative analysis that the innovation systems approach has already set the groundwork as a powerful framework for analyzing LCSEs' external sources of learning, knowledge and innovative capability building.

Borrowing from these three literatures, we elaborate our discussion and develop four propositions. We map the LCSEs' innovation system and we theorize that by being embedded in latecomer innovation systems, LCSEs are often subject to knowledge-related systemic failures. Thus, empirically examining LCSEs should account for the distinct nature of their innovation systems. Drawing from the international business literature and based on ownership structure, we provide a typology of domestic and foreign LCSEs, multinational SEs (MNSEs) and emerging – latecomer – country MNSEs (EMNSEs). This typology emphasizes that different types of ownership lead to different governance structures for building operational and innovative capabilities necessary to achieve their dual mission.

In Section 10.2, we present the defining characteristics of the LCSEs. In Section 10.3, we compare the innovation systems and innovation ecosystems approaches and we present the LCSE innovation systems. We discuss the

LCSEs' domestic innovation system's inherent sustainability disadvantages. In Section 10.4, we highlight the importance of the innovation systems approach for studying the LCSE-level technological capability building process. Through a normative analytical process, in Section 10.5, we typify and exemplify foreign and domestic LCSEs and MNSEs and we highlight selected future research agendas for international business, social entrepreneurship and innovation studies. We conclude in Section 10.6.

10.2   DEFINING CHARACTERISTICS OF LCSEs

The term latecomer was first coined by the historian Gerschenkron (1952), who put forward the notion of latecomer development based on his studies of nineteenth-century latecomer European economies relative to the then leader, Great Britain (Mathews, 2005). Latecomer economies are in essence "backward economies", due to their institutions and technological infrastructures being less developed than those of advanced economies. His approach to development sparked the awareness that capability building is a precondition for economic catch-up by latecomer economies. This evolved into the social capability approach (e.g. Abramovitz, 1986), the innovation systems approach (e.g. Nelson, 1993; Freeman, 1987) and the technological capability approach (Kim, 1980, 1997; Lall, 1987). While the former two approaches focused on the country level, the latter involved enterprise-level studies, whereby the term latecomer became attached to enterprises. Thus, we define LCSEs as SEs that operate in emerging, developing and less developing economies.

Second, LCSEs pursue a social mission either through non-profit business models or through the adoption of some form of commercial activity to generate revenue in the pursuit of social goals (Doherty, Haugh & Lyon, 2014).

Third, our definition also includes LCSEs which are "ordinary entrepreneurs" (Tobias, Mair & Barbosa-Leiker, 2013, p. 730) who tend to subsist in conditions of desperate poverty and entrenched conflict and who engage in transformative entrepreneuring. Tobias et al. (2013) exemplify ordinary entrepreneurs as rural dwellers in Rwanda's specialty coffee sector, who perpetuate and enact economic and social value generation. They argue that existing empirical evidence has largely ignored such ordinary entrepreneurial protagonists. Integrating them in our definition is key as their socio-economic and political realities are exclusively relevant to the LCSEs' innovation systems.

Fourth, our proposed definition of LCSEs extends on Voltan and De Fuentes' (2016) definition. They define SEs as entities which represent social innovators working toward finding new solutions to existing social problems. We elaborate that LCSEs are those which represent social innovators working towards finding new solutions, or *imitating existing solutions from advanced or other latecomer economies* to solve social problems.[3] SEs' definitions abound in the social entrepreneurship literature (Iraci de Souza, Charbel & Simone, 2017; Doherty et al., 2014; Kerlin, 2012). By extending Voltan and De Fuentes' (2016) characterization in our definition, we reconcile the heterogeneity of SEs under one unifying theme, namely innovation. Thus, the main premise is that LCSEs, irrespective of their organizational form and logic, must learn and accumulate knowledge to become innovative over time, in order to be financially self-sufficient and generate social impact. Furthermore, Voltan and De Fuentes' (2016) definition is extended since LCSEs can be launched by existing developed-country SEs or LCSEs from other latecomer locations, in which situations they are required to apply or imitate existing solutions from elsewhere to solve domestic social problems (Wang, Alon & Kimble, 2015; Bruton, Khavul & Chavez, 2011).

Lastly, LCSEs tend to face three sets of intrinsic "sustainability disadvantages" which are related to the nature of their domestic innovation systems. In the next section, we describe the LCSEs' innovation systems and these sustainability disadvantages by drawing from existing innovation studies and specifically those related to national innovation systems (e.g. Nelson, 1993), latecomer capabilities (e.g. Hobday, 1995, 1998) and innovation systems for social inclusion (e.g. Dutrénit & Sutz, 2014).

10.3   LATECOMER INNOVATION SYSTEMS VERSUS INNOVATION ECOSYSTEMS

10.3.1   The Origins

The innovation systems approach evolved from the national innovation systems (Freeman, 1987, 1995; Lundvall, 1988, 1992; Nelson, 1993; Nelson et al., 1988; Dosi et al., 1988), regional (Asheim & Isaksen, 2002) and global systems (Binz & Truffer, 2017). The systemic approach emphasizes the role of context for fostering or inhibiting an innovative environment. The system is composed of domestic and foreign economic actors (enterprises), non-economic actors (e.g. government agencies, universities, bridging organizations) and institutions (e.g. policy regimes, international institutions) that connect them both within and across countries (Narula, 2004). These actors define the stock of knowledge within any given location because they determine the knowledge available within an innovation system. The system centers on the interrelationships between these actors for understanding the dynamics of innovation and its connection to development processes.

The role of foreign firms and foreign technology flows for domestic technological capability building in latecomers (Malerba & Nelson, 2012) is also an integral aspect of innovation systems (Kim, 1980, 1997; Lall & Streeten, 1977). Even though foreign sources of technology might be readily available to different countries, the identification, use and adoption differs from country to country. Thus, innovation systems can be functional or dysfunctional which explains the difference in innovative capacity between various developing countries (Cirera & Maloney, 2017).

The innovation systems literature has emphasized the role of country and regional characteristics (e.g. institutions, firms, industries, trade agreements) and path dependencies (Lundvall & Borrás, 2004) for transforming the innovation process and sourcing foreign technologies to build further innovative capabilities. Malerba and Nelson (2012), for example, indicate that country characteristics are highly relevant to analyzing capacity building. However, most of these studies focus on the economic aspect of innovation, i.e. showing that innovation contributes to economic growth (Cirera & Maloney, 2017). But these studies do not address how this economic growth generates social inclusion.

Recently, studies have emphasized the need to link innovation systems and enterprise-level technological capabilities for generating social value (Cozzens & Sutz, 2014; Dutrénit & Sutz, 2014). Just as commercial enterprises exist as part of innovation systems into which they are embedded through historical, social and economic ties to other economic units (Narula, 2004), it is necessary to view SEs as part of innovation systems as well. Cozzens and Sutz (2014) and Dutrénit and Sutz (2014), particularly, were among the first to link knowledge, innovation systems, inclusion and development.

Contrastingly, the terms ecosystem (Moore, 1993) and innovation ecosystem emerged from the practitioner and strategy literatures. Regarding innovation ecosystems specifically, Autio and Thomas (2014) and Cameron's (2012) comprehensive works focus on enterprises within a system that has already achieved a certain level of knowledge stock and innovation capacity. This literature does not examine the activities that enterprises engage in, or resources they use, to accumulate knowledge and learn prior to building innovative capabilities.

Our depiction of the LCSE's innovation system serves to highlight the domestic and potential foreign sources of knowledge and learning to LCSEs. It complements Foster and Heeks' (2013) modified systems of innovation framework for inclusive innovation, but it additionally highlights formal science and technology institutions and foreign actors as knowledge sources. As shown in Figure 10.1, the LCSE is at the center of the system. It regroups traditional and formal actors encountered in the innovation studies literature, while adding idiosyncratic formal and informal domestic and foreign actors (e.g. beneficiaries, volunteers, foundations).

Thus, unlike the innovation ecosystem discussed above or Bloom and Dees' (2008) socially entrepreneurial ecosystem, the LCSE innovation system proposed here focuses on the key potential providers of knowledge and learning

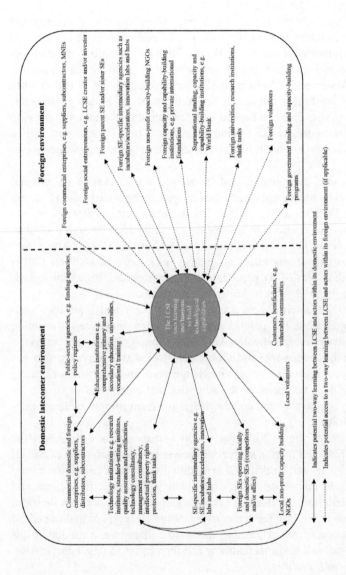

Source: Authors' own elaboration based on review of existing studies.

Figure 10.1 *Actors within the LCSE's innovation system*

to LCSEs, and not necessarily on the other actors within the general social entrepreneurial ecosystem. It is focused on the external linkages for innovative capability development, and can be applied to individual or the sum of LCSEs in the system.

Hence, LCSEs are part of larger innovation systems shaped by the domestic and foreign contexts. Nevertheless, to assess LCSEs' potential for sustainability, it is crucial to consider the domestic context first, i.e. the local actors, the activities they perform and the linkages established amongst them to share and build knowledge (Carlsson, Jacobsson, Holmén & Rickne, 2002).

Figure 10.1 depicts an ideal scenario where knowledge and information are readily available and freely flowing between actors. Thus, it indicates potential two-way learning links between LCSEs and the actors within its domestic and foreign environments. However, as explained in Section 10.3.2, systemic failures (Soete, Verspagen & Weel, 2009; Nelson, 1993) within innovation systems will often hinder these links and lead to one-way or even no learning links. We discuss these systemic failures and the LCSE's sustainability disadvantages by drawing from existing innovation studies and specifically those related to national innovation systems (e.g. Nelson, 1993), latecomer capabilities (e.g. Hobday, 1995, 1998) and innovation systems for social inclusion (see Dutrénit & Sutz, 2014).

10.3.2 Innovation Systems Address Systemic Failures

Unlike the innovation ecosystems framework within the social entrepreneurship literature, the innovation systems literature addresses the systemic failures which impede innovation and development (Chaminade, Intarakumnerd & Sapprasert, 2012; Soete et al., 2009; Nelson, 1993).

Building on the existing foundations set by the innovation systems literature, and linking them to the idiosyncrasies of SEs, we propose that LCSEs face three sets of intrinsic knowledge-related "sustainability disadvantages" in their domestic environments. LCSEs that have connections to foreign and/ or developed country actors in their innovation systems must first overcome cultural, administrative, geographic and economic differences and barriers (Ghemawat, 2007) to harness knowledge through linkages.

The first set of sustainability disadvantages is related to the knowledge–institutions nexus. Dutrénit and Sutz (2014) argue that one of the marks of underdevelopment in latecomer economies for reducing the social divide and inequalities is the weak level of knowledge demand from both the public and private sectors. They (2014, p. 4) posit that in these economies, there is a need for "stronger" knowledge and innovation generation directed towards solving problems that lead to social exclusion. In other words, latecomers' domestic innovation systems are viewed as being inherently weaker than that of developed countries. This leads to our first proposition.

Proposition 1: LCSEs are often disconnected from leading-edge international sources of knowledge, skills, technology and other resources (financial, political and social capital), and they need access to brokers or intermediaries that channel these resources which are key for achieving their dual mission.

Thus, in general the LCSEs' innovation systems lag behind those of more advanced economies. Their universities, for example, which function as a knowledge producer in finding scalable, system-changing ways to sustain existing social entrepreneurs (Cameron, 2012), may be weaker epistemologically and/or technologically. Other educational and technical institutions may be poorly equipped. Consequently, this impacts their access to quality human and intellectual resources. Wang et al. (2015) state that there are no courses or training on social entrepreneurship provided by business schools in China, which is one of the best performing latecomer economies in the world. The LCSEs can also be isolated from or lag behind in accessing information on good practice. Other aspects of the LCSE innovation systems can hinder access to financial, social and political resources when compared to that of developed countries. Institutional conditions which are key for supporting or undermining access to knowledge for the practice of social entrepreneurship such as public policy and politics, governance, media, economic and social conditions are often absent or limited. While the existing social entrepreneurship literature (e.g. Autio & Thomas, 2014; Bloom & Dees, 2008; Martin & Osberg, 2007) describes the importance and characteristics of a healthy innovation ecosystem for SEs in general, it also overlooks its inherent edge for developed-country SEs' sustainability over that of LCSEs. In a deficient latecomer innovation system, the LCSE will be technologically disadvantaged with limited ability to learn from the limited available pool of knowledge and skills to create and accumulate operational and then innovative capabilities. The LCSE must therefore devise and implement strategies to overcome its system's technological disadvantage by either tapping into ways to create and accumulate innovative capabilities to meet its double bottom line or by accessing those resources through linkages from other sources and/or advanced locations.

The second set of sustainability disadvantages concerns the nature of the above-mentioned linkages. Several studies (e.g. Peerally & Cantwell, 2011, 2012; Dutrénit, 2000) have shown the importance of linkages for learning and acquiring operational and innovative capabilities in commercial latecomer businesses. Moreover, echoing Dutrénit and Sutz (2014), innovation systems need to take onboard people with differing levels of skills and education and enable them to interact for the co-production (Ostrom, 1996) of knowledge for social problem solving: a process which they concede is challenging even for the latecomer Latin American economies. Thus, LCSEs will also confront less sophisticated actors in their domestic innovation systems. This can inhibit their learning potential and therefore their development of innovative capabilities through linkages.

Linkages can be with the different actors in Figure 10.1. In latecomer countries, these actors are often less sophisticated than those of advanced countries, and their propensity for impacting LCSEs in terms of knowledge and skills creation as well as spillover effects can be significantly lower. Allies of LCSEs (Peerally et al., 2019) can take many forms including domestic/foreign suppliers, sister affiliates/subsidiaries when the LCSE is part of an MNE, or even the suppliers to the MNE parent. In cases where there exist interactions between the customers/beneficiaries – namely the actors who benefit from LCSE activities – and the LCSEs, linkages for learning can be low due to the former's less sophisticated nature and more importantly because they are poorer, undereducated and/or unhealthy.

The LCSE's sustainability, therefore, partly hinges on finding key domestic and foreign sources of knowledge and developing learning linkages with them.

The final set of sustainability disadvantages applies to the LCSE markets. Chan, Lau, Lo and Ni (2010), for example, state that the market scope of SEs remains limited in China, despite it being a major emerging economy and market. Thus, we elaborate our second proposition as follows.

Proposition 2: LCSEs will often confront underdeveloped and/or small local markets, sometimes with slim growth prospects and weak delivery infrastructure, which will in turn exacerbate their challenges related to scalability and the potential to achieve their dual mission.

Furthermore, the LCSEs' capabilities in product development, marketing and other areas – especially when they lack absorptive capacity – can be less cutting-edge than those from more advanced innovation systems. Since, in general, SEs do not operate in isolation from each other, we can posit that advanced innovation systems regroup more sophisticated SEs capable of generating – collectively or individually – knowledge, skills and, thus, innovation for social impact. Furthermore, in advanced markets, SEs deal with more sophisticated buyers and/or beneficiaries – even if these are vulnerable members of the population – and the SEs will more likely have access to better market feedback into their knowledge and skills bases.

It can be argued that LCSEs have labor and country-related cost advantages which make their market entry or sustainability less challenging. However, they will still need to devise and implement strategies for overcoming initial market entry barriers, but also for continuously and systematically upgrading their knowledge stock needed for scaling social impact and delivering value to society.

10.4   LCSE-LEVEL TECHNOLOGICAL CAPABILITY BUILDING FOR SOCIAL IMPACT

LCSEs should therefore benefit from domestic but also regional and global innovation systems that include foreign actors. They must tap into different knowledge sources to benefit from a wide range of learning mechanisms. As with commercial enterprises, SEs also need to engage in technological learning and technological capability building to achieve sustainability.

Technological learning is defined as the processes by which individual learning is converted into organizational learning and involves the processes through which enterprises accumulate technological capabilities over time (Figueiredo, 2002). Due to the heterogeneity of LCSEs that produce physical goods, provide services and achieve their social mission with a combination of both, we refer to their technological capabilities as the knowledge, skills and experience required to produce goods and/or services, and to achieve their social mission. More specifically, the LCSE's technological capability refers to the knowledge, skills and experience needed to generate and manage innovation (Peerally et al., 2019; Bell & Pavitt, 1995). The technological capability approach holds that learning by latecomers – through a wide range of mechanisms and resources for acquiring knowledge and skills from external and internal sources – leads to the building and deepening of capabilities to innovate (Bell & Pavitt, 1993).

Bell and Figueiredo (2012) list the several internal and external learning mechanisms that commercial enterprises rely on, to build and accumulate technological capabilities. These learning mechanisms are relevant for research in LCSEs. However, as shown in Figure 10.1, the LCSEs' innovation systems add idiosyncratic external sources of knowledge such as funding organizations, volunteers and vulnerable communities which ought to be accounted for, when applying Bell and Figueiredo's (2012) mechanisms.

As Cozzens and Sutz (2014), George, McGahan and Prabhu (2012) and Peerally et al. (2019) highlight, innovative capability-building processes are necessary for achieving social impact. These authors posit that learning, human capital and capability building are some of the crucial factors for enhancing the emergence of innovations that address social problems. They also emphasize that research is required to further understand the role of capabilities as drivers of inclusive growth.

In line with previous studies that focus on the analysis of technological capability building in latecomer countries (Bell & Figueiredo, 2012), we emphasize that LCSEs have access to technologies from outside the organization, but not necessarily the knowledge to identify, use or adapt them. Or as per Cohen and Levinthal (1990), they do not have the required level of absorptive capacities to fully benefit from external sources of knowledge. This gives rise to our third proposition.

Proposition 3: LCSEs begin mainly as technology users and the creation of low-cost, pro-poor, frugal innovations by them do not occur automatically or in a vacuum.

The knowledge, skills and resources available in their innovation systems provide them with the basic inputs to operate and create a set of embryonic technological capabilities (Dutrénit, 2000) that are required to perform basic operations, have basic social impact and achieve the preliminary steps towards reaching financial self-sufficiency. Through continued purposive learning efforts and by gradually engaging in a network of linkages LCSEs, firstly, build operational capabilities. This involves, for example, the capability to identify a social problem and conceptualize solutions by engaging in linkages for shaping the product, defining social impact and raising funds.

By increasingly engaging in networks of linkages and searching and combining knowledge from different internal sources and their innovation systems, LCSEs can further accumulate technological capabilities and upgrade from operational capabilities to basic innovative capabilities. Moreover, the identification of external actors and further engagement by LCSEs to build formal or informal linkages differ from commercial enterprises, in the sense that many of these external actors may not have economic motivations (Bloom & Smith, 2010), but they may instead be more socially driven and interested in scaling social impact. Therefore, building diverse and even hybrid networks of linkages with external actors in the innovation system is necessary to achieve a basic level of innovative capabilities in the LCSE.

LCSEs need to build market channels to overcome one of the sustainability disadvantages previously discussed, so as to scale social impact wide. This can only be achieved by further upgrading their technological capabilities to a higher, more intermediate level (Peerally et al., 2019). For scaling deep, LCSEs need to develop advanced innovative technological capabilities to innovate in product and process and achieve sustainability.

Technological capability building therefore requires LCSEs to constantly improve techniques, technologies and/or processes through actively engaging in learning processes internally and externally through linkages with actors within their innovation systems. Thus, the nature of LCSE innovation systems will bear on their innovative, sustainability and social impact levels. The interplay of internal and external sources of learning within the LCSE's innovation system can lead to various innovative outcomes for social impact by the LCSEs, such as low-cost or frugal innovations (George et al., 2012), social and/or inclusive innovations (Cozzens & Sutz, 2014), pro-poor innovations, below-the-radar innovations and more (Foster & Heeks, 2013). It can also result in innovations that are embodied within the LCSE's physical systems and employees or are combinational (physical systems with human capital) in nature. Finally, it may also result in unpredicted positive spillovers into the larger community, and not just the targeted vulnerable community (Peerally et al., 2019). Hence the reason we argue that the innovation systems approach is a much larger framework that accounts for the developmental impacts of LCSEs, when compared to the innovation ecosystems approach within the social entrepreneurship literature which focuses on SEs' strategic objectives. As shown in this section, research has not yet examined how different types of SEs, based on ownership structure, learn and build basic operational followed by innovative capabilities through interactions with actors within their innovation systems.

10.5   TYPIFYING LCSEs BY OWNERSHIP STRUCTURE

Based on ownership structure and from a normative analytical process, we elaborate a detailed typology of domestic and foreign-owned LCSEs, as shown in Table 10.1. The typology refines previous ideas on how SEs are organized and innovate on existing analysis by bridging the international business and innovation studies areas, both of which are increasingly relevant to understanding SEs. Indeed, the international business and innovation studies literatures mutually focus on ownership structure to assess the developmental impacts of foreign versus domestic enterprises in latecomer economies. Thus, it adds to a better comprehension of not only the sustainability issues and developmental impacts of SEs, but also their internationalization strategies and their cross-border value-adding equity and non-equity structures.

Moreover, the typology readily denominates LCSEs' knowledge and learning sources within innovation systems. In a first instance, it highlights whether LCSEs are part of an MNE with connection to foreign innovation systems, thus benefitting from internal and foreign flows of specialized knowledge and resources; or whether they are loosely connected to other domestic and/or foreign SEs and sources of knowledge through regular market channels; or if they are mostly engaged with domestic actors within their innovation systems, with limited links to foreign actors.

The typology, therefore, allows for properly framing future studies on LCSEs' role in development. In other words, what can often be viewed as successful endemic LCSEs can in fact be LCSEs launched by foreign social entrepreneurs, foreign investors or foreign parent companies belonging to

Table 10.1   Typifying and exemplifying LCSEs

Types of LCSEs **Examples; country/SE creator(s)' origin and/or country of financial/ strategic control**	Attributes of ownership structure	Selected research questions
	Domestic LCSEs	
Purely domestic micro LCSE E.g. women's communities in the shea butter sector, rural dwellers in specialty coffee sector of Africa.	Launched and operated in latecomer countries by locals. They are fully owned and controlled – financially and strategically – by local nationals and operate locally only. They can: • be "ordinary" domestic entrepreneurs;	• How do they learn to build capabilities? • At what innovative capability level are they operating?
Purely domestic LCSE E.g. Grupo OEZ, Mexico; Selco, India.	• be created by locals but be funded by foreign organizations without any control or ownership ties; • internationalize to other countries through non-equity modes, such as export-ing. Foreign intermediaries handling exports will therefore likely be foreign-owned.	• What are their key learning sources and knowledge interactions? • How do they overcome inherent knowledge-related sustainability disadvantages within their innovation systems?
	Foreign non-equity-based SEs	
Foreign DCSE E.g. Dialogue Social Enterprise franchise, Germany.	Latecomer social franchisee/licensee of foreign social franchises/licenses. The social franchisors/licensors are headquartered in developed countries. The social franchisors use non-equity modes to internationalize, therefore there are no ownership ties between the cross-country entities. The latecomer social franchisee/licensee is domestic-owned but accountable to the foreign social franchisor/licensor based on their contract terms. Even though the parent social franchisor/licensor does not own the LCSEs or cross-border value-adding activities for social impact, the LCSE is considered foreign, since the concept – hence knowledge – originates from a foreign source.	• What is the significance of idiosyn-cratic formal informal institutions in this process? • Does their level of technological capability or the quality of interac-tions within their innovation systems affect their scope for generating social impact?

Types of LCSEs Examples; country/SE creator(s)' origin and/or country of financial/strategic control	Attributes of ownership structure	Selected research questions
	Foreign and domestic multinationals: equity-based	
Foreign commercial MNE with LCSE affiliates E.g. Grameen Danone Foods Limited, France and Bangladesh.	Commercial MNEs originating from the developed world but launched and operate SE affiliates/subsidiaries in latecomer countries with the potential to do so globally. There are ownership ties between the cross-country entities. The LCSE affiliates/subsidiaries are either fully owned by the foreign MNE or are in shared ownership with local partners in the cases of joint ventures. The commercial MNE owns and/or controls cross-border value-adding activities for social impact. The nature and scope of their value-adding activities are comparable to other similar commercial MNEs.	• From a development perspective, what capabilities do these MNEs impart to the actors within the latecomer innovation systems? • Do they upgrade innovative capacity in latecomer innovation systems?
MNSE with LCSE affiliates E.g. Grameen Foundation, America; KickStart International, America/Europe.	• Foreign investors and/or foreign social entrepreneurs – often from developed countries – own and control LCSEs that operate in latecomer countries, leading to ownership ties between the cross-country entities. The LCSE is foreign-owned and the investors/entrepreneurs are proxy parent companies. They can even own/control multiple value-adding LCSE affiliates/subsidiaries across several latecomer countries.	• Is their scope for generating social impact related to their level of interactions in global innovation systems? • What is the nature, scope and various features of these MNEs' internal and cross-border arrangements and workings?
	• MNSEs originate from either developed or developing countries, but are head-quartered in and controlled from a developed country, have LCSE affiliates/subsidiaries in latecomer countries and potentially globally. There are owner-ship ties between the cross-country entities. Their parent companies are 100% foreign-owned. LCSE affiliates/subsidiaries are either fully owned by the foreign MNSE parent companies or in shared ownership with local partners. The MNSEs own and/or control cross-border value-adding activities for social impact.	• Where are high-level social impact offerings created and adapted within these MNE networks, i.e. global innovation systems?

Types of LCSEs Examples; country/SE creator(s)' origin and/or country of financial/ strategic control	Attributes of ownership structure	Selected research questions
EMNSE E.g. Unidentified; latecomer (emerging, developing and less developing) countries.	They originate, are headquartered and operate in latecomer countries but internationalize to other countries through equity modes, i.e. investing hierarchies. Their parent company is 100% latecomer-owned and controlled.	• Why do some LCSEs abandon their innovation systems for more advanced ones when they evolve into MNEs?

Source: Based on the authors' own elaboration of evidence from existing studies and from publicly available information.

more advanced innovation systems. Thus, to comprehensively understand the nature and success of LCSEs, studies should jointly examine their ownership structures, sources for learning and linkages and technological capability creation paths. This leads to our final proposition.

Proposition 4: The resources available to LCSEs and their ability to use and recombine these resources to create and upgrade their technological capabilities, are jointly determined by their ownership structures and the key stakeholders in their innovation systems.

Dunning and Lundan (2008) use ownership structure to compare MNEs with other types of international enterprises. According to them (2008, p. 3), the threshold definition of an MNE is an enterprise that engages in foreign direct investment and owns or, in some way, controls value-added activities in more than one country. Hence, without ownership or control of some cross-border value-adding activities through foreign direct investment, an international enterprise is not an MNE. We use this aspect as a first step, to typify the MNSE.

Additionally, Dunning (1989, p. 5) states that the MNE engages in cross-border value-adding activities which may lead to the production of tangible goods, intangible services or a combination of both. In other words, by engaging in foreign direct investment and owning affiliates/subsidiaries across national borders, MNEs are able – through majority equity stake – to maintain ownership and control of decision making over the use of the transferred resources, including knowledge, to those affiliates/subsidiaries. Control – interpreted as financial control combined with strategic control of decision making over how the affiliates/subsidiaries operate – is the second step in typifying the MNSE (Caves, 2007; Geringer & Hebert, 1989).

Conversely, international enterprises are those that engage in a variety of cross-border non-equity cooperative ventures such as licensing and franchising agreements, strategic alliances, partnerships and trade, which may give the parent enterprise some, but not complete control over the foreign activities associated with those ventures.

In Section 10.5.1, we exemplify the LCSE typologies and discuss their relevance to the innovation systems approach. Our analysis generates key selected research avenues, which we present as an initial premise for future studies.

10.5.1 Domestic LCSEs

This classification includes the domestic *micro* LCSE and the domestic LCSE. It is conceptually essential to separate these two, as the former relates to Tobias et al.'s (2013, p. 730) "ordinary entrepreneurs" while the latter are usually launched by social entrepreneurs who do not subsist in conditions of desperate poverty and are not entrenched in conflict. They generally have had access to better life opportunities and to both domestic and foreign actors in their innovation systems.

The purely domestic micro LCSE evolves, for example, within the agri-cultural sector of latecomer economies such as the women's group and communities of the shea butter sector or rural dwellers in specialty coffee sectors of Africa. The study of technological change in agriculture has already been ascertained as being key for those who are in vulnerable economic and social positions (Clark, 2002). Studies (Devaux, Torero, Donovan & Horton, 2018; Rousseau, Gautier & Wardell, 2015; Zylberberg, 2013) are increasingly focusing on the position of these ordinary entrepreneurs within the global value chain (GVC) thereby indirectly revealing the domestic and foreign actors within their spheres. These include, for example, local government and domestic technology institutes (Mohammed, Boateng & Al-Hassan, 2013), MNEs (Rousseau et al., 2015), international institutions such as the United Nations and foreign governments (UN Women-Africa, 2017). While inclusion of ordinary entrepreneurs in GVCs through better production methods can improve their productivity and income (Mohammed et al., 2013), it is unclear whether their positioning within the GVC is subject to an increased scope for major skills upgrades and movement into higher value-adding activities. Thus, without novel research on the nature and depth of their interactions with actors within their innovation systems and on their domestic micro LCSE-level tech-nological capability-building paths, it cannot be ascertained if ordinary entre-preneurs are trapped, or not, at the lower end of the GVC with little or ample scope for moving upwards. Addressing this lacuna represents an important future research agenda which bridges the inclusive development and inclusive innovation literatures.

The social entrepreneurship literature abounds with cases on purely domes-tic LCSEs. Grupo EOZ[4] and Selco India (Pai & Hiremath, 2016) are examples of domestic LCSEs, created and launched within latecomer countries by local social entrepreneurs. The founders are often depicted as having had access to more advanced innovation systems, and they often created their offerings with support from foreign actors. The founder of Grupo EOZ, for example, is Mexican-born but has volunteered with Doctors Without Borders in Russia and studied at the University of California Berkeley. Grupo EOZ's product offerings based on the UVeta technology were developed and patented in the United States (US) and are manufactured there. Similar inferences about interacting domestic and foreign innovation systems can be made when examining cases on Selco India and its Indian founder (Pai & Hiremath, 2016). Nevertheless, empirical evidence on how such domestic LCSEs create and upgrade their technological capabilities to the level of introducing a new-to-the-world innovation, or accumulated other innovative capabilities in manufacturing, exporting, training, setting up institutes and so on, are lacking. Thus, research is needed to inform LCSEs, policymakers as well as private/ public institutions on how to nurture and develop their innovation systems.

10.5.2   Foreign Non-Equity-Based LCSEs

Foreign non-equity-based LCSEs include the social franchising and licensing models, created and launched in a developed country and later launched to other countries. This is exemplified by Germany-based Dialogue Social Enterprise. It operates Dialogue in the Dark SE franchises across several developed and developing countries. Dialogue in the Dark's aims are to empower the blind and to raise public awareness of the problems associated with blindness. While the social franchising and licensing models are well established in the developed world (Tracey & Jarvis, 2007), they are still a novelty in latecomer economies (Wang et al., 2015).

The social franchise/license being conceptualized in a developed country implies that the latecomer social franchisee or licensee is connected to its parent enterprise's more advanced innovation system. Wang et al. (2015) reveal that Dialogue Social Enterprise provides the core concepts and expertise to the Dialogue in the Dark China franchise in return for a fee, implying knowledge and learning flows from the parent enterprise to its social franchisee, but through the external market and not through an investing hierarchy. They also state that the founder of the China franchise had lived, studied and worked overseas, including at Dialogue Social Enterprise itself. We additionally propose that her access to foreign sources of knowledge and innovation systems could be significant factors that enabled her and the LCSE to build the technological capabilities for making successful changes to the China franchise. In other words, our contention is that to comprehensively understand the nature and success of similar LCSEs, studies are required to examine their knowledge sources, innovation systems, learning processes and technological capability creation paths in conjunction with their ownership structure.

10.5.3   Foreign Commercial MNEs with LCSE Affiliates/Subsidiaries

The third type of LCSEs takes equity form and is the LCSE affiliate/subsidiary of a foreign commercial MNE. This is exemplified by Grameen Danone Foods Limited (GDFL) located in Bangladesh, and operated as a 50–50 joint venture between Danone (France) and four Bangladesh-based Grameen partners. GDFL's mission involves amongst other things developing a product that has high nutritional value and is affordable for the poorest individuals, the Shokti Doi yoghurt. This LCSE has been studied extensively, however, a recent study by Peerally at al. (2019) examines how GDFL has evolved from having embryonic technological capabilities to creating and accumulating innovative capabilities through various learning mechanisms, to meet its dual mission. The authors observe several forms of innovation which are embodied within the LCSE affiliate but are also generated as products to beneficiaries and other actors within its various innovation systems.

10.5.4   The MNSE versus the EMNSE

Due to its large size and expansive presence across all continents, and the fact that it self-reports owning two subsidiaries and two affiliates, Grameen Foundation is viewed as an MNE. Grameen Bank was originally established in Bangladesh in 1997 by Professor Muhammed Yunus. Due to being first established in Bangladesh, the Grameen network is often mistaken as being an EMNSE. The Grameen Foundation, however, is in fact headquartered in and controlled from the US through its board of directors and executive staff (Grameen Foundation website) and is therefore typified as a foreign MNSE with LCSE affiliates/subsidiaries.

Another example of an MNSE easily mistaken for an EMNSE includes KickStart International, originally launched in Africa by foreign social entrepreneurs and later headquartered in the US. KickStart International designs and promotes low-cost, high-quality irrigation pumps to poor farmers, which significantly increases yields, incomes and provides a real path out of poverty. It was created by US-born and educated Martin Fisher and Nick Moon. Moon was born in India, from European parents and he spent most of his life in Europe. Together, in 1991, Fisher and Moon founded Kickstart in Kenya, which made it a foreign LCSE created and controlled by foreigners but launched and operated in a developing country.

In 2000, Kickstart expanded to Tanzania and in 2015 it expanded to several countries across West Africa. At this point, Kickstart was renamed KickStart International with its main head office relocated to the US. Thus, it evolved from being a foreign LCSE to a foreign MNSE with LCSE affiliates/subsidiaries. It can be inferred from secondary sources (Galvin & Iannotti, 2015; KickStart International website) that this MNSE has amassed an enormous base of technological capabilities. However, empirical evidence on the processes for creating technological capabilities by such MNSEs, through interactions with – possibly global – innovation systems, is lacking. Such evidence, as mentioned before, is key for informing all stakeholders within global innovation systems.

In the literature, we have encountered several cases of LCSEs which have evolved into MNSEs by moving the parent company, and strategic/financial controls from a latecomer to a more advanced innovation system. Thus, the

EMNSE – i.e. originating, headquartered in and controlled from latecomer countries, with operations in latecomer countries and potentially globally – remains elusive. This opens several research avenues for exploring the LCSEs which have evolved into MNEs, by abandoning their latecomer innovation systems and relocating to more advanced ones. While differing conceptual lenses can be applied to examine this, the integration of the innovation systems approach can provide a richer and more comprehensive investigation.

The typology, LCSE exemplifications and key selected research avenues emerging from the above discussion are presented in Table 10.1.

10.6   CONCLUSIONS

In this chapter, we assert that LCSEs must learn and create knowledge in the first place, to then build and accumulate technological capabilities for achieving innovation and sustainability. We build on existing concepts from the international business, social entrepreneurship and innovation studies literatures to provide an alternative and multidisciplinary conceptual tool for examining LCSEs within their idiosyncratic innovation systems. We synthesize these three strands of research to explain alternative types of LCSE based on ownership structure.

In addition to the research avenues presented in the previous section, the ideas presented in this chapter are useful for guiding future research. First, the ownership-based typology provides predictive power for future research, because it facilitates visualizing and denominating LCSE innovation systems and their inherent sustainability disadvantages and LCSEs' potential, if any, for international expansion. By viewing LCSEs as entities representing social innovators working towards finding new solutions, or imitating existing solutions from advanced or other latecomer economies to solve social problems, we highlight the importance of building knowledge stock within the SEs and their innovation systems for sustainability.

Second, the creation of a typology based on ownership structure provides an additional example of taking existing conceptual tools from other disciplines and extending them to generate alternative classifications of SEs. Most of the literature that relates the performance of SEs to their business models or organizational forms tends to build on management theories, while in this chapter we show that this can also be done from an evolutionary economics perspective on knowledge and innovative capability building.

Third, by bringing country contexts and systemic failures into the discussion, we add heuristic concepts which offer a broader framework for organizing and interpreting both qualitative and quantitative research based on LCSEs' performance. In this chapter, we proposed that not all LCSEs are created equal, and an examination of their performance must account for their access to foreign sources of knowledge through linkages with foreign founders, foreign investors or foreign parent/sister companies and other foreign actors within their innovation system.

Fourth, the international business literature stipulates that MNEs engage in the direct internal transfer of assets, resources and products through and within their investing hierarchies and their efficiency essentially depends on their ability to achieve economics of common governance, to leverage knowledge within and between the different constituents of its international network, through efficient internal markets and well-structured cross-border hierarchies. How relevant are these attributes to MNSEs? Future studies should investigate the implications of traditional international business theories and frameworks for the MNSE.

Finally, the ownership-based typology sets the premise for a discussion on and empirical investigation of the attributes of the LCSE's home country innovation system for, on the one hand, propelling it to an MNE status, but on the other hand inhibiting its location within the same innovation system. LCSEs' move to more advanced innovation systems once they evolve into MNEs could be based on the nature of financial and taxation institutions of the Global North, rather than the search for more advanced sources of knowledge. Still, it is unclear whether these MNSEs can have as much significant social impact when managing their cross-border value-adding activities under such willfully imposed cultural, administrative, geographic and economic distances. The preferred location of more advanced innovation systems for housing the parent company of *bona fide* LCSEs that evolve into MNSEs requires exploring in more detail how, and if conditions of their home countries' innovation systems push them to move abroad.

NOTES

1. See Caves (2007) for a comprehensive literature review.
2. The wording "socially desired outcomes" is used interchangeably with "social impact". It implies – as per Martin and Osberg (2007) – the achievement of (or additionally we suggest "the progress towards achieving") a new, stable socio-economic equilibrium that releases trapped potential or alleviates the suffering of a targeted group, and ensures a better future for the targeted group and even society at large through the activities of SEs.
3. Social problems are those that afflict underserved, neglected or highly disadvantaged populations or targeted groups who lack the financial means or political clout to achieve the transformative benefit on their own (Martin & Osberg, 2007).
4. Information on Grupo EOZ was gathered from its website www.agualimpia.mx/.

REFERENCES

Abramovitz, M. (1986). Catching up, forging ahead, and falling behind. *Journal of Economic History*, *46*(2), 385–406.

Asheim, B. T., & Isaksen, A. (2002). Regional innovation systems: the integration of local "sticky" and global "ubiquitous" knowledge. *Journal of Technology Transfer*, *27*(1), 77–86.

Autio, E., & Thomas, L. (2014). Innovation ecosystems: implications for innovation management. In: M. Dodgson, D. M. Gann & N. Phillips (Eds), *The Oxford Handbook of Innovation Management* (pp. 204–28). Oxford: Oxford University Press.

Batillana, J., Lee, M., Walker, J., & Dorsey, C. (2012). In search of the hybrid ideal. *Stanford Social Innovation Review*, Summer, 51–5.

Bell, M., & Figueiredo, P. N. (2012). Innovation capability building and learning mechanisms in latecomer firms: Recent empirical contributions and implications for research. *Canadian Journal of Development Studies*, *33*(1), 14–40.

Bell, M., & Pavitt, K. (1993). Technological accumulation and industrial growth: Contrasts between developed and developing countries. *Industrial and Corporate Change*, *2*(2), 157–211.

Bell, M., & Pavitt, K. (1995). The development of technological capabilities. In: I. ul Haque, M. Bell, C. Dahlam, S. Lall & K. Pavitt (Eds), *Trade, Technology and International Competitiveness* (pp. 69–102). Washington, DC: World Bank.

Binz, C., & Truffer, B. (2017). Global innovation systems: A conceptual framework for innovation dynamics in transnational contexts. *Research Policy*, *46*, 1284–98.

Bloom, P. N., & Dees, G. (2008). Cultivate your ecosystem. *Stanford Social Innovation Review*, Winter, 47–53.

Bloom, P. N., & Smith, B. (2010). Identifying the drivers of social entrepreneurial impact: Theoretical development and an exploratory empirical test of SCALERS. *Journal of Social Entrepreneurship*, *1*(1), 126–45.

Bruton, G. D., Khavul, S., & Chavez, H. (2011). Microlending in emerging economies: Building a new line of inquiry from the ground up. *Journal of International Business Studies*, *42*(5), 718–39.

Cameron, H. (2012). Social entrepreneurs in the social innovation ecosystem. In: A. Nicholls & A. Murdock (Eds), *Social Innovation* (pp. 199–220). London: Palgrave Macmillan.

Carlsson, B., Jacobsson, S., Holmén, M., & Rickne, A. (2002). Innovation systems: Analytical and methodological issues. *Research Policy*, *31*, 233–45.

Caves, R. E. (2007). *Multinational Enterprise and Economic Analysis*. Cambridge: Cambridge University Press.

Chaminade, C., Intarakumnerd, P., & Sapprasert, K. (2012). Measuring systemic problems in national innovation systems: An application to Thailand. *Research Policy*, *41*, 1476–88.

Chan, K. F., Lau, T., Lo, C., & Ni, N. (2010). An exploratory study on the development of social enterprises in China: Does context matter? Proceedings from ICSB World Conference. Washington, DC: International Council for Small Business.

Cirera, X., & Maloney, W. (2017). *The Innovation Paradox: Developing-country capabilities and the unrealized promise of technological catch-up*. Washington, DC: World Bank.

Clark, N. (2002). Innovation systems, institutional change and the new knowledge market: Implications for third world agricultural development. *Economics of Innovation and New Technology*, *11*(4–5), 353–68.

Cohen, W., & Levinthal, D. (1990). Absorptive capacity: A new perspective on learning and innovation. *Administrative Science Quarterly*, *35*(1), 128–52.

Cozzens, S., & Sutz, J. (2014). Innovation in informal settings: Reflections and proposals for a research agenda. *Innovation and Development*, *4*(1), 5–31.

Devaux, A., Toreiu, M., Donovan, J., & Horton, D. (2018). Agricultural innovation and inclusive value-chain development: A review. *Journal of Agribusiness in Developing and Emerging Economies*, *8*(1), 99–123.

Doherty, B., Haugh, H., & Lyon, F. (2014). Social enterprises as hybrid organizations: A review and research agenda. *International Journal of Management Reviews*, *16*, 417–36.

Dosi, G., Freeman, C., Nelson, R., Silverberg, G., & Soete, L. (Eds) (1988). *Technical Change and Economic Theory*. London: Pinter.

Dunning, J. H. (1958). *American Investment in British Manufacturing Industry*. London: Allen and Unwin.

Dunning, J. H. (1970). *Studies in International Investment*. London: Allen and Unwin.

Dunning, J. H. (1989). Multinational enterprises and the growth of services: Some conceptual and theoretical issues. *Service Industries Journal*, *9*(1), 5–39.

Dunning, J. H., & Lundan, S. M. (2008). *Multinational Enterprises and the Global Economy*, 2nd ed. Cheltenham, UK and Northampton, MA, USA: Edward Elgar Publishing.

Dutrénit, G. (2000). *Learning and Knowledge Management in the Firm: From knowledge accumulation to strategic capabilities*. Cheltenham, UK and Northampton, MA, USA: Edward Elgar Publishing.

Dutrénit, G., & Sutz, J. (Eds) (2014). National Innovation Systems, Social Inclusion and Development: The Latin American experience. Cheltenham, UK and Northampton, MA, USA: Edward Elgar Publishing.

El Ebrashi, R. (2017). Typology of growth strategies and the role of social venture's intangible resources. *Journal of Small Business and Enterprise Development*, *25*(5), 818–48.

Figueiredo, P. N. (2002). Does technological learning pay off? Inter-firm differences in technological capability-accumulation paths and operational performance improvement. *Research Policy*, *31*(1), 73–94.

Foster, C., & Heeks, R. (2013). Conceptualising inclusive innovation: Modifying systems of innovation frameworks to understand diffusion of new technology to low-income consumers. *European Journal of Development Research*, *25*(3), 333–55.

Freeman, C. (1987). *Technology Policy and Economic Performance*. London: Pinter.

Freeman, C. (1995). The national system of innovation in historical perspective. *Cambridge Journal of Economics*, *19*(1), 5–24.

Galvin, M. D., & Iannotti, L. (2015). Social enterprise and development: The KickStart model. *Voluntas*, *26*(2), 421–41.

George, G., McGahan, A., & Prabhu, J. (2012). Innovation for inclusive growth: Towards a theoretical framework and a research agenda. *Journal of Management Studies*, *49*(4), 661–83.

Geringer, J. M., & Hebert, L. (1989). Control and performance of international joint ventures. *Journal of International Business Studies*, *20*(2), 235–54.

Gerschenkron, A. (1952). Economic backwardness in historical perspective. In: B. Hoselitz (Ed.), *The Progress of Underdeveloped Areas*. Chicago, IL: University of Chicago Press.

Ghemawat, P. (2007). Managing differences: The central challenge of global strategy. *Harvard Business Review, 85*, 58–68.

Grameen Foundation website accessible at https://grameenfoundation.org/.

Hobday, M. (1995). *Innovation in East Asia: The challenge to Japan*. Cheltenham, UK and Northampton, MA, USA: Edward Elgar Publishing.

Hobday, M. (1998). Latecomer catch-up strategies in electronics: Samsung of Korea and ACER of Taiwan. *Asia Pacific Business Review, 4*(2–3).

Hockerts, K. (2015). How hybrid organizations turn antagonistic assets into complementarities. *California Management Review, 57*(3), 83–106.

Iraci de Souza, J., Charbel, J. C. J., & Simone, V. R. G. (2017). What is a social enterprise? Revising old concepts and interviewing social entrepreneurs. *Journal of Organisational Transformation and Social Change, 14*(2), 127–47.

Kerlin, J. A. (2012). Defining social enterprise across different contexts: A conceptual framework based on institutional factors. *Nonprofit and Voluntary Sector Quarterly, 42*(1), 84–108.

KickStart, International website accessible at http://kickstart.org/.

Kim, L. (1980). Stages of development of industrial technology in a developing country: A model. *Research Policy, 9*, 254–77.

Kim, L. (1997). *Imitation to Innovation: The dynamics of Korea's technological learning*. Cambridge, MA: Harvard Business School Press.

Lall, S. (1987). *Learning to Industrialise: The acquisition of technological capability by India*. Basingstoke: Macmillan.

Lall, S., & Streeten, P. (1977). *Foreign Investment, Transnationals and Developing Countries*. London: Macmillan.

Lorenzen, M. (2019). How early entrants impact cluster emergence: MNEs vs. local firms in the Bangalore digital creative industries. *Management and Organization Review*, 1–37.

Lundvall, B.-Å. (1988). Innovation as an interactive process: From user producer interaction to national systems of innovation. In: G. Dosi, C. Freeman, R. Nelson, G. Silverberg & L. Soete (Eds), *Technical Change and Economic Theory* (pp. 61–84). London: Pinter.

Lundvall, B.-Å. (Ed.) (1992). *National Systems of Innovation: Towards a theory of innovation and interactive learning*. London: Pinter.

Lundvall, B.-Å., & Borrás, S. (Eds) (2004). Science, technology and innovation policy. In: J. Fagerberg, D. C. Mowery & R. R. Nelson (Eds), *The Oxford Handbook of Innovation* (pp. 599–631). Oxford: Oxford University Press.

Malerba, F., & Nelson, R. (2012). *Economic Development as a Learning Process*. Cheltenham, UK and Northampton, MA, USA: Edward Elgar Publishing.

Martin, R. L., & Osberg, S. (2007). Social entrepreneurship: The case for definition. *Stanford Social Innovation Review, 5*, 28–39.

Mathews, J. (2005). The intellectual roots of latecomer industrial development. *International Journal of Technology and Globalisation, 14*, 433–50.

Miller, T. L., Grimes, M. G., McMullen, J. S., & Vogus, T. J. (2012). Venturing for others with heart and head: How compassion encourages social entrepreneurship. *Academy of Management Review, 37*(4), 616–40.

Mohammed, F., Boateng, S., & Al-Hassan, S. (2013). Effects of adoption of improved shea butter processing technology on women's livelihoods and their microenterprise growth. *American Journal of Humanities and Social Science*, *1*(4), 244–50.

Moore, J. (1993). Predators and prey: A new ecology of competition. *Harvard Business Review*, *71*(3), 75–86.

Narula, R. (2004). Understanding absorptive capacities in an "innovation systems" context: Consequences for economic and employment growth. DRUID Working Papers 04-02, DRUID, Copenhagen Business School, Department of Industrial Economics and Strategy/Aalborg University, Department of Business Studies. https://ideas.repec.org/p/aal/abbswp/04-02.html

Nelson, R. (Ed.) (1993). *National Innovation Systems: A comparative analysis*. New York: Oxford University Press.

Nelson, R., Freeman, C., Lundvall, B.-Å., & Pelikan, P. (1988). National systems of innovation. In: G. Dosi, C. Freeman, R. Nelson, G. Silverberg & L. Soete (Eds), *Technical Change and Economic Theory* (pp. 309–98). London: Pinter.

Ostrom, E. (1996). Crossing the great divide: Coproduction, synergy, and development. *World Development*, *24*(6), 1073–87.

Pache, A. C., & Santos, F. (2012). Inside the hybrid organization: Selective coupling as a response to competing institutional logics. *Academy of Management Journal*, *56*, 972–1001.

Pai, V. S., Hiremath, C. V. (2016). SELCO India: Solar energy for the underserved. *South Asian Journal of Business and Management Cases*, *5*(2), 145–54.

Peerally, J. A., & Cantwell, J. (2011). The impact of trade policy regimes on firms' learning for innovation from suppliers. *International Journal of Innovation Management*, *15*(1), 29–68.

Peerally, J. A., & Cantwell, J. (2012). Changes in trade policies and the heterogeneity of domestic and multinational firms' strategic response: The effects on firm-level capabilities. *World Development*, *40*(3), 469–85.

Peerally, J. A., De Fuentes, C., & Figueiredo, P. N. (2019). Inclusive innovation and the role of innovative technological capability-building: The social business Grameen Danone Foods Limited in Bangladesh. *Long Range Planning*, *52*(6). doi:https://doi .org/10.1016/j.lrp.2018.04.005

Rousseau, K., Gautier, D., & Wardell, A. (2015). Coping with the upheavals of globalization in the shea value chain: The maintenance and relevance of upstream shea nut supply chain organization in western Burkina Faso. *World Development*, *66*, 413–27.

Smith, W. K., Gonin, M., & Besharov, M. L. (2013). Managing social-business tensions: A review and research agenda for social enterprises. *Business Ethics Quarterly*, *23*(3), 407–42.

Soete, L., Verspagen, B., & Weel, B. (2009). Systems of innovation. In: B. H. Hall & N. Rosenberg (Eds), *Handbook of the Economics of Innovation*, Vol. 2 (Chapter: 27). Amsterdam: North-Holland.

Tobias, M. J., Mair, J., & Barbosa-Leiker, C. (2013). Toward a theory of transformative entrepreneuring: Poverty reduction and conflict resolution in Rwanda's entrepreneurial coffee sector. *Journal of Business Venturing*, *28*(6), 728–42.

Tracey, P., & Jarvis, O. (2007). Toward a theory of social venture franchising. *Entrepreneurship Theory and Practice*, *31*(5), 667–85.

Tracey, P., Phillips, N., & Jarvis, O. (2011). Bridging institutional entrepreneurship and the creation of new organizational forms: A multilevel model. *Organization Science*, *22*, 60–80.

UN Women-Africa (2017). Powering up women's income in the Ivory Coast through climate-smart shea butter production. http://africa.unwomen.org/en/news-and -events/stories/2017/12/powering-up-womens-income-in-the-ivory-coast

Voltan, A., & De Fuentes, C. (2016). Managing multiple logics in partnerships for scaling social innovation. *European Journal of Innovation Management*, *19*(4), 446–67.

Wang, H., Alon, I., & Kimble, C. (2015). Dialogue in the dark: Shedding light on the development of social enterprises in China. *Global Business and Organizational Excellence*, *34*(4), 60–9.

Yunus, M., Moingeon, B., & Lehmann-Ortega, L. (2010). Building social business models: Lessons from the Grameen experience. *Long Range Planning*, *43*(2–3), 308–25.

Zylberberg, E. (2013). Bloom or bust? A global value chain approach to smallholder flower production in Kenya. *Journal of Agribusiness in Developing and Emerging Economies*, *3*(1), 4–26.

11. Entrepreneurial ecosystems as a mechanism to promote economic formality in emerging economies: The case of Bogota

Andres Guerrero Alvarado and Vinciane Servantie

11.1 INTRODUCTION

Since the seminal article of Moore (1993), the concept of entrepreneurial ecosystems (EE) has been studied for over 20 years with an important recent boom. EE are considered to be a set of actors that interact with each other to promote entrepreneurship in a specific geographical area (Mason & Brown, 2014; Stam, 2015). They have traditionally been studied in consolidated economies, which present high levels of economic growth associated with opportunity entrepreneurship and economic formality. Some examples of these are the technological EE in Silicon Valley, Singapore and Boston and the industrial and services EE in Barcelona and Israel (Cheng & Low, 2006; Loossens, García, Llisterri & Kamiya, 2008; OECD, 2009; Roberts & Eesley, 2009).

EE in emerging economies, in contrast, have not been widely studied. In such contexts, necessity-driven entrepreneurship (Maritz, 2004) and lower rates of formal entrepreneurship (ILO, 2018) pose a challenge for economic development. Based on a case study of the EE in Bogota we seek to understand how – in a context with high rates of informality and necessity-driven entrepreneurship – the city's EE contributes to economic development and formality. The city of Bogota is an interesting case because not only does it have the highest rate of economic formality in the country's economy, but its EE is arguably the most developed, with Rappi – the Colombian unicorn that recently came to fame – hosted there as well as most of the incubators and accelerators. Additionally, the EE in Bogota is not geared towards a particular type of economic activity. Instead, it is varied in terms of organizations, types of entrepreneurs, types of entrepreneurial motivation and types of enterprises that are part of it.

This chapter discusses the structure of Bogota's EE, contributing to a deeper understanding of the organizational dynamics within an EE. We apply network analysis to characterize the EE and analyze it with respect to necessity versus opportunity entrepreneurship and according to the stage of the entrepreneurial process. By doing so, we seek to evaluate the support of the EE for start-ups in their transition towards formality. This analysis contributes to both the theoretical advancement of the issue and to the management of public policies that affect the economic development of cities and regions.

The chapter is structured into five sections. Section 11.2 offers the conceptual framework of EE and emerging economies; Section 11.3 explains the method of analysis used for the case; and Section 11.4 presents the results of the case study for Bogota's EE. Section 11.5 presents the conclusions and a discussion of the results, together with the implications and value for academic and practical development.

11.2   CONCEPTUAL FRAMEWORK

The theoretical framework has been divided into two sections. The first presents the concept of EE, and the second builds on the types of entrepreneurship in emerging economies such as Bogota and the role of support institutions in fostering formality.

11.2.1   The Entrepreneurial Ecosystem Concept

The concept of an EE is taken from the concept of an ecosystem in biology (Auerswald, 2015). Moore (1993) presented an early application of its use transplanted to the business field: analogous to the effect of sunlight, water and soil nutrients in the emergence of species, based on the combination of capital and customer interest talent for new innovations is generated (Brown & Mason, 2017). Bahrami and Evans (1995) invoke the term "Ecosystems" related to entrepreneurship for the first time in the academic literature. The term relates to the characteristics identified in Silicon Valley, particularly the availability of venture capital, trained personnel, research institutions, professional services infrastructure and lead users of innovations. Subsequently, Spilling (1996) describes the EE as one where actors, roles and environmental factors interact to determine a region's business performance. From this moment on, the concept of an EE has proliferated in the literature on development and entrepreneurship policies and has been studied in different parts of the world (Zacharakis, Shepherd & Coombs, 2003). However, there is still no single definition accepted in the theoretical field that serves as a mandatory reference point (Jacobides, Cennamo & Gawer, 2016). In general terms, EE have been described rather than defined.

Based on a review of 90 published studies on the topic of management, Tsujimoto, Kajikawa, Tomita and Matsumoto (2017) groups the definitions of EE into four approaches: industrial ecology, business ecosystem, platform management and network approach. The network approach is based on social network theory and has been developed the most, focusing on the description of the actors of the network as the framework of the EE (Feld, 2012; Isenberg, 2010; Singer, Amoros & Moska, 2015; Vogel, 2013). When understood as a social network, the entrepreneur benefits from the ecosystem and the fate of the individual depends, largely, on the wealth of resources available in the area where the entrepreneur performs the operation. The resources are provided and generated by the organizations in the EE. The individuals who operate within resource-rich environments will have greater possibilities of success in the task of creating companies to solve their needs in each of the aspects involved in company creation. They also demonstrate better abilities to adapt to the demands of the environment through learning (Breslin, 2008). Thus, entrepreneurs move amidst a range of agents and institutions, with which they maintain a complex web of interactions. Institutions, particularly accelerators, universities, funders and government agencies, are particularly important as the wealth of the resources in the environment takes on a concrete form through them, particularly when institutions meet the needs of entrepreneurs. In this way, in regions or localities where there are institutions that supply entrepreneurs with capital, knowledge and qualified human resources, there is a greater probability of entrepreneurial success (Wessner, 2004).

Although studies on the network approach have focused on the theoretical development of the characterization of ecosystems, there is recent interest in the analysis of relationships and effects beyond the entrepreneur. Motoyama and Knowlton (2017), for example, focused more directly on the connections between agents in an EE and found that the identification of the coherence and consistency of this connectivity is fundamental for the proper functioning of the ecosystem. This has meant that the analysis of EE is receiving more and more academic, professional and political attention due to its potential as a source of economic growth and revitalization. This is particularly true when empirical evidence of the effect of the characteristics of the EE on the economic dynamics begins to come to light (Arruda, Nogueira & Costa, 2013; Autio & Fu, 2015; Breznitz & Taylor, 2014; Isenberg, 2010; Neck, Meyer, Cohen & Corbett, 2004; Spigel, 2016).

11.2.2 Types of Entrepreneurship

In this chapter, we refer to entrepreneurship as the action of creating a business or the process of establishing a new organization. Entrepreneurship is a potential driver of job growth and economic development, especially in developing countries (Autio & Fu, 2015). It enables poor people to create their own income, and provides a potential tool for redressing poverty and alleviating income inequality (Bruton, Ketchen & Ireland, 2013; Tebaldi & Mohan, 2010). In order to better understand EE, the diversity and complexity of entrepreneurship should be recognized. Two categories come up when trying to do so; first, necessity and opportunity entrepreneurship can be distinguished according to the type of entrepreneurial motivation (Van Stel, Storey & Thurik, 2007; van der Zwan, Thurik, Verheul & Hessels, 2016). Second, entrepreneurship takes place both in the formal and informal economy (Williams, 2007). Below we review these categorizations.

11.2.2.1 Necessity and opportunity entrepreneurship

Necessity-driven entrepreneurs are those that are pushed into entrepreneurship because other employment options are absent or unsatisfactory (Hechavarria & Reynolds, 2009). Opportunity entrepreneurs, on the other hand, are those who become entrepreneurs out of choice, pulled by, for example, their wish for independence, self-realization or to own a business (Carter, Gartner, Shaver & Gatewood, 2003; Williams & Nadin, 2010), and by taking advantage of a perceived entrepreneurial opportunity (Hechavarria & Reynolds, 2009). Necessity-driven entrepreneurships are more likely to emerge in countries where gross domestic product (GDP) per capita is lower (Fuentelsaz, González, Maícas & Montero, 2015; Wennekers, Wennekers, Thurik & Reynolds, 2005) in periods of rising and high unemployment (Deli, 2011) and in populations with low educational levels (Poschke, 2013). In contrast, opportunity entrepreneurship shows a positive correlation with innovative capacities (Wennekers et al., 2005), higher education (Van Stel et al., 2007), GDP per capita (Wennekers et al., 2005) and economic conditions (Deli, 2011; Jaén, Fernández-Serrano & Liñán, 2013). Opportunity entrepreneurs may have higher growth expectations (Poschke, 2013; Van Stel et al., 2007) and are more likely to be involved in product innovation (Darnihamedani & Hessels, 2016).

In emerging economies like Colombia's, both pull- and push-motivated entrepreneurs are present and while opportunity-driven entrepreneurship is generally related to economic growth, necessity-driven entrepreneurship may also contribute to value creation in the developing country. While opportunity-driven entrepreneurship creates value and brings creativity, dynamism and innovation to society (Williams, 2008), necessity-driven entrepreneurship is a strong alternative to unemployment and limited opportunities in the wage market (Oxenfeldt, 1943). Moreover, Williams and Round (2007) showed that the primary motives for endeavoring in business creation might change from necessity- to opportunity-driven factors as the business grows and matures. In this context, political and economic institutions need to understand both opportunity and necessity entrepreneurship, their drivers, profile, characteristics and needs. The advice, support and funds they provide to scale up entrepreneurial endeavors should be differentiated according to the type of entrepreneurship (Van Stel et al., 2007; van der Zwan et al., 2016). And, more importantly, as the institutional environment influences the relative presence of opportunity and necessity entrepreneurship (Fuentelsaz et al., 2015), it is important to understand its structure to understand the EE as a whole.

11.2.2.2 Formal and informal entrepreneurship
The process of the emergence of any organization occurs before it formally exists (Gartner, 1995) and evolves according to specific stages (Kazanjian, 1988). First comes the idea. Then follows business conceptualization and resource gathering, which is eventually formulated through business planning. The start-up stage is third and it begins with the company's first sales. Finally, the acceleration stage is when the organization begins to create value for society. Registering the organization with the authorities implies its formalization (Webb, Bruton, Tihanyi & Ireland, 2013). This generally occurs during the start-up stage. However, some entrepreneurs develop their activities within the informal economy, also known as businesses that are "off-the-books", "undeclared", "shadow", "cash-in-hand" or "hidden". As a result, informal entrepreneurs emerge. They are defined as all those entrepreneurs that have "started a business or are the owner/manager of a business that is less than 36 months old which engages in the remunerated production and/or sale of licit goods and services that are not declared to the state for tax, benefit and/or labor law purposes when they should be declared" (Williams & Nadin, 2012).

Informal economies – and as a result informal entrepreneurs – exist in all countries regardless of their level of economic development (Thai & Turkina, 2012) and can be highly prevalent in specific countries. For instance, 90 percent of Ukraine's business start-ups operate partially or wholly in the informal economy (Williams & Round, 2007). In emerging Latin American countries, such as Colombia, informality covers 55 percent of the total economy, which is much higher than developed countries with an average of 20 percent of informality (ILO, 2018). Informal entrepreneurs have generally been characterized as being forced into this circumstance by their inability to find formal employment, and involvement in such activities is viewed as a survival strategy and a last option (Castells & Portes, 1989; Gallin, 2001; Portes & Walton, 1981; Raijman, 2001; Sassen, 1997; Williams, 2008). However, other studies point out that entrepreneurs perceive that, by operating informally, they incur lower costs and/or they do not perceive the benefits of being formal (Autio & Fu, 2015). For example, and according to Williams and Nadin (2012), they fear the loss of social benefits, they perceive tax-related injustice or unfairness and they face barriers in terms of registering as formal companies. Sometimes, they choose to participate in the informal economy because they find that they can be more autonomous, flexible and enjoy greater freedom in this sector (Gerxhani, 2004), or because they find that they can create an alternative space in which they can transform their work identity and/or reveal their true selves such as by establishing informal lifestyle businesses (Snyder, 2004).

Although informal entrepreneurship is legitimate (Webb, Tihanyi, Ireland & Sirmon, 2009), undeclared remunerated production and/or sale affects tax, employees' social security and can involve unethical practices (e.g. corruption, worker exploitation, natural environment abuse, etc.) (William & Nadin, 2010). For society, an informal organization in the acceleration stage represents a missed value. On the other hand, Williams (2008) points out that the informal economy acts as an incubator for business potential and is a transitional base for accessibility and graduation to the formal economy. In such contexts, the main role of the EE is to enhance formality. This implies that support institutions need to help organizations that intend to become formal and to encourage informal organizations to do so too (Williams & Nadin, 2012). For this to happen, the benefits of being formal should be more visible for entrepreneurs, in order to persuade them to advance to the later stages of entrepreneurship.

11.2.2.3 Opportunity and necessity entrepreneurship in the formal and informal economy

It might be assumed that the ratio of necessity to opportunity entrepreneurship would be much greater among informal entrepreneurs than among entrepreneurs starting up legitimate business operations, as shown by Lozano (1989) in the context of flea markets. However, Williams (2007) found that the ratio between necessity and opportunity entrepreneurship in the informal and formal economies was approximately the same in the context of England. Also, Snyder (2004) found that most of the informal entrepreneurs that she studied were informal out of choice or opportunity-driven. Williams (2007) explains that, in fact, necessity and opportunity-driven entrepreneurship shouldn't be seen as a dichotomy. At the end of the day, the decision to undertake such an endeavor is a balance and a mix of rationales. The decision to self-employ is one into which informal entrepreneurs feel both pushed, for example, when dissatisfied with their formal employment, and pulled because of their interest in the activity involved (Williams, 2007). Moreover, motivations change over time. Necessity-driven entrepreneurship might change into opportunity-driven entrepreneurship when the organization grows and matures (Aidis et al.,

2006; Williams, 2009). Finally, as explained earlier, the entire entrepreneurial process begins in informality. The main challenge for the EE is to foster and drive entrepreneurs towards opportunity-driven entrepreneurship and formality.

11.3   METHOD

A case study based on a network approach was conducted for Bogota in order to understand whether the structure of the EE supports both opportunity and necessity entrepreneurship and fosters the development of the formal economy. As the capital of Colombia, Bogota contributes 20 percent to the GDP and concentrates the largest number of organizations supporting entrepreneurship in the country. However, its rates of formality have not changed significantly in recent years. The case study analyzes the structure of the city's EE, according to the types of organization that comprise it and the types of entrepreneurship that they supported between 2010 and 2012. The case was analyzed using network analysis constructed from surveys and in-depth interviews with the directors of entrepreneurial support institutions.

The initial process began with the identification and selection of the actors of the ecosystem. To this end, all entities that fulfilled three criteria were considered potential actors: (1) the mission of the organization is related to entrepreneurship, whether providing services to the entrepreneurs themselves or acting as a catalyst for the system; (2) its area of activity is the city of Bogota; and (3) its entrepreneurship programs have been active during the last two years. The actors were identified in the database of the Economic Development Secretariat of the Mayor's Office of Bogota and were complemented by researchers using a viral marketing method, which resulted in a preliminary database of 300 organizations. This information was validated considering the aforementioned criteria and using means such as information from press articles available on the organizations' web pages, phone calls and, in some cases, visits to the institutions. At the end of the validation process, a refined database of 155 organizations represented the initial sample for the following process of surveys and interviews.

We contacted each organization formally via email and telephone to encourage participants to complete a paper-and-pencil survey. The survey was structured with 22 questions to obtain information on five general topics such as general characterization of the organization, characterization of the beneficiaries of the organization, type of entrepreneurship supported, organization size and organization networks. At the end of the process, 91 valid surveys were obtained. Subsequently, in-depth interviews were conducted with the organizations that reported the greatest number of contacts in the surveys and/ or others that had not been previously identified but that were reported by other organizations as relevant in the ecosystem. The objective of these interviews was to deepen the understanding of the purpose of the organization and its role in the ecosystem. A total of 28 in-depth interviews were conducted, of which 20 had also responded to the survey and eight were new organizations identified in the process. At the end of the process, 128 organizations were identified as active actors in the city's EE (99 contacted directly and 29 organizations not contacted directly but referred by the organizations participating in the study) and 76 were selected for the analysis because they presented the complete information required for the analysis.

The information obtained from this process of surveys and interviews allowed us to build statistics on the number of beneficiaries that each organization had supported and to classify the ecosystem's organizations according to three main variables: role in the ecosystem, type of supported entrepreneurship and type of support stage. The first variable identifies the role of the organization based on the support activities it carries out in the ecosystem. We classified it as follows: (1) *assistance*, for those organizations that provide assistance services and technical support to entrepreneurs, particularly incubators and accelerators; (2) *knowledge and training*, for those organizations that offer education and training programs to entrepreneurs, as well as research activities, particularly universities and research centers; (3) *regulation and public policy* that includes public organizations that support the entrepreneur through support programs or activities to promote conditions for business development; (4) *financing*, for those organizations that provide financing to entrepreneurs either under credit, capital or donations; and (5) *trade unions*, for those organizations that develop associative support activities for entrepreneurs. The second variable identifies the type of entrepreneurship supported by the organization: *necessity* and *opportunity*; and the third variable is the stage of entrepreneurship on which the organization focuses its support activities: *ideation, business plan, start-up* and *acceleration*.

The results for Bogota's EE are presented in network maps and analyses of the variables selected to characterize it. The information about beneficiaries is compared with data from the Global Entrepreneurship Monitor (GEM) (Quiroga & Vesga, 2010) for the city and with the Bogota Chamber of Commerce's registers of new businesses constituted, when information from the three sources mentioned was available.

11.4   FINDINGS

11.4.1   Ecosystem Beneficiaries

The year 2010 is taken as the reference year to analyze the characteristics of the beneficiaries of Bogota's EE. For this year, there is complete information from various sources related to entrepreneurship and economic formality. Comparisons between these data should be made with caution, since they come from different sources and were created for different purposes, but in general, they offer a rough measure of the effort and results of the EE. According to GEM Bogota, about 670,000 people participated in an early stage of entrepreneurial activity, that is they had the intention to start or had started a business in the past three years; without a differentiation whether they had registered the business (formal) or not (informal) (Quiroga & Vesga, 2010). According to our survey, the support organizations report that they served 116,500 people as beneficiaries, whereas the city's Chamber of Commerce reports the creation of 64,250 new companies.

Comparing these three sources, the total number of entrepreneurs supported by the city's EE falls within the range of the total number of entrepreneurs reported by the GEM (Early Stage Business Activity) and the total number of companies created reported by the city's Chamber of Commerce. The wide gap is due to a very different way to measure entrepreneurial activity. Whereas GEM measures entrepreneurial activity and intentions, the Chamber of Commerce only reports those enterprises that have already been formally registered. Hence the stark difference in terms of numbers.

GEM Bogota reported that 75 percent of the entrepreneurs in the city were motivated by an opportunity, whereas 25 percent initiated entrepreneurial activity due to necessity. The surveyed support organizations report that of the supported start-ups, 27 percent of the entrepreneurs are necessity-driven (31,500 beneficiaries) and 73 percent opportunity-driven (85,000 beneficiaries). In 2010, the city's level of economic informality reached 49.89 percent, the lowest rate in Colombia, while the country average reached around 55 percent (DANE, 2011). In the following section, we analyze the characteristics and composition of the ecosystem that supports entrepreneurship in Bogota.

11.4.2 Ecosystem Characterization

Bogota's EE was characterized according to the following aspects: diversity, centrality, quantity, support stage and density. *Diversity* represents the classification of organizations in the five categories established for the ecosystem; *centrality* represents the location of the organization in the network (those of greater relevance in the ecosystem are in the center, and those of minor relevance are in the periphery); *quantity* establishes the proportion of ecosystem organizations dedicated to opportunity entrepreneurship and necessity entrepreneurship; *support stage* refers to the entrepreneurship stage supported by the organization; and finally, *density*, as a characteristic of articulation, measures the existing relationships between organizations and their relationship potential. These characteristics allow us to analyze the ecosystem in terms

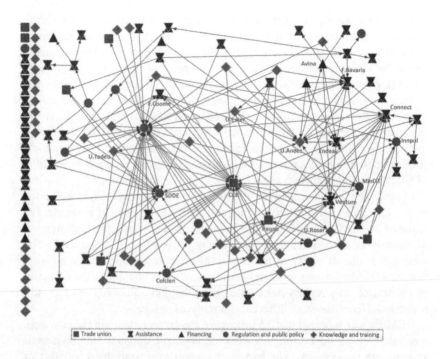

Figure 11.1   Bogota's entrepreneurial ecosystem structure

of its approach, the participation of organizations, their articulation and, in general, their functioning.

11.4.2.1 Diversity

Bogota's EE consists of 76 organizations divided into the five categories described in the method section with the following dispersion: knowledge and training (about 45.5 percent of the organizations identified within the ecosystem), assistance (36.4 percent), regulation and public policy (13.2 percent), financing (3.9 percent) and trade unions (3.9 percent) (see Figure 11.1). The organizations dedicated to assistance, knowledge and training present the greatest participation in the ecosystem, reaching 80 percent of the total. At the same time, the financing and trade union organizations have a low participation in the ecosystem (less than 5 percent each).

11.4.2.2 Quantity

Opportunity entrepreneurship is supported by organizations in all the different categories, with those engaged in knowledge and training and assistance having the greatest participation. At the same time, opportunity entrepreneur-

Table 11.1   Distribution of the organizations in Bogota's EE according to type of entrepreneurship supported

Activities	Opportunity (%)	Necessity (%)
Assistance	21	55
Knowledge and training	52	35
Regulation and public policy	10.5	10
Financing	5.2	0
Trade unions	7.8	0
Total distribution	73.2	26.8

Source: Guerrero & Garcia (2014).

ship is targeted by most actors; on average, 73 percent of the organizations that are part of the ecosystem are geared towards this type of entrepreneurship, compared to 27 percent of organizations that are dedicated to necessity entrepreneurship. Necessity entrepreneurship is supported by organizations mainly focusing on assistance followed by knowledge and training, and regulation and policy. There are no organizations under the financing and trade union categories supporting necessity entrepreneurship (see Table 11.1). The opportunity-driven entrepreneurship network is three times larger than the necessity entrepreneurship network which is consistent with the structure of the beneficiary's population reported by GEM according to the entrepreneurship orientation: 73 percent opportunity-driven and 27 percent necessity-driven.

11.4.2.3 Support stage

Organizations in the EE support different stages of the entrepreneurial process: ideation, business plan, start-up and acceleration. By definition, the first two stages are developed before the company creation. The next two stages, after the company launches its commercial activities, can occur in both informal and formal ways. The stages that receive the greatest support are the ideation and business plan stages, accounting for 56.7 percent of the organizations, while start-up and acceleration stages are supported by 43.3 percent of the organizations (see Table 11.2).

The proportion of beneficiaries within the ecosystem is 28/72 (necessity/ opportunity entrepreneurship beneficiaries). Opportunity-driven entrepreneurship is supported in all the stages of its entrepreneurial process while, in the case of necessity-driven entrepreneurship, support is concentrated in the three initial stages and not in the acceleration stage. For opportunity entrepreneurship, the institutional organizations predominantly support the business plan and start-up stage (respectively 25 percent and 30.2 percent). It is important to note that support tools in acceleration processes are generally designed for

Table 11.2   Distribution of the organizations in Bogota's EE according to support stage

Stage		Proportion of support organization (%)	Type of beneficiaries attended		
			Formal/informal	Necessity (%)	Opportunity (%)
Before launching	Idea	25.4	100% informal beneficiaries	14.3	5.3
	Business plan	31.3		7.2	24
After launching	Start-up	20.4	Mixed formal / informal	6.5	30.2
	Acceleration	22.9	100% formal		12.5
Total		*100*		*28*	*72*

Source: Guerrero & Garcia (2014).

opportunity-driven entrepreneurship, which may explain the lack of attention at this stage for necessity-driven entrepreneurship. In the case of opportunity entrepreneurship, the two stages of greater attention are precisely those that are found before and after company creation, something that does not occur with necessity-driven entrepreneurship that focuses on the first stage.

11.4.2.4 Centrality
The centrality of the organizations in the network was analyzed as a characteristic of articulation, which is, in turn, important in an ecosystem as it allows entrepreneurs to connect with different institutions according to the progress of their enterprise, and as such, support company growth. For example, an entrepreneur who is supported by a university in the idea stage has access to a potential investor for a later stage through university contacts. The average number of relationships per organization in the ecosystem is 6.6; however, the range is very wide and can go from 46 to 0 relationships. There are three levels of centrality, high for organizations with more than 30 relationships, average for organizations with between 15 and 30 relationships and low for organizations with less than 15 relationships. The first level of centrality includes the ecosystem's core organizations. For Bogota, only two organizations appear at this level: Chamber of Commerce (also one of the few existing trade unions in the ecosystem) and SENA (a public organization geared towards business training). These organizations become the main pillars of the ecosystem.

The second level of centrality includes the node organizations that were identified as those that, despite lacking a significant number of relationships, have a much higher number than the average and are connected with different types of organization. These organizations have the potential to become core organizations in the ecosystem. Bogota has seven of them, mainly

Table 11.3   *Network characteristics according to type of entrepreneurship supported in Bogota's EE*

Type of entrepreneurship	Diversity	Quantity	Centrality	Density
Opportunity	High	High	High	High
Necessity	Low	Low	Low	Low

Source: Guerrero & Garcia (2014).

involved in technical assistance. It is important to highlight that 51 percent of ecosystem organizations are in the lower level of centrality, with very few interconnections with the ecosystem; these organizations are usually new in the ecosystem or they address very specific needs of certain types of entrepreneurs, such as the vulnerable population. Organizations dedicated to opportunity entrepreneurship are located in the center, while those focusing on necessity organizations are located in the periphery of the network. The core support organizations of the ecosystems are different according to the type of entrepreneurship. The Chamber of Commerce (trade union organization[1]) and SENA (assistance – government organization) are at the core of the network focusing on opportunity entrepreneurship, whereas with no apparent core node the economic development secretary of the Mayor's Office is considered the main node in charge of necessity-driven entrepreneurship.

Overall, these figures present a nascent ecosystem, with few articulators but with great growth potential given the number of organizations. The main articulation in the ecosystem is given by the organizations that support opportunity entrepreneurship more than the organizations that support necessity entrepreneurship.

11.4.2.5 Density

In terms of density, the opportunity entrepreneurship network is almost double the necessity entrepreneurship network. Organizations dedicated to supporting opportunity entrepreneurship have an average of 8 percent of the total possible links with other organizations in the ecosystem, while those dedicated to supporting necessity entrepreneurship have an average of 4.7 percent of the total possible links in the ecosystem. It is possible that, as the number of organizations in a network grows, the density of the network also increases given the organizations' possibilities of establishing more relationships. These levels of connection are characteristic of young EE (Isenberg, 2015).

To conclude, the network focusing on opportunity entrepreneurship reaches significantly higher values for these variables compared to the network for necessity entrepreneurship (see Table 11.3).

11.5   DISCUSSION AND CONCLUSIONS

The challenge for an EE in an emerging economy, such as Bogota, is twofold: (1) to achieve entrepreneurial growth and consolidation; and (2) to achieve greater formality. Bogota has a structured and diversified EE with a lower level of informality than the rest of the country. The ecosystem is composed of entrepreneurs (beneficiaries) and support organizations (assistance, knowledge and education, regulation and government, financing and trade unions). In Bogota, the EE in general supports entrepreneurs regardless of whether they are opportunity entrepreneurs or necessity ones, as advocated by Fuentelsaz et al. (2015). However, the support organizations assist entrepreneurs according to their profile; that is, whether they are necessity-driven, opportunity-driven or both. They also support organizations' segment entrepreneurs according to the stage in which they are in their entrepreneurial process and focus their support activities on a selected group of entrepreneurs in specific stages.

In the idea and business plan stages, support organizations assist informal organizations because the companies have not yet been created (Gartner, 1995). In these stages, the organizations support opportunity and necessity entrepreneurship to the same extent, mainly in terms of technical assistance and education. They aim to prepare the entrepreneurial processes for formalization. In the start-up and acceleration stages, all kinds of supportive organizations are active, and it is in these stages that the beneficiary companies are formally created.

The organizations of the ecosystem support the entrepreneur in their development process, but as entrepreneurs grow and formalization is not achieved, accompaniment is reduced and instead geared towards formal companies. Thus, while the ecosystem supports the same proportion of necessity and opportunity entrepreneurs in the early and later stages of company creation, there is a clear focus during later stages on opportunity entrepreneurs that are more closely related with economic formality. In this sense, we argue that the more the ecosystem satisfies entrepreneurs in the ideation stage, the more entrepreneurs will identify the benefits of staying connected to the ecosystem and the more they will tend to reach a formal start-up stage and pursue the acceleration stage.

Consistent with the idea proposed by Fuentelsaz et al. (2015), our study reveals consistency between the ecosystem and its environment. In particular, the ratio of support organizations according to the type of beneficiaries served is the same as the ratio between the type of beneficiary entrepreneurs; i.e. opportunity entrepreneurs to necessity entrepreneurs (75% versus 25 percent, respectively). At the same time, we observe that in Bogota, networks of support organizations that promote opportunity entrepreneurships that are close to economic formality or in advanced stages of entrepreneurship engage with more diverse organizations which are, in turn, more solidly articulated, with the main organizations being at the center of the network. Networks of the ecosystem that support necessity entrepreneurship engage with fewer organizations, have low levels of articulation and diversity and focus on public and private technical assistance and education, but do not provide financing or trade union support.

Institutional articulation is fundamental to the accompaniment to entrepreneurship (Fuentelsaz et al., 2015). Enterprises grow and transform, and each institution's portfolio of services caters to the beneficiary's level of development and requirements. Once the enterprise reaches a higher level of development, the articulated work between institutions allows it to be accompanied by another institution with adequate services for that level. In emerging economies, this is essential when transforming necessity entrepreneurship into formal entrepreneurship. Supporting necessity entrepreneurship is a step that could potentially lead to formality and institutional articulation favors this transition towards formality. The network that supports necessity entrepreneurship must have more organizations and be more closely articulated to the network that supports opportunity entrepreneurship given the formality challenge in this kind of entrepreneurship.

A single type of support institution does not generate an impact on entrepreneurship because entrepreneurship is dynamic and varied. Different types of institutions are required for the needs of different types of entrepreneurship and stages (van der Zwan et al., 2016). The transition from informal to formal economies can be supported by EE with networks that provide benefits to opportunity and necessity entrepreneurs. The integration of these networks is fundamental for the transition, particularly in emerging economies. These institutions must focus on providing greater support for the entrepreneurship process than for a particular type of entrepreneurship.

Finally, contrasting network measures such as quantity, diversity, density and centrality with the support stage and motivation behind the start-up helps us to understand the ecosystem and the potential dynamics behind the lack of formalization for many of the start-ups in this context. Although the study does not present an explicit relationship between type of entrepreneurship (necessity/opportunity) and economic formality, ecosystem measures provide clues regarding this relationship. Thus, the measures showed low levels of indicators for necessity entrepreneurship and high levels for opportunity entrepreneurship. Table 11.3 shows that a way to encourage formality through the ecosystem is to increase the levels of quantity, diversity, support stage and centrality in the support networks for necessity entrepreneurship. This clue opens up a whole possibility of academic research such as public policy management for strengthening the EE.

11.6   IMPLICATIONS, VALUE, LIMITATIONS

The analysis of networks in EE can help us to understand how ecosystems are related to economic formality. Generally, formality has been related to the type of entrepreneurship, particularly opportunity entrepreneurship, but there are other entrepreneurial characteristics that can better demonstrate this relationship such as the stage of the entrepreneurial process. Although the main study was developed in reference to ecosystem organizations, the comparison with studies that characterize the entrepreneur (such as the GEM), and its results (such as the analysis of the creation of companies), help to provide a comprehensive vision of the entrepreneurial process and the functioning of an EE. Future studies on EE should include both support organizations and entrepreneurs.

This case study provides many potential research questions and questions that public policy makers should ask. For example, what happens with entrepreneurs who do not formalize and continue with their economic activities? Should EE in emerging economies prioritize particular types of entrepreneurship? How can we identify these entrepreneurs within the entrepreneurship stages and link them to the ecosystem to help them grow and consolidate? From the perspective of support organizations, there is a great support network. Yet, the ecosystem does not capture the totality of entrepreneurs in the city. Do we need more organizations or different forms of relationships in the EE? Likewise, formality in emerging economies does not occur as it does in consolidated economies, so what kind of value should support organizations provide for the transition from informality to formality? It is evident that tangible benefits are needed for the entrepreneur to link with the ecosystem and perceive the value of formalization. Another important aspect is the formalization of support institutions. The study has focused on the relationship with the formal institutional support to entrepreneurship, but there are also informal supports for entrepreneurs such as family and friends who, under informal structures, also support the entrepreneur's development, an aspect that has not yet been analyzed. It could be interesting to examine the structure of informal network support to entrepreneurship in a subsequent study.

It is important for studies on EE in emerging countries to include the relationship with economic formality, either from the perspective of support from organizations or from the perspective of entrepreneurs' interest in formalization. The case study of the EE in Bogota contributes to the theoretical development of the EE concept from the network approach. The results offer elements for the design of public policies that support entrepreneurship and formality, such as the identification of the absence of financing and trade union organizations to support early stages, the limitations involved in the formalization of necessity entrepreneurship and the characterization of the organizations and beneficiaries that constitute the EE.

NOTES

1. The Chamber of Commerce is classified as a trade union organization because the first criteria to classify the organizations in this study is based on their mission. In any case, the Chamber of Commerce develops different activities in the ecosystem, like providing technical assistance, promoting public policy and education, among others.

REFERENCES

Arruda, C., Nogueira, V. S., & Costa, V. (2013). The Brazilian entrepreneurial ecosystem of startups: An analysis of entrepreneurship determinants in Brazil as seen from the OECD pillars. *Journal of Entrepreneurship and Innovation Management, 2*(3), 17–57.

Auerswald, P. E. (2015). Enabling entrepreneurial ecosystems: Insights from ecology to inform effective entrepreneurship policy. *Kauffman Foundation Research Series on City, Metro, and Regional Entrepreneurship*.

Autio, E., & Fu, K. (2015). Economic and political institutions and entry into formal and informal entrepreneurship. *Asia Pacific Journal of Management, 32*(1), 67–94.

Bahrami, H., & Evans, S. (1995). Flexible re-cycling and high-technology entrepreneurship. *California Management Review, 37*(3), 62–89.

Breslin, D. (2008). A revolutionary approach to the study of entrepreneurship. *International Journal of Management Reviews, 10*(4), 399–423.

Breznitz, D., & Taylor, M. (2014). The communal roots of entrepreneurial–technological growth–social fragmentation and stagnation: Reflection on Atlanta's technology cluster. *Entrepreneurship and Regional Development, 26*(3–4), 375–96.

Brown, R., & Mason, C. (2017). Looking inside the spiky bits: A critical review and conceptualization of entrepreneurial ecosystems. *Small Business Economics, 49*(1), 11–30.

Bruton, G. D., Ketchen, Jr., D. J., & Ireland, R. D. (2013). Entrepreneurship as a solution to poverty. *Journal of Business Venturing, 28*(6), 683–89.

Carter, N. M., Gartner, W. B., Shaver, K. G., & Gatewood, E. J. (2003). The career reasons of nascent entrepreneurs. *Journal of Business Venturing, 18*(1), 13–39.

Castells, M., & Portes, A. (1989). World underneath: The origins, dynamics and effects of the informal economy. In: A. Portes, M. Castells & L. A. Benton (Eds), *The Informal Economy: Studies in advanced and less developed countries* (pp. 11–37). Baltimore, MD: Johns Hopkins University Press.

Cheng, K., & Low, P. (2006). Cultural obstacles in growing entrepreneurship: A study in Singapore. *Journal of Management Development, 25*(2), 169–82.

Darnihamedani, P., & Hessels, J. (2016). Human capital as a driver of innovation among necessity-based entrepreneurs. *International Review of Entrepreneurship, 14*(1), 1–23.

Deli, F. (2011). Opportunity and necessity entrepreneurship: Local unemployment and the small firm effect. *Journal of Management Policy and Practice, 12*(4), 38–57.

Departamento Administrativo Nacional de Estadística (DANE) (2011). Press bulletin, February.

Feld, B. (2012). *Startup Communities: Building an entrepreneurial ecosystem in your city*. Hoboken, NJ: John Wiley & Sons.

Fuentelsaz, L., González, C., Maícas, J. P., & Montero, J. (2015). How different formal institutions affect opportunity and necessity entrepreneurship. *Business Research Quarterly*, *18*(4), 246–58.

Gallin, D. (2001). Propositions on trade unions and informal employment in time of globalization. *Antipode*, *19*(4), 531–49.

Gartner, W. B. (1995). Aspects of organizational emergence. In: I. Bull, H. Thomas & G. Willard (Eds), *Entrepreneurship: Perspectives on Theory Building*, pp. 67–86. Oxford: Pergamon Press.

Gerxhani, K (2004). The informal sector in developed and less developed countries: A literature survey. *Public Choice*, *120*(2), 267–300.

Guerrero, A., & García, O. (2014). *Retos en la Transformación del Ecosistema de Emprendimiento de Bogota, 2010–2012*. Bogota: School of Management, Universidad de los Andes and Secretaría de Desarrollo Económico de Bogotá.

Hechavarria, D. M., & Reynolds, P. D. (2009). Cultural norms and business start-ups: The impact of national values on opportunity and necessity entrepreneurs. *International Entrepreneurship and Management Journal*, *5*(4), 417.

International Labour Office (ILO) (2018). *World Employment Social Outlook 2018: Greening with jobs*. Geneva: ILO, Recommendation 204.

Isenberg, D. J. (2010). How to start an entrepreneurial revolution. *Harvard Business Review*, *88*(6), 40–50.

Isenberg, D. J. (2015). The entrepreneurship ecosystem strategy as a new paradigm for economic policy: Principles for cultivating entrepreneurship. Based on a presentation at the Institute of International and European Affairs, May 12, 2011, Dublin.

Jacobides, M., Cennamo, C., & Gawer, A. (2016). Towards a theory of ecosystems. *Strategic Management*, *2018*(39), 2255–76.

Jaén, I., Fernández-Serrano, J., & Liñán, F. (2013). Valores culturales, nivel de ingresos y actividad emprendedora. *Revista de economía mundial*, *35*, 35–51.

Kazanjian, R. K. (1988). Relation of dominant problems to stages of growth in technology-based new ventures. *Academy of Management Journal*, *31*(2), 257–79.

Loossens, R., García, J., Llisterri, J. J., & Kamiya, M. (2008). *High Growth SMEs, Innovation Entrepreneurship and Intellectual Assets*. Washington, DC: Multilateral Investment Fund, Inter-American Development Bank.

Lozano, B. (1989). *The Invisible Work Force: Transforming American business with outside and home-based workers*. New York: Free Press.

Maritz, A. (2004), New Zealand necessity entrepreneurs. *International Journal of Entrepreneurship and Small Business*, *1*(3–4), 255–64.

Mason, C., & Brown, R. (2014). Entrepreneurial ecosystems and growth-oriented entrepreneurship. Final Report to OECD, Paris, *30*(1), 77–102.

Moore, J. F. (1993). Predators and prey: A new ecology of competition. *Harvard Business Review*, *71*(3), 75–86.

Motoyama, Y., & Knowlton, K. (2017). Examining the connections within the startup ecosystem: A case study of St Louis. *Entrepreneurship Research Journal*, *7*(1).

Neck, H. M., Meyer, G. D., Cohen, B., & Corbett, A. C. (2004). An entrepreneurial system view of new venture creation. *Journal of Small Business Management*, *42*(2), 190–208.

Organisation for Economic Co-operation and Development (OECD) (2009). *Promoting Entrepreneurship, Employment and Business Competitiveness: The experience of Barcelona*. LEED Program Local Development Review Series. Paris: OECD.

Oxenfeldt, A. R. (1943). *New Firms and Free Enterprise*. Washington, DC: American Council on Public Affairs.

Portes, A., & Walton, J. (1981). *Labor, Class and the International System*. New York: Academic Press.

Poschke, M. (2013). Entrepreneurs out of necessity: A snapshot. *Applied Economics Letters, 20*(7), 658–63.

Quiroga, R., & Vesga, R. (2010). *Global Entrepreneurship Monitor Reporte Anual Bogotá 2010–2011*. Bogota: Universidad de Los Andes, Facultad de Administración, Cámara de Comercio de Bogotá.

Raijman, R. (2001). Mexican immigrants and informal self-employment in Chicago. *Human Organization, 60*(1), 47–55.

Roberts, E. B., & Eesley, C. (2009). *Entrepreneurial Impact: The role of MIT*. Kansas City, MI: Kauffman Foundation.

Sassen, S. (1997). *Informalisation in Advanced Market Economies*. Issues in Development Discussion Paper 20. Geneva: International Labour Office.

Singer, S., Amoros, E., & Moska, D. (2015). *Global Entrepreneurship Monitor: 2014 global report*. London: Global Entrepreneurship Research Association.

Snyder, K. A. (2004). Routes to the informal economy in New York's East Village: Crisis, economics and identity. *Sociological Perspectives, 47*(2), 215–40.

Spigel, B. (2016). Developing and governing entrepreneurial ecosystems: The structure of entrepreneurial support programs in Edinburgh, Scotland. *International Journal of Innovation and Regional Development, 7*(2), 141–60.

Spilling, O. R. (1996). The entrepreneurial system: On entrepreneurship in the context of a mega-event. *Journal of Business Research, 36*(1), 91–103.

Stam, E. (2015). Entrepreneurial ecosystems and regional policy: A sympathetic critique. *European Planning Studies, 23*(9), 1759–69.

Tebaldi, E., & Mohan, R. (2010). Institutions and poverty. *Journal of Development Studies, 46*(6), 1047–66.

Thai, M. T. T., & Turkina, E. (2012). Determinants of formal entrepreneurship versus informal entrepreneurship at the macro level. In: *Academy of Management Proceedings*. New York: Academy of Management, August.

Tsujimoto, M., Kajikawa, Y., Tomita, J., & Matsumoto, Y. (2017). A review of the ecosystem concept: Towards coherent ecosystem design. *Technological Forecasting and Social Change, 139*, 49–58.

Van der Zwan, P., Thurik, R., Verheul, I., & Hessels, J. (2016). Factors influencing the entrepreneurial engagement of opportunity and necessity entrepreneurs. *Eurasian Business Review, 6*(3), 273–95.

Van Stel, A., Storey, D. J., & Thurik, A. R. (2007). The effect of business regulations on nascent and young business entrepreneurship. *Small Business Economics, 28*(2–3), 171–86.

Vogel, P. (2013). *The Employment Outlook for Youth: Building entrepreneurship ecosystems as a way forward*. Conference Proceedings of the G20 Youth Forum.

Webb, J. W., Bruton, G. D., Tihanyi, L., & Ireland, R. D. (2013). Research on entrepreneurship in the informal economy: Framing a research agenda. *Journal of Business Venturing, 28*(5), 598–614.

Webb, J. W., Tihanyi, L., Ireland, R. D., & Sirmon, D. G. (2009). You say illegal, I say legitimate: Entrepreneurship in the informal economy. *Academy of Management Review, 34*(3), 492–510.

Wennekers, S., Van Wennekers, A., Thurik, R., & Reynolds, P. (2005). Nascent entrepreneurship and the level of economic development. *Small Business Economics, 24*(3), 293–309.

Wessner, C. (2004). *Entrepreneurship and the Innovation Ecosystem Policy Lessons from the United States.* US Discussion Papers on Entrepreneurship, Growth and Public Policy # 4604. National Academies and Max Planck Institute for Research into Economic Systems.

Williams, C. C. (2007). Entrepreneurs operating in the informal economy: Necessity or opportunity driven? *Journal of Small Business and Entrepreneurship, 20*(3), 309–19.

Williams, C. C. (2008). Beyond necessity-driven versus opportunity-driven entrepreneurship: A study of informal entrepreneurs in England, Russia and Ukraine. *International Journal of Entrepreneurship and Innovation, 9*(3), 157–65.

Williams, C. C. (2009). Informal entrepreneurs and their motives: A gender perspective. *International Journal of Gender and Entrepreneurship.*

Williams, C. C., & Nadin, S. (2010). Entrepreneurship and the informal economy: An overview. *Journal of Developmental Entrepreneurship, 15*(4), 361–78.

Williams, C. C., & Nadin, S. (2012). Tackling the hidden enterprise culture: Government policies to support the formalization of informal entrepreneurship. *Entrepreneurship and Regional Development, 24*(9–10), 895–915.

Williams, C. C., & Round, J. (2007). Entrepreneurship and the informal economy: A study of Ukraine's hidden enterprise culture. *Journal of Developmental Entrepreneurship, 12*(1), 119–36.

Zacharakis, A. L., Shepherd, D. A., & Coombs, J. E. (2003). The development of venture-capital-backed internet companies: An ecosystem perspective. *Journal of Business Venturing, 18*(2), 217–31.

12. Epilogue: The systems perspective on economic development: The past, the present and the future

Rhiannon Pugh, Jana Schmutzler and Alexandra Tsvetkova

Schumpeter (2003 [1911]) in his early work envisioned an "entrepreneur as innovator" to be a key figure in driving economic development. As a result, entrepreneurial and innovation processes have been of interest not only for academics, but also for public policy makers.

In this context, systemic approaches to economic development – such as national (Lundvall, 2007) and regional innovation systems (IS) (Cook, 1998), entrepreneurial (Spigel, 2017; Stam, 2015) and innovation ecosystems (Adner & Kapoor, 2010) as well as business (Moore, 1996) and knowledge ecosystems (Clarysse, Wright, Bruneel & Mahajan, 2014) – have gained popularity. Containing elements of previous concepts such as industrial districts (Marshall, 1920 [1890]) or clusters (Porter, 2000), learning regions and the industrial milieu (Camagni, 1995), the (eco)system perspective is mainly based on the analogy to the natural ecosystems (Audretsch, Cunningham, Kuratko, Lehmann & Menter, 2019). As such, it reflects the assumption that economic agents interact among themselves and with their environment and these interactions explain differential economic outputs and outcomes of a region (Acs, Stam, Audretsch & O'Connor, 2017).

The interest in the systemic view on innovation, entrepreneurship and economic development is clearly growing in academic and policy circles. This is not surprising given the long-standing efforts to better account for the interconnectedness, dynamism and the complex nature of economic and social processes as advocated by the heterodox economists, economic geographers, innovation management researchers and development scholars.

As of today, the IS and entrepreneurial ecosystems (EE) literatures are highly popular but separate concepts. Despite the obvious linkages and overlap in the topics and approaches, the dialog between the two has been limited (Alvedalen & Boschma, 2017; Stam & Spigel, 2018). This edited book aims to bridge the two traditions through the lessons one perspective can learn from the other. To do so, it systematizes similarities and differences between the approaches and explores synergies and the limitations in the concepts' ability to jointly explain various dimensions of regional socio-economic performance and to guide economic development policies.

The national IS framework was originally introduced more than 30 years ago (e.g. Lundvall, 1988) and evolved over time considerably giving rise to a variety of its sectoral, regional and local modifications. Most importantly, the IS frameworks were rigorously tried and tested globally (Uriona-Maldonado, dos Santos & Varvakis, 2012), most notably (but not exclusively) by members of the Globelics community (Cassiolato & Lastres, 2008; Dutrénit & Sutz, 2014). In contrast, the newly popular EE perspective is still largely untested outside of the large urban or otherwise successful centers in Europe and North America (Spigel, 2018).

In this collection, we do not attempt to delineate or impose divisions among different approaches within this broad church of systemic thinking on innovation, entrepreneurship and economic development. Instead, our aim is to unite differing perspectives, but with underlying principles of interconnectivity, dynamism and evolution when examining socio-economic processes. Our keyword was inclusivity: inclusivity on the basis of theoretical perspectives, nationality, mother tongue, gender and ethnicity. On the topic of diversity, we need to expand the knowledge field along an array of dimensions, which include nationality, ethnicity, culture, religion, language, gender, education, experience, occupation, knowledge mix and industrial mix, among others (Karlsson, Rickardsson & Wincent, 2019). We, of course, cannot claim that this edited book comprehensively covers all of these issues but it takes clear steps in contributing to this agenda.

Overall, this collection goes beyond the mainstream narrow approach to the economy, considering alternative perspectives such as environmental, social and necessity entrepreneurship. Here we see considerations of diaspora communities (Andonova et al.), social entrepreneurs (Peerally & De Fuentes; Gonzalez et al.), the sustainability view (Cassiolato et al.) and alternative Global South-situated perspectives (Kantis et al.; La Rovere et al.). This wide range of epistemologies, viewpoints and cases illustrate just how far we can go in employing systemic approaches to our understanding of entrepreneurship, innovation and development.

Conceptually, the contributions are broad. Some authors have taken methodologies from the extant literature on IS and EE and followed these quite closely in applying them to their cases. Others have taken a more blended approach, picking and choosing elements of the theory that speak best to their cases and orientations. What this shows is how flexible we can be in applying the systems perspectives proposed in the literature. We can wholesale replicate the existing formulations and test them in our own cases, or we can perform some contortions to adjust theory in order to fit specific contexts. Through this diversity of approaches, our bridging potential increases. We can see the similarities and differences between various approaches when they are applied "on the ground" in different places, and we can start to draw out the interconnections.

An increasing theorization of the differently evolving IS and EE perspectives was clearly a hot topic for the community, and we received several contributions that attempted, on a theoretical plane, to establish the similarities and differences between the older IS approaches and the newer EE approaches. Initially we intended to perform a unification of diverse perspectives and give some indication as to the future of (eco)systemic thinking. However, upon curating this collection, such a task looks increasingly like a fool's errand. Instead, we luxuriate in the diversity and differences and move away from trying to rationalize or unify too much. The evolution of theory is clear to see: the earlier IS approaches, whilst still popular and valid as this collection attests, have arguably evolved and diversified, and recombined with other ideas from neighboring fields, into (eco)systemic perspectives. Whilst bridging, drawing out similarities and differences and cross-examining the links in the theoretical evolutions and shifts is an interesting and valuable task, focusing overly on a singular and simplistic narrative may not be wise. If this book shows anything, it is that theory can be applied in a variety of places in a variety of ways, and a concept developed in one context can, and indeed should, be interrogated and tested in diverse contexts, be they geographical, sectoral or epistemological.

A task for us as editors, or perhaps curators, of this diverse collection of work is to offer some thoughts on the future directions in IS and EE research. This feels like a tall mountain to climb, and we can only partially cover the possibilities and potentials that this mode of investigation and policy practice could entail. Of course, we do not have a crystal ball. However, from reading the works in this book collection, but also immersing ourselves in the literature pertaining to the IS and EE more broadly, we see a number of future possible pathways or directions we could take in pushing forward these theories, updating them, making them more relevant to the lived experiences on the ground in different global settings and bridging them further.

The first pathway we have addressed in this book is the bridging issue. We have attempted to bring IS and EE under one roof and consider them holistically and complementarily rather than as opposing or competing viewpoints on innovation and entrepreneurship.

Thinking more broadly and long term, however, we highlight a handful of other directions that work in IS and EE could be taken in. Firstly, we highlight the possibility of the (eco)systemic frameworks on entrepreneurship and innovation, when viewed and applied through a policy lens, to unite the top-down and bottom-up approaches to economic development in a more harmonious manner. A more place-based policy view (Barca, McCann & Rodriguez-Pose, 2012; Morgan, 2013) has recently gained in popularity, especially as a part of research and policy practice focused on entrepreneurship and innovation within the smart specialization perspective. Both research and policy interventions increasingly acknowledge the value of a more context-specific and less one-size-fits-all approach to economic development. Within the dichotomy of the place-based versus place-neutral policy approaches to economic development (Barca et al., 2012), the systemic approaches, both IS and EE, clearly lean towards the locally derived, context-specific and potentially more bottom-up angle that can be tailored specifically to local circumstances, needs and capabilities. The chapters in this collection go a long way in showing how systemic approaches can be reinterpreted and reapplied in local settings in interesting ways, drawing on the same core principles but producing policies and perspectives that are very different from one another.

That said, the process of adapting frameworks and blueprints, such as IS and EE, to the local circumstances throws up clear challenges and issues, which this collection has also started to unpack. For instance, what happens to our approaches and frameworks when we take them out of their comfort zones and apply them in new and different settings? How relevant and tenable are they then? In the particular case of EE, how do we create approaches and frameworks for the highly informalized settings, which do not have the organizations and institutions listed in the main guiding literatures (for example, Isenberg, 2010)? Many important questions arise when we start thinking about applications of the IS and EE frameworks in the informal economy settings (Sheikh & Bhaduri, 2019). The IS approaches, in contrast to the EE, were tested in such circumstances. The chapter by Guerrero Alvarado and Servantie analyzes the role of the EE in transforming informal entrepreneurs into formal ones, which is likely to be an important research question for countries with high degrees of economic informality.

When we do transpose theory and policy approaches into very different settings from those in which they originated and have been tested, it is not only specific concepts and tools that need to be examined and re-examined, but also our underlying ideas and outlooks as well. To be specific, when we try to apply the IS and EE perspectives in very diverse settings, we need to take a step back and think about the basic concepts of innovation and entrepreneurship and how they can be applied in these contexts. As highlighted above, in many parts of the world just thinking about entrepreneurs and innovation in a high-tech mode can be unsuitable (Tsvetkova, Pugh & Schmutzler, 2019), especially in situations of high informality and quite a basic nature of many entrepreneurial ventures. The chapters by Gonzalez et al. and Guerrero Alvarado and Servantie in this collection illustrate this point. In such settings, shifting our ideas of entrepreneurship and innovation towards the concepts of social innovation and entrepreneurship may hold promise. The latter offers the possibility to unite and combine economic growth and development with more social elements, which might be much more relevant in many parts of the world.

Social entrepreneurship is a promising concept to investigate further within the domain of the EE work because of its potential to combine social justice and solidarity with market activities (Defourny & Nyssens, 2010; Benneworth & Cunha, 2015), to create and implement social change (van der Have & Rubalcaba, 2016) or to create "better futures" (Pol and Ville, 2009). As with any rapidly evolving field containing new or different perspectives, the work on social entrepreneurship and innovation requires further theorization and testing in diverse contexts to increase its conceptual clarity, empirical validity and to better define its contributions to theory and practice (Isaksen and Trippl, 2016; Martin and Osberg, 2007; Cajaiba-Santana, 2014).

Much of what these discussions about adjusting our theoretical constructs and exploring alternative conceptualization come down to is whether we need different methods and approaches to studying economic development in different geographical contexts, or whether we can use the same theories globally. An important avenue for future research is thinking about this transplantation process from a theoretical perspective – how we use and adjust our frameworks depending on the context – but also considering the methods and tools we employ in different settings. Do we need to develop a new range of approaches when taking innovation and entrepreneurship theories into new environments, or can we rely on the "usual suspects" (Nordling & Pugh, 2019) that have already been tried and tested extensively? The literature has already started to explore this question; for instance, a recent special issue in the *African Journal of Science, Technology and Innovation* (Raunio, Pugh, Sheikh & Egbetokun, 2019) includes many contributions by the members of the Globelics community on the issue. It is clearly an issue that will require much attention and empirical research going forwards, not least by researchers interested in the IS and EE approaches.

In addition to these future directions that we have identified as a result of undertaking this book project, there are other gaps in the current EE and IS literatures that researchers have highlighted. For instance, more evolutionary and dynamic perspectives are required to understand how systems change over time (Mack and Meyer, 2016). Also, we need to more centrally place learning into our conceptualization of EE, because without learning, the system cannot evolve and grow (Pugh, Soetanto, Jack & Hamilton, 2019). Alvedalen and Boschma (2017), in their review of the EE framework, identify four particular areas for development, which we also see as relevant to the evolution of the IS concepts: clarifying the analytical framework; integrating insights from the network theory; understanding how and what institutions impact upon the ecosystem; and incorporating comparative and multi-scalar perspectives. We add our future pathways discussion on top of these, not instead of.

Overall, it is very clear that there is a massive amount of work to be done in theorizing and rendering the IS and EE approaches more useful for policy interventions. This is good news for the research community: this work will keep us occupied for a while and there is clearly more scope for special sessions, special issues, books, collections, blogs and conversations on these topics. Without doubt, more future pathways will open up, into an overlapping and interweaving maze, as we progress with this project. For now, we embrace this complexity and look forward to seeing how the EE and IS frameworks will evolve, shape each other and be shaped by other concepts and ideas while applied in an increasing array of locations and sectors.

REFERENCES

Acs, Z. J., Stam, E., Audretsch, D. B., & O'Connor, A. (2017). The lineages of the entrepreneurial ecosystem approach. *Small Business Economics*, *49*(1), 1–10.

Adner, R., & Kapoor, R. (2010). Value creation in innovation ecosystems: How the structure of technological interdependence affects firm performance in new technology generations. *Strategic Management Journal*, *31*(3), 306–33.

Alvedalen, J., & Boschma, R. (2017). A critical review of entrepreneurial ecosystems research: Towards a future research agenda. *European Planning Studies*, *25*(6), 887–903.

Audretsch, D. B., Cunningham, J. A., Kuratko, D. F., Lehmann, E. E., & Menter, M. (2019). Entrepreneurial ecosystems: Economic, technological, and societal impacts. *Journal of Technology Transfer*, *44*(2), 313–25.

Barca, F., McCann, P., & Rodriguez-Pose, A. (2012). The case for regional development intervention: Place-based versus place-neutral approaches. *Journal of Regional Science,* *52*(1), 134–52.

Benneworth, P., & Cunha, J. (2015). Universities' contributions to social innovation: Reflections in theory and practice. *European Journal of Innovation Management*, *18*(4), 508–27.

Cajaiba-Santana, G. (2014). Social innovation: Moving the field forward. A conceptual framework. *Technological Forecasting and Social Change*, *82*, 42–51.

Camagni, R. P. (1995). The concept of innovative milieu and its relevance for public policies in European lagging regions. *Papers in Regional Science*, *74*(4), 317–40.

Cassiolato, J. E., & Lastres, H. M. (2008). *Discussing Innovation and Development: Converging points between the Latin American school and the innovation systems perspective?* Georgia Institute of Technology.

Chataway, J., Hanlin, R., & Kaplinsky, R. (2014). Inclusive innovation: An architecture for policy development. *Innovation and Development*, *4*(1), 33–54.

Clarysse, B., Wright, M., Bruneel, J., & Mahajan, A. (2014). Creating value in ecosystems: Crossing the chasm between knowledge and business ecosystems. *Research Policy*, *43*(7), 1164–76.

Cooke, P. (1998). Introduction: Origins of the concept. SSRN. https://ssrn.com/abstract=1497770

Defourny, J., & Nyssens, M. (2010). Conceptions of social enterprise and social entrepreneurship in Europe and the United States: Convergences and divergences. *Journal of Social Entrepreneurship, 1*(1), 32–53.

Dutrénit, G., & Sutz, J. (Eds) (2014). *National Innovation Systems, Social Inclusion and Development: The Latin American experience.* Cheltenham, UK and Northampton, MA, USA: Edward Elgar Publishing.

Isaksen, A., & Trippl, M. (2016). 4 path development in different regional innovation systems: A conceptual analysis. In: M. D. Parrilli, R. D. Fitjar & A. Rodriguez-Pose (Eds), *Innovation Drivers and Regional Innovation Strategies* (pp. 82–100). London: Routledge.

Isenberg, D. J. (2010). How to start an entrepreneurial revolution. *Harvard Business Review 88*(6), 40–50.

Karlsson, C., Rickardsson, J., & Wincent, J. (2019). Diversity, innovation and entrepreneurship: Where are we and where should we go in future studies? *Small Business Economics.*

Lundvall, B.-Å. (1988). Innovation as an interactive process: From user-producer interaction to the national innovation systems. In: G. Dosi, C. Freeman, R. Nelson, G. Silverberg, & L. Soete (Eds), *Technology and Economic Theory.* London: Pinter.

Lundvall, B.-Å. (2007). *Innovation System Research: Where it came from and where it might go.* Globelics Working Paper 2007-01.

Mack, E., & Meyer, H. (2016). The evolutionary dynamics of entrepreneurial ecosystems. *Urban Studies, 53*(10), 2118–33.

Marshall, A. (1920 [1890]). *Principles of Economics.* London: Macmillan.

Martin, R. L., & Osberg, S. (2007). Social entrepreneurship: The case for definition. www.ngobiz.org/picture/File/Social%20Enterpeuneur-The%20Case%20of%20Definition.pdf

Moore, J. F. (1996). *The Death of Competition: Leadership and strategy in the age of business ecosystems.* New York: HarperBusiness.

Morgan, K. (2013). The regional state in the era of smart specialisation. *EKONOMIAZ: Revista vasca de Economía, 83*(2), 103–26.

Nordling, N., & Pugh, R. (2019). Beyond the "usual suspects": Alternative qualitative methods for innovation policy studies. *African Journal of Science, Technology, Innovation and Development,* 1–10.

Pol, E., & Ville, S. (2009). Social innovation: Buzz word or enduring term? *Journal of Socio-Economics, 38*(6), 878–85.

Porter, M. E. (2000). Location, competition, and economic development: Local clusters in a global economy. *Economic Development Quarterly, 14*(1), 15–34.

Pugh, R., Soetanto, D., Jack, S. L., & Hamilton, E. (2019). Developing local entrepreneurial ecosystems through integrated learning initiatives: The Lancaster case. *Small Business Economics,* 1–15.

Raunio, M., Pugh, R., Sheikh, F. A., & Egbetokun, A. (2019). Introduction: Importance of methodological diversity for innovation system studies. *African Journal of Science, Technology, Innovation and Development, 11*(4), 465–67. doi:10.1080/20421338.2018.1530406

Schumpeter, J. (2003 [1911]). *Theorie der wirtschaftlichen Entwicklung.* In: *Joseph Alois Schumpeter* (pp. 5–59). Boston, MA: Springer.

Sheikh, F. A., & Bhaduri, S. (2019). Policy space for informal sector grassroots innovations: Towards a "bottom-up" narrative. *International Development Planning Review,* 1–24.

Spigel, B. (2017). The relational organization of entrepreneurial ecosystems. *Entrepreneurship Theory and Practice, 41*(1), 49–72.

Spigel, B. (2018). Envisioning a new research agenda for entrepreneurial ecosystems: Top-down and bottom-up approaches. In: J. A. Katz & A. Corbett (Eds), *Reflections and Extensions on Key Papers of the First Twenty-Five Years of Advances* (pp. 127–47). London: Emerald Publishing.

Stam, E. (2015). Entrepreneurial ecosystems and regional policy: A sympathetic critique. *European Planning Studies, 23*(9), 1759–69.

Stam, E., & Spigel, B. (2018). Entrepreneurial ecosystems. In: R. Blackburn, D. de Clercq & J. Heinonen (Eds), *The SAGE Handbook of Small Business and Entrepreneurship*. London: SAGE.

Tsvetkova, A., Pugh, R., & Schmutzler, J. (2019). Beyond global hubs: Broadening application of systems approaches. *Local Economy, 34*(8), 755–66.

Uriona-Maldonado, M., dos Santos, R. N., & Varvakis, G. (2012). State of the art on the systems of innovation research: A bibliometrics study up to 2009. *Scientometrics, 91*(3), 977–96.

van der Have, R. P., & Rubalcaba, L. (2016). Social innovation research: An emerging area of innovation studies? *Research Policy, 45*(9), 1923–35.

Index